Anger in the East

2nd Edition

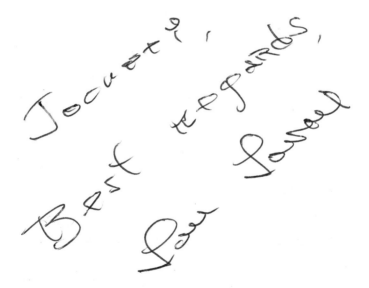

Published by
Louis Lavoie
1300 W. Medicine Lake Dr. # 211
Plymouth, MN 55441

Library of Congress Control Number 2008926525

ISBN 978-0-9791018-1-6

Printed in the United States by Morris Publishing
3212 East Highway 30
Kearney, NE 68847
1-800-650-7888

iv

Anger in the East

Historic Sources
of Muslim Discontent

**Second Edition
Revised and Expanded
2008**

Louis Lavoie

Dedicated to

Christopher Lavoie

My Son

Contents

Figures & Maps

Figures

Maps

Acknowledgments

I am especially pleased to acknowledge the help I have received in researching and writing this book. Those mentioned here will never truly know how grateful I am and how important their contributions have been. The staffs and students at Anoka/Ramsey and Century Colleges, the Science Museum of Minnesota, and the Elderhostels where I first tried out my ideas were very supportive and constructive. Mark Lindberg and Alan Willis at the University of Minnesota Cartography Laboratory were particularly helpful with the map preparations. I wish especially to note Pat Lockyear at Lakewood Community College and Karen Engler, née Laun, at the Science Museum. My family has been profoundly influential in this enterprise; thanks to my late father Louis Sr., my late mother Mary, my sister Harriet Showah, and my son Chris. I am deeply grateful for Connie Lavoie's special editorial help and particularly her questions and suggestions about the sharī'a. Jim Delaney, and Rick Turner, my friend of more than forty years, read the manuscript and materially helped me to improve it. Ann Weiblen, Roger Berg and especially Galen Sneesby were kind enough to read parts of the manuscript and offer excellent suggestions. The many conversations with Esam Aal helped me understand not only the modern Egyptian's view of Islām but some of the broader currents within his faith. Shakil Siddiqui was also helpful with some translations. My very good friend Professor Paul Weiblen at the University of Minnesota was especially helpful and encouraging. Professor John Woods at the University of Chicago was very helpful in clarifying some issues in Islāmic history and the Arabic language as was Professor Iraj Bashiri at the University of Minnesota. Dr. Muhammad Isa Waley of the British Library was uniquely helpful with information on Persian miniatures.

Historic Sources of Muslim Discontent

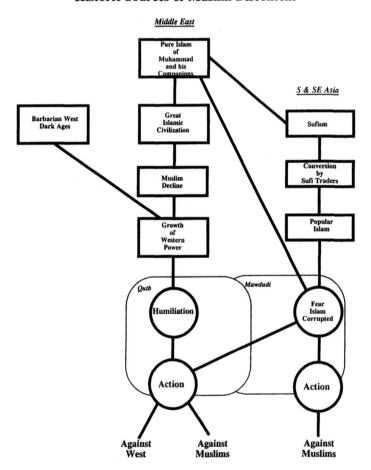

Preface

What is going on in the Muslim world? Why do they seem to hate America so? What are Muslims, anyway? Americans are surprised, bewildered, and frightened by events of the past few decades *vis-a-vis* the Muslim world, and especially that part traditionally known as the Levant, the area clustered around the eastern Mediterranean. They are hugely ignorant, if not indeed misinformed and prejudiced about this world. However, it is symptomatic of Western confusion that so many atlases and histories of Islām treat only the Middle East when the majority of the world's Muslims live elsewhere. The misinformation comes from everywhere, deep cultural biases, the government, the media, and a host of well-meaning but wanting experts writing nonsense at the drop of a hat. And some experts are, alas, really experts, but with flawed expertise. In 1978 the late Edward Said tried to correct this sorry state of affairs with his book, *Orientalism*.[1] Or at least he tried to alert us to the presence of a significant distortion of our knowledge of the "Orient." Unfortunately, Said, a man of prodigious learning and equally prodigious anger, allowed these characteristics to obscure his message: The West has categorized, pigeonholed, oversimplified, misrepresented, and dehumanized the peoples and cultures of the Arabs, the Middle East, and the Muslim world. For convenience he gathered them into the term, "Orient" and its study in the West into "Orientalism." While cooler heads will avoid his distracting passion and obscure erudition, they may also agree with his righteous thesis, we don't know the peoples of the East (read, Islām.) It is on this matter that I present here a very brief and focused account of some of the sources of Muslim discontent. This book is intended to summarize some of the relevant Islāmic history that has positioned the 'East' of my title where it is, opposite the 'West.' I believe understanding the sources and varieties of Islām can disarm the fear and misunderstanding latent in such writings as Huntington's *Clash of Civilizations*[2] while not denying that Muslims do indeed intensely dislike and react to the West's (US) actions. Though I don't see any 'Clash of Civilizations', I don't see Said's very intense 'Orientalism' either, notwithstanding the reality of many elements of each. Thus I hope to navigate safely between the Scylla of Orientalism and the Charybdis of Clash... I trust we wont be wrecked in the venture.

Said detested dehumanizing categories. Though he carried this dislike much too far, it is understandable. Yet, I will categorize the "East" and beg some leniency by easing its breadth to include the Mediterranean with extensions to the Arabian peninsula and Persia. I will also treat other Easts, South and Southeast Asia. The diversity of cultures and Islāmic beliefs within and beyond the areas I treat is dazzling. It is one of the breathtaking failures of Western (US) knowledge of the East to not appreciate this. For those seeking a broader picture of Islāmic societies one might begin with Lapidus.[3]

A little more about the title of this book, *Anger in the East: Historic Sources of Muslim Discontent.* For the most part I will address Muslim anger with the West springing from relevant world history. However, this is not to say that there are not other sources of Muslim discontent or anxiety. Indeed, I touch on one important example that is very often confused with their hate of us, that is, the natural objection of ridged believers, often called fundamentalists, to the practices of popular and folk Islām common to the Muslim masses. Muslims who indulge in these practices are often seen as apostate by fundamentalists who would destroy them if they could. The US government gives every indication of being opaque to the distinction of these sources of discontent. As for the 'anger' we need look no further than Said himself, a Palestinian American rightly and deeply unhappy with his adopted country's obtuseness. And Said's anger is mild compared to the statements and actions of Osama bin Laden and Abu Musab al-Zarqawi that seethe with frustrated hatred of America and its power over them.

The limitations of my presentation in service of maintaining focus are also met in the absence of the definite article "the" preceding "Historic Sources." I might have said, 'Some' Historic Sources, for Muslim discontent springs not only from affairs within Islām that I will treat here but from external sources as well. The economic exploitation of the Muslim world, and the growing license in Western social behavior, particularly as related to the sexes and projected globally by modern media, revolt the conservative sensibilities of Muslims everywhere.

As for "Discontent", I might have used "Malcontent", particularly after having chosen, "Anger in the East." This distinction gets at the core of much of today's conflict, for it seems to me that for the most part Muslims do not inherently hate us and wish us ill (malcontent) so much as they resent and complain of our arrogance and dominance (discontent) and wish we would stop. The problem is that the West (US) does not understand that it is discontent, and fears that they hate us and that it is implacable malcontent. Yes, al-Zarqawi implacably hated us, but there are a billion other Muslims who would probably accept us if we would simple respect them.

This is not a book for scholars, nor is it a book about the religion of Islām; it is more in the nature of a survey of Muslim history and its inevitable impact on the present. In the process I have had to leave out much about the religion and its manifestations around the world. My selection criteria have been relevance to current events, and narrative coherence. Beyond these I have merely striven for factual accuracy and interpretive integrity with occasional garnishes to preserve the natural interest of the subject. From time to time you will encounter caveats in the text, a useful precaution in view of my desire for a focused and concentrated presentation. There are also some personal asides and opinions which are obvious enough to detect immediately and with which one may wish to argue. Such arguments with a book are always good. The last part of Chapter 5 and especially the concluding essay of Chapter 6, *Tides of History,* are of a more reflective sort and include some guesses about the future based on the past treated in the preceding chapters. Nevertheless, nothing presented here will have to be unlearned if the curious decide to explore these matters further. Indeed, apart from the central focus of the 'historic sources of Muslim discontent' one will find that this short presentation is well suited as an introduction to all of Muslim history in general.

In order to maintain narrative flow I have put a somewhat more detailed treatment of *jihād,* the Sharī'a, Sufism, the Assassins, the term 'fundamentalism', and the meaning and role of popular religion at the end in appendices. Though one may read them at any time, they will be best understood after reading the chapter in which they are first referenced. Many of the endnotes have been provided as a reference guide for those who are curious beyond my limited treatment. A guide is included at the end to help with the pronunciation of Arabic words.

In this second edition, in addition to correcting the inevitable typos, I have updated and added figures as well as two maps. Several sections have been partially rewritten and an entire chapter added where before there was only a more or less passing reference to South and Southeast Asia.

Chapter 1

In the Beginning

In the *Muqaddimah*,[4] written in 1377, the Muslim historian Ibn Khaldūn reveals a pattern of history: comfort is at once the pinnacle and death knell of a nation or civilization. Almost precisely 400 years later Edward Gibbon observed in his celebrated, *The Decline and Fall of the Roman Empire* that, "If a man were called to fix the period in the history of the world during which the condition of the human race was most happy and prosperous, he would, without hesitation, name that which elapsed from the death of Domitian to the accession of Commodus."[5] Together, Ibn Khaldūn and Edward Gibbon are telling us that with the death of the philosopher emperor Marcus Aurelius and the accession of his son Commodus in 180 A.D. the onset of the European Dark Age was coming into view, and that major changes in civilization could be expected.

Barely a century later the Emperor Constantine converted to Christianity thrusting aside not only Roman polytheism, but the Roman capital as well, transferring the Empire's political and geographical focus from Rome to Byzantium 900 miles east on the forested hills overlooking the Bosporus. By 395 the Roman Empire had permanently fractured into east and west. The west lingered in confusion another 81 years during which time Rome was captured by the Visigoths in 410 and sacked by the Vandals in 455. After 476 all that remained of the Western Roman Empire was a memory and the religious influence of Christianity.

The surviving Eastern Roman Empire found that its political power had also evaporated. The distant provinces of Britannia,

Chapter 1

Hispania, Gallia, and Mauretania, as well as most of the rest of Europe and the coast of North Africa were no longer hers. What remained was what today constitutes Greece, Egypt, Turkey, Israel, Lebanon, Syria, and the western part of Iraq. By the early seventh century the Eastern Roman Empire had long since ceased to be either an Empire or Roman. Known by then as the Byzantine Empire it had its own parochial interests including commerce with the Orient and the protection of its borders farther east where the Sasanids of Persia (Map 1) were constantly contesting its claims and slowly draining its resources in a never ending stream of little wars.

The early seventh century was a transition time for Sasanid Persia that put it in the same vulnerable position as the Byzantine Empire. Heir to a tradition over 2,000 years old, it's kings and wars are still read about in the Greek classic, *The Persian Wars* by Herodotus. By 620 the Sasanian dynasty had achieved considerable military and political success, but the next dozen years of war with Byzantium, and internal political chaos, finally exhausted it. Persian territories extended from modern Afghanistan in the east through the Iranian Plateau, down upon the fertile plains of Mesopotamia and across the Tigris and the Euphrates rivers right up to the border of the Byzantine Empire. North and northeast lay the gut of Eurasia always ready to debouch its seemingly endless supply of barbarians upon the civilized world, and to the south, the arid frontier disappearing into the deserts of Arabia out of which troubling but manageable Bedouin raiders periodically pestered.

In a quirk of history it was these insignificant Bedouin tribes bursting out of the desert, unified and driven by religion and the promise of easy plunder, that changed the course of history more profoundly than any Hun, Vandal, or Gothic horde from the north.

Arabia. Did ever any name conjure an image more remote, of empty, trackless, sandy, stony wilds than Arabia. Arabia stood then as it stands now, a rectangular plateau, 700 miles by 1,200 miles, rising abruptly in the west along the Red Sea and sloping eastward to the Persian Gulf with a narrow fringe of fertile land here and there along the coasts and in the nearby mountains.

In the Beginning

Encompassing an area as large as the United States west of Denver with a Spain-size spur on its southeast corner, it has not a single permanent river or stream. The dotted blue water courses shown on maps merely show the *wādīs*, depressions along which water flows when it rains. The annual rainfall is comparable to one or two good summer thunderstorms in Iowa. Temperatures range beyond 120 degrees in the summer sun to below freezing on winter nights. Like the plains of South Dakota the wind blows constantly, and the Bedouin take what little advantage they can of its dryness and evaporative cooling qualities. In the central Nejd plateau, the great deserts of the An Nafūd to the north, and the Rub' al-Khālī to the south, sand and rock dominate, although the careful observer or hungry animal can still find some pasturage. Yet, even for man and animal accustomed to these climes life remains hard and hardening.

Millennia of struggle had produced a lean and hearty people. Tough, generous, proud, hospitable, loyal, and fiercely tribal, blood truly was thicker than water, a significant matter in a land so parched. Part of the tribal identity was also in its gods. Bedouin polytheism was as rich as tribal imagination, geography, and geology demanded with spirits identified with many rocks, springs, stars, and places. The desert tribes known then as the Kalb, Ghatafān, Hawāzin, Aus, Hārith and others, as well as the Quraysh, had unique pantheons sharing little with their neighbors except perhaps a principal deity or two, among them one known as *al-ilah*. Intertribal conflict over water, pasturage, and honor, always a fact, was exacerbated further by religious loyalties.

Mecca was the one place in Arabia free of this constant tribal conflict, a place of pilgrimage where many tribal gods including *al-ilāh* were represented in the Ka'bah. The Ka'bah is the central shrine of Islām but predates Islām by at least 700 years. The first known mention of it about 60 B.C. was by the Roman historian Diodorus Siculus. It is a stone building,[6] roughly cubic, 40 feet

7

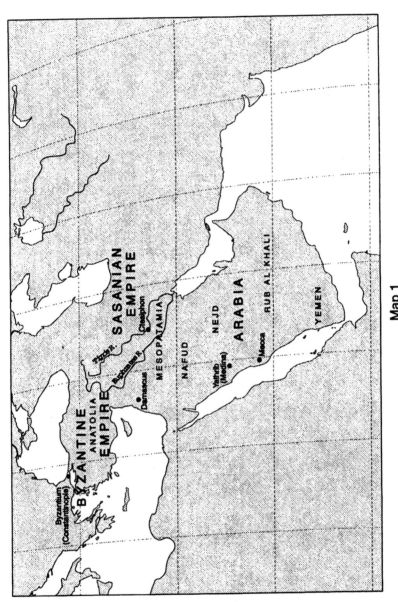

Map 1
The Middle East of Muhammad's Time

long, 35 wide and 50 high with no windows and a single double leaf door seven feet above the ground. The door is accessible by a wheeled, steep wooden staircase brought over from the nearby mosque as needed. Outside, at the southeast corner, embedded shoulder high in the wall is the sacred Black Stone, possibly of meteoric origin, that has been revered by the Bedouin as their most holy object since before the birth of Christ. And so it continues to this day with the world's Muslims.

Mecca, located 50 miles inland from the Red Sea and 650 miles south from the tip of the Sinai, was by the late sixth century not only the center of pilgrimage in Arabia but an important trading center as well. It was well located to take advantage of the instability in Persia and Byzantium where constant warfare had forced commerce away from the direct routes to the Orient to a circuitous path down the length of Arabia to Yemen, where goods were shipped by sea to and from India and China.

The Quraysh tribe, who about the year 500 had moved into the area, were very successful in their forceful control of the spice trade. Their technique reminds us of modern mobsters or corrupt politicians who sell 'protection' and influence. For a fee the Quraysh would see to it that the caravans passing through their area were free of bandit or tribal harassment. Other fees would get you the benefit of their contacts with merchants up north in Damascus and shippers down south in Yemen. The situation turned out so profitable that many of the Quraysh moved to town and settled in Mecca, where naturally enough, they were also in control.

About this time a feud broke out in the tribe between two otherwise anonymous figures, Hāshim and his nephew, Umayyah, that has had ramifications even into the 20th century. The followers of each split into the separate clans Hāshim and Umayyah. The Umayyah clan became dominant in Mecca, and eventually one of its members founded the Umayyad Caliphate, the first ruling dynasty in Islāmic history. The Banū Hāshim lost influence and became rather second class citizens of Mecca as the animosities between clans continued. Nevertheless, the Banū Hāshim have had at least two illustrious sons, the most recent, the late King Hussain of the Hāshemite Kingdom of Jordan. The other was Hāshim's great grandson, Abū Al-Qāsim Muhammad Ibn 'Abd Allāh Ibn 'Abd Al-Muttalib Ibn Hāshim, known to history simply as Muhammad.

Who could have guessed that the child Muhammad, fatherless at birth and orphaned by six, member of an inferior if not oppressed clan in a backwater town deep in the wastes of a land barely on the fringe of civilization, would become among the two or three most significant persons in human history? Born in Mecca about 570, he came to an Arabia seething with unharnessed energy. The Bedouin tribes were raiding each other and the empires to the north at the same time they were facilitating the caravans between Damascus and Yemen, and between Mecca and the Persian Gulf. The polytheistic paganism of the tribes boiled in a stew laced with many messianic prophets predicting the coming of one who would destroy the tribal pantheons and replace them with the one true god. The *hanīfs*, neither Christian nor Jew, were preachers of monotheism that was beginning to weaken tribal polytheism. Jews and Christians with their monotheistic religions were also no strangers to Mecca or to Yathrib (Medīna), the other principal town in the region.

Some evidence suggests the young Muhammad was exposed to Jewish and Christian beliefs while accompanying his uncle on caravan to Syria, but the potential for local exposure was entirely adequate to account for his later knowledge of the Old and New Testament however fragmented and imperfect that knowledge may have been. Moreover, Waraqah ibn Maufal, a cousin of Muhammad's first wife, Khadīja, was a well known *hanīf* who must have spoken often with Muhammad, and probably influenced him. Nevertheless, for the first 40 years of his life what Muhammad saw and heard was simply absorbed, provoking no action, only thought.

He appears to have had a contemplative habit, for he was known to frequently retire to a cave in the hills outside of Mecca where he would go to think. Judging from later traditions and the Qur'ān he must have been troubled by the constant intertribal blood feuds as well as the religious conflicts driven by tribal loyalties to unique gods. Some have also suggested that his later revelations may have been influenced by a growing disregard of the poor by the increasingly prosperous mercantile class of Mecca. Muhammad himself was in a good position to appreciate both worlds, coming as he did from a modest background and eventually progressing, through talent and luck, to a comfortable living.

"Oh, Muhammad thou art the messenger of Allāh, and I am Gabriel." Thus Muhammad learned of his mission in the year 610. This first vision occurred while on retreat at his mountain cave. The words come down to us in the *hadīth* or traditions of the Prophet's life collected and recorded by his followers.[7] Just preceding this utterance Muhammad was commanded in a vision to read some Arabic writing on a silk cloth. He protested that he couldn't read. The archangel insisted thrice more, and miraculously, Muhammad read, "Read in the name of your Lord who created .." These are the first words collected and later written in the Qur'ān, a book whose influence in human history is comparable only to that of the Bible. (However, for reasons that are not clear these words appear in the Qur'ān very late in the book, in the 96th chapter, "The Surāh of the Clot.")

For three years Muhammad said nothing publicly about his vision or any of the others he subsequently had. But privately he did persuade his wife and a few friends and relatives to discard their traditional tribal beliefs, accept the message of Allāh, and submit to His will ("islām" means submission/surrender in Arabic.)

About 613 he began public preaching and slowly gathered converts in Mecca. At first he was ignored by the town leaders, then looked upon as a harmless eccentric. But as his message that there is "no god but Allāh" got wider public attention the mercantile interests began to feel threatened. It simply would not do, religiously or commercially, to have the sacred deities of the Ka'bah thrown out. Business would be ruined. (Indeed, some modern scholars have conjectured that had not Mecca been the religious center that it was it might have gone the way of Petra, that amazing ghost city carved out of stone in a rocky basin and surrounding gorges in southwestern Jordan and largely abandoned one and a half thousand years ago.) At one point in trying to accommodate the Meccans Muhammad had a revelation telling him that it was alright to continue worshiping three other deities, the very popular al-Lat, Manat, and al-Uzza, thought to be the 'daughters' of *al-ilāh*. However, he very quickly appreciated this inconsistency with Islām's central idea that "There is no god but Allāh" and recanted, telling his followers that he had been deceived by the Devil. Accordingly, these verses of the Qur'ān were expunged, and have ever since been known as the 'satanic' verses. Of modern relevance, Salman Rushdie's 1989 novel "Satanic Verses" deals in part with these dethroned goddesses. The extremely zealous Shī'a of Iran were so offended by "Satanic Verses" that they declared a death sentence on the author. The recantation almost had similar results for Muhammad for it precipitated a final rapid decline in his relations with Mecca's ruling class until he and his followers were forced to flee town. He arrived in Yathrib on September 24, 622. This emigration is called the *hijra* (hegira) and marks the year from which Muslims record all subsequent events in history. Accordingly, the date of Muhammad's death in A.D. 632 is recorded by Muslims as A.H. 11 (Anno Hegirae), and the year A.D. (February 2006 to January 2007) is A.H. 1427.[8]

Fortunately, by 622 Muhammad was sufficiently well known in the surrounding area that he was welcomed at Yathrib. Indeed, he was invited there by representatives of several Arab clans to mediate a local blood feud. Within a short time a seminal event occurred, driven by the necessities of the situation, which has, arguably, more characteristically imprinted Islāmic culture than any other thing. In resolving the blood feud, many had joined the emigrants from Mecca and converted to Islām. In order to maintain this group with any hope of long term harmony Muhammad declared that henceforth all believers form a single community, the *umma* (the community of believers) and that commitment to this community and its rules superseded all previous allegiances to family, tribe, or nation. The shift of allegiance from blood ties to Allāh was profound; this was at once a religious and a political commitment, a fusion of loyalties that was unique and quite contrary to that generally accepted in the

West of Christ's distinction when He said, "Render to Caesar the things that are Caesar's, and to God the things that are God's." This commitment by Muslims, at least in principle, to the unity of religion and politics, and indeed, to the unity of all of life's endeavors has had consequences for Muslims and non-Muslims of historic scope which we shall encounter again and again in our story.

As his influence and following grew he came into conflict with the Jews of Yathrib who rejected his assertion of being the latest of a long line of biblical prophets, and alas, as so often happens in history, the zealous advocate of God's will resorted to the sword. The subsequent shock to the city's economy in destroying the vitally productive Jewish clans drove Muhammad to another decision; thereafter, he and his followers were to give captured unbelievers a choice of conversion, death, or tribute. Uncounted thousands of Christians and Jews chose to pay, and having paid, were left to go about their lives unmolested as continuing residents of the conquered lands. Through the next 12 centuries this was generally the policy of Islāmic states, a remarkable historic fact in view of our 20th-century experience otherwise.

The sword also served Muhammad beyond the environs of Medīna ("the city", for so Yathrib was becoming known) as his Muslim raiders began to attack caravans bound for Mecca 200 miles to the south. Naturally the merchants of Mecca were upset by this; in the first place they were losing money, and secondly, they were becoming keenly sensitive to Muhammad's growing power. Eight years of occasional battle between the cities, with armies sometimes amounting to more than 10,000, each side alternately winning and losing, finally decided the issue in favor of Muhammad and his followers. A treaty was signed and eventually a triumphant Muhammad returned to Mecca in 630.

There followed a nobly mild reprisal against his onetime enemies as well as the reassuringly good example of his Muslims treating tribal sensitivities at the Ka'bah with at least some tact and discretion. The Ka'bah was indeed purged clean of its pantheon of idols, save two, the sacred Black Stone and *al-ilāh*, known ever after as Allāh; "the god" had now become "God."

13

Chapter 1

Word of Muhammad's military successes over the decade 622 to 632 became known to the tribes the length and breadth of Arabia. At the cost of much blood some learned of it first hand. Others heard the message and voluntarily chose to submit. Nothing succeeds like success, and in a land like medieval Arabia success at arms was especially successful. Not only did such success bring power, it also brought booty and the message and promise of Islām. When contrasted with the tribal religions, Islām presented a unity, harmony, and simplicity totally beyond the vague offerings of polytheism. However, above all else stood Islām's prodigious power to politically unify the tribes. In the harsh, elemental world of the Bedouin the prospects of Islām, power, and booty must have seemed irresistible. When Muhammad died of natural causes in 632 in Medīna all of Arabia was Muslim, and the empires of Byzantium and Persia were on the threshold of disaster.

"There is no god but Allāh, and Muhammad is his Prophet." This declaration, sincerely made before a Muslim, is all that is required to become a Muslim. The practice of Islām is almost as simple, including what are known as the "five pillars"[9]; 1./ the declaration of faith given above, called the *shahādah*, 2./ prayer five times daily, called the *salāt*, 3./ pilgrimage to Mecca at least once in one's lifetime, called the *hajj*, 4./ the fast of the month of Ramadan where neither food nor water are taken nor sexual intercourse indulged in from sun up to sun set, called the *sawm*, and 5./ alms of 2½ to 10 percent of one's income given to charity, called the *zakāt*. This is a small price to pay for everlasting pleasure in Paradise. But of course, there are a few other details determining a Muslim's behavior.

The Qur'ān is the supreme authority in Islām.[10] It is the eternally existing book transmitted from God by the angel Gabriel to Muhammad in the Arabic language.[11] Unlike the Bible, which was <u>inspired</u> by God, the Qur'ān is <u>directly</u> God's word (brought by Gabriel). <u>The distinction is the essence</u>; the "inspired" may be modified, for example through translation from original texts. The Qur'ānic word of God cannot be modified in any way because it would be tampering with Allāh Himself.[12] That is one reason why the Arabic language was so universal and essential in Islām, and why for centuries translation of the Qur'ān was not encouraged. The Qur'ān originally existed in fragments, some written, some only in the memory of those who heard Muhammad's revelations. The fragments were first collected and committed to writing about a year after Muhammad died. The standard version we know today with its peculiar arrangement of chapters (*surāhs*), not chronologically but by length with the longest first, was put together about 20 years later.[13]

The *hadīth* is a record of the words and actions of the Prophet as remembered by those around him, a kind of composite biography.[14] It is composed of many thousands of episodes, each like a short reminiscence; for example, the story of Muhammad's first vision of the angel Gabriel mentioned earlier. The *hadīth* is second only to the Qur'ān in authority among Muslims. In the centuries following Muhammad's death *hadīth* were frequently counterfeited so that by the ninth century the number of *hadīth* had grown to more than half a million items. Muslim scholars at that time made several independent, critical reviews of the *hadīthic* literature and settled on the *hadīth* known and accepted by Sunnī Muslims today. It is the basis for establishing the *sunna*, the orthodox customs and practices for the Muslim community. A somewhat different version is accepted by Shī'ī Muslims.

The *sharī'a* is the law of Islām. It is the divinely supported, indistinguishably religious and secular Law of behavior. Although based on the Qur'ān and the *hadīth*, it was man made and often developed in the absence of specific Qur'ānic or *hadīthic* guidance. Nevertheless, it is seen as an expression of God's will concerning Muslim behavior. This is quite the opposite of Western law which is experience-based, pragmatic, and claims no divine authority. Saudi Arabia and Iran are examples of late 20th-century Islāmic States living under strict compliance to the *sharī'a*. The *sharī'a* illustrates the principle that in Islām there can be no distinction between church and state; the Qur'ān and the *hadīth*, through the *sharī'a* determine what is lawful and what is not for all actions. On the other hand most Islāmic states do not, and have not, strictly adhered to the *sharī'a*.

Chapter 1

There is no clergy in Islām the way there is in Christianity. Muslim leaders never have a sacerdotal role, even in the mosque. They never intervene between the believer and Allāh (here too, the Shī'a believe somewhat differently with their Imām playing a special role). In the West the term "clergy" or "cleric" is sometimes applied to Muslim leadership, especially those aggressively practicing their faith and therefore involving themselves in all aspects of public life. There are also scholars, teachers (mullahs), lawyers (*muftīs*), and judges in the *sharī'a* courts (*qādis*) that collectively are known as the *ulamā,* a group often influential in Muslim affairs. There are and have been other figures that have had public influence and leadership functions, the historic nature of which can be understood by their titles, such as caliph, sultan, imām, and ayatollāh. The Caliph was the successor and deputy of Muhammad, the leader of the Muslim state with complete religious and secular powers. He led the prayers in the mosque as well as the army in the field. As we shall see later, the caliphate declined and died, gradually being replaced by the sultanate. The Sultan was mainly a military/political and rather secular ruler though at times some tried to assume religious leadership as well. The imām was a special kind of leader with the term having strong associations with divine favor or mission.

Muslims trace their traditions back through the Old Testament to Adam who is supposed to have received the Black Stone from God as a token of forgiveness when he was expelled from Paradise. Further tradition has it that the first Ka'bah was built by Abraham and Ishmael. Another link with the Old Testament is seen when Muhammad was in Medīna; he first enjoined his followers to turn to Jerusalem to pray, and only later, after his conflict with the Jewish tribes, did he change the direction to Mecca. With these examples and those mentioned earlier it is clear that, contrary to the belief of many Christians and Jews, Islām is a natural continuation of the Judeo-Christian tradition. It has certainly always been viewed as such by Muslims. (The Muslim position is strikingly reminiscent of a much later development within Christianity, the appearance of The Church of Jesus Christ of Latter-day Saints (Mormons) with its prophet and holy book, Joseph Smith and the Book of Mormon.) Muslims view Christians and Jews as, "People of the Book." They cherish and revere the Old Testament and its prophets just as Christians and Jews do. Indeed, they believe Muhammad is the most recent of the long line of prophets that includes Jesus. And therein lies Islām's chief quarrel with Christianity; Muslims are scandalized by the Christian deification of Jesus, and they are even more scandalized by the trinitization of God...... there is only <u>one</u> God .....i.e., "There is no god but Allāh..."[15] As for the Jews, historically the Muslim quarrel has been with Jewish refusal to acknowledge Muhammad's primacy among the prophets.

Muslims do not regard Muhammad as divine nor do they pray to him. Muhammad himself always insisted that he was just an ordinary mortal chosen to act as God's messenger, and he took great pains to discourage those who wanted to elevate him beyond this level.[16] His immediate successor, the first caliph, Abū Bakr, thoroughly understood this and articulated it to reduce the confusion and panic at Muhammad's death; "Whoever worships Muhammad, know that Muhammad is dead. But whoever of you worships God, know that God is alive and does not die."

Chapter 2

Expansion and
the Golden Age of Islām

"Muhammad is dead!" Imagine the confusion of these simple, seventh-century Arabs who had surrendered their lives and their very souls to the guidance of one man. His message and promise of Paradise were contingent only on this surrender, and though he had frequently warned that he was merely the messenger, his listeners could not help but revere him, the tangible manifestation of an abstract idea. Some did not believe that he was dead. Others were at a loss at what to do with their lives now that he was gone.

Amongst Muhammad's inner circle a deeper and clearer vision of his role was apparent, "Muhammad is dead. But ... Allāh is alive and does not die." How then should the community carry on? Muhammad had not even mentioned the matter of a successor. A gathering at Muhammad's house produced a quick consensus that his father-in-law Abū Bakr was the best man to succeed in Muhammad's role as leader of the Muslim community, especially as he was what would eventually be called a Sunnī, a strong and respected follower of Muhammad's practices, the *sunna*. Only the day before he had been asked by The Prophet to lead the prayers of the day in his stead. This successor or deputy (*khalīfa*) we call the Caliph.

The consensus was not unanimous. Alī, cousin of Muhammad, who had also been adopted by Muhammad, and later also married his daughter Fātima, bitterly resented being passed over. He and his followers, later known as Shī'a or Shī'ites (the party of Alī, *shī'at 'Alī*) felt that the succession should stay in the family. Once again the powerful Bedouin notion of blood ties was

19

about to seed conflict, this time not only by shadowy tribes in the nameless deserts fringing recorded history, but at the very center of history. And the fruit would reappear again and again and again for more than 1,300 years up to our own time; Sunnīs against Shī'as.

Like all movements, Islām was very vulnerable in its early stages and might easily have fragmented and disintegrated without continued strong leadership. The vigorous move of the Muslim leadership in appointing Abu Bakr protected the movement and directed its energy. Like a lens gathering the sun's rays and focusing them to create a very hot spot, Arab energy was coming to a focus through the unifying power of Islām. The caliphate was the lens for this energy, the natural consequence of the need to have it controlled and directed.

Alī put aside his disappointment and joined the Arab armies in their conquests. In a short time given the comparatively small size of their army, they attacked, subdued, and pillaged Sasanid Persia, and much of the Byzantine Empire. Palestine and Syria were conquered by 640, Persia and Egypt a year later. Eastward expansion continued to the edge of China crossing the Oxus river in 667, through fabled Bukhara and Samarkand to the Jaxartes river in 712, and down into India in 713. It appeared nothing could stop the sword of Islām. Further conquests continued in the west along the coast of North Africa all the way to the Atlantic and across the Straights of Gibraltar up into Spain, parts of which would remain under Muslim domination for more than 700 years. Not until 732, a hundred years after Muhammad's death, were the Muslims finally stopped with their defeat by Charles Martel, Charlemagne's grandfather, at Poitiers, less than 200 miles from Paris. It may have been the depth of the Dark Ages for Europe, but it was a heady time for the Arabs and the Middle East (Map 2).

While all this was happening at the expanding edges of the Muslim Empire there was almost as much action at the center. The first four caliphs were variously known as the "Rightly Guided" or the "Companion" caliphs, because they had known the Prophet personally. Abu Bakr was elected in 632, and died two years later of a fever. Umar lasted 10 years before being assassinated by a Christian slave. Uthmān lasted 12 years before being assassinated by a group of unhappy Muslim soldiers. Alī finally became caliph in 656, but survived only five years before being assassinated in 661 by another unhappy Muslim.[17] In the first 29 years after the Prophet's death three of the four caliphs were murdered. What is particularly revealing is that two of them were murdered by fellow Muslims, yet the Prophet had specifically forbidden Muslims from killing Muslims. Muhammad's moral prohibitions have been no more a deterrent to Muslims than "Thou shalt not kill" has been to Christians and Jews. Like the moral power of Christianity and Judaism, the moral power of Islām has always been notably limited in the face of politics or passion.

However, not only caliphs were being slaughtered by fellow Muslims. In 656 Alī and his forces fought the "Battle of the Camel," against other Muslims in order to subdue those that didn't want him as caliph. (It was called the "Battle of the Camel" because the influential Ā'isha, one of Muhammad's later wives, urged Alī's defeat while watching the fight from a litter atop her camel.) For the remainder of his caliphate the story is the same, battles between Muslims over who will lead the Empire. Coincidentally or not, many of Alī's adversaries were of the clan of Umayyah who 150 years before had feuded with Alī's clan Hāshim. By 659 the Umayyads, under the leadership of Mu'āwiyah, then governor of Syria, not only controlled Mecca but Syria and Egypt. Mu'āwiyah was a nephew of Uthmān and claimed the caliphate over Alī. Alī's murder probably saved the Islāmic world from considerably more bloodshed in the short run, but in the long run saved nothing, for Sunnīs and Shī'as would continue the bloodletting even to the Iran/Iraq War of the 1980s, the persecution of the Iraqi Shī'as by Saddam Hussein in the early 1990s, and the vengeance killings of Iraqi Sunnīs by Shī'as in the 2000s.

Alī's death permanently ended the possibility of a Shī'ī reign

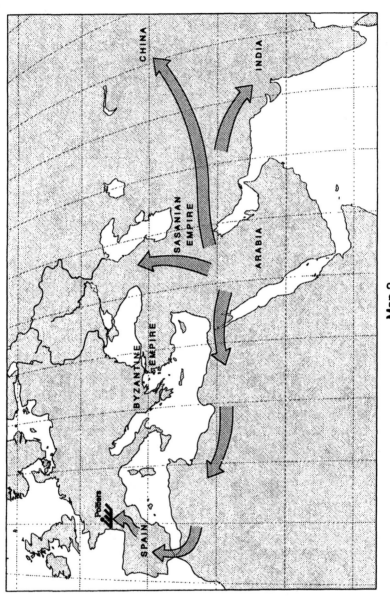

Map 2
Muslim Conquests

over the Muslim world. Mu'āwiyah founded the Umayyad caliphate, and moved the administrative capital of Islām north out of Arabia to Damascus. It would never return. The first unconscious step had been taken removing the Arabs and Arabia from control of the Muslim world. Simultaneously, the followers of Alī and his sons declared the caliph in Damascus unlawful, thus creating the first major split in Islām as they shifted their religious allegiance to Alī's descendants, the Imāms. While the supporters of Alī from 632 onward planted the seeds of schism, one may plausibly argue that it was the disaster at Karbalā in 680 that gave Shīī Islām autonomous life. Alī's son, Husayn, was traveling from Mecca to Kufā, a center of proto-Shīī sympathies, when confronted by an Umayyad army. In the ensuing Battle of Karbalā his entire family but one were killed. The reaction precipitated the birth of Shīīsm. In view of this history it is easy to understand Shī'ī reverence for Husayn, his martyrdom, and the shrine at Karbalā in modern Iraq.

The Imāmate is one of the features distinguishing Shī'ī and Sunnī Islām. For the Shī'as the leader of Islām, the Imām, must be of Muhammad's family, and was, accordingly, divinely appointed. He is also viewed as sinless, the possessor of special, divine knowledge, and the sole and infallible interpreter of doctrine.

For Sunnīs, the term "Imām" was synonymous with "caliph" (it was first used in the Qur'ān as "pattern," to be followed as an example; a leader) and later often used as an honorific title or for any leader of the Muslim community. He was the prayer leader in the mosque. The Sunnī Imām was appointed by men, not God, and was accepted as a sinner and liable to error like the rest of us. Community consensus, not the Imām, determined and interpreted doctrine. Nevertheless, he was an authority figure and was expected to be obeyed.

Accordingly, while the caliph reigned in Damascus and elsewhere for the majority of Muslims, the Imām ruled for the Shī'ī minority, and just as there existed the institution of the caliphate, there simultaneously existed the institution of the Imāmate for the Shī'as. The most fertile ground for Shī'ism was at various times in Yemen, North Africa and Egypt, as well as in

Iraq, and in Persia where it eventually became, and remains, the belief of the overwhelming majority. Its dominance in Egypt during the 10th through 12th centuries was manifest as the Fātimid caliphate.

The conflict between the caliph and the Imām was not merely a religious affair, it was also political and social. Since religion and politics were in principle indistinguishable in Islām it has never been totally clear which drives the social engine on a given issue, religion or politics. Islāmic states are in theory a theocracy in which God is the sole source of power and law, so it was natural that political factions would take the form of religious sects. They have acted ever since in ways faintly reminiscent of our political parties.

The Umayyad caliphate survived less than 100 years. During that time Islām's political boundaries expanded to the Atlantic in the west and to the border of China in the east; it probed India and Europe and established itself in Spain, not to be ejected till 1492. The Muslim state of Pakistan exists today as a direct result of the Umayyad conquests 1,200 years ago.

The Sūfī movement (see Appendix C) emerged during the Umayyad Caliphate, and thereafter fully permeated the Muslim world. To varying degrees the Sūfīs were persecuted, ignored, or courted, depending on the fears and needs of the ruler at hand. Paradoxically, the movement on occasion played an important role in the survival of Islām, for Sūfī brotherhoods provided social coherence when central government weakened. The Sūfīs (from the Arabic, *sūf,* for the wool of the simple garments worn in the beginning) originated with ascetics rebelling against the materialism and mechanical observances into which the Muslim faith rapidly fell as military and political successes mounted. Sūfīs preached a loved and loving God directly accessible through mystical experience. This was in contrast to orthodoxy's view of a coldly formal God demanding the worshiper's submission, and in the case of the Shī'as, to be approached only indirectly through the Imām. Sūfī practices eventually evolved from asceticism into mysticism, and from individual practice into membership in "orders" with study under a master and housed together in a 'lodge'. The Sūfīs are of interest to us because they were among the most influential in making converts to Islām, principally because they were very flexible in what they demanded often allowing the converts to retain substantial portions of their preexisting faith. This led to a widespread informal, popular practice of Islām (see Appendix F) far removed from the practices and beliefs of the *ulamā*, the religious leadership, and in the process put considerable psychological distance between the two, palpably weakening the unity of the *umma*, the Muslim community. This is one reason why Indonesia, the most populous Muslim nation in the world, is so little involved with the Muslim travails in the Middle East today. In the past few hundred years Sufism has become quite conservative losing much of its energy, and where active, it has tended to political involvement as the Naqshbandī have in Turkey. It is not clear what role Sūfīsm will play in the decades to come, but it has the historic potential for bridging the religious divide.

The age of the sword, and Arab expansion and influence was about to end, and the most glorious age of Muslim culture about to begin. The link, alas, was more blood.

Why is slaughter so constant in this narrative? It is not an artifact of selection, for no historian could write this history without acknowledging it. Nor is it an aberration of the peoples of the Middle East, for Europe, the Far East, and the Americas have similar histories of conflict. Nor is it merely an artifact of the time, for men have killed men with appalling constancy from time immemorial. And what about the paradox we are about to reveal where the most wonderful products of man and his culture will spring from this blood saturated ground, a phenomenon not unique to the time and place of this narrative either. Are blood, conflict, and suffering prerequisites for growth and development? Are pain and suffering inextricably linked to fulfillment and happiness? This is not the place to treat these issues, but we might mention in passing Arnold Toynbee's conjecture that civilizations grow, fail, or succeed in accordance with their ability to respond to surrounding challenges. The dynamics of optimized challenge and response produce the most successful civilizations.[18] Ibn Khaldūn 600 years ago contributed the idea that cultural success springs out of conflict, and having succeeded, becomes weak and unable to resist subsequent competition. In the 20th century the Nobel Prize winning physicist, Max Plank, observed that, "A new truth does not triumph by convincing its opponents and making them see the light, but rather because its opponents eventually die, and a new generation grows up that is familiar with it." Though Plank was referring to the genteel world of science, the essence of his idea may be applicable to history in general; there may be limits to evolutionary social change beyond which only revolution can be effective. So let us not judge too harshly the Muslim engine of history for there is ample evidence that it runs on the same energy that drives us all.

The Umayyads were conquerors, not rulers, and it showed. Converts to Islām in the conquered territories, called *mawālī*, were in principle the equal of any Arab Muslim in the eyes of the *sharī'a* law. But in fact Arab racial arrogance seldom allowed real equality.[19] Even the word, "*mawālī*," reflected this, for it means helper, freed slave, or client. The implied inferior rank is clear. Since many of the *mawālī* were Persians of relatively high sophistication compared to their Arab 'masters', and since the Arabs treated them as second class citizens, it was inevitable that before long the *mawālī* would become exceedingly unhappy with their lot under the Umayyads. Add to this the embittered Shī'as and the still strong independent tribal instinct of the Bedouin to disregard central authority, even of the Caliph, and you get a situation too unstable to last.

In the late 740s resistance to the Umayyads grew and coalesced around Abū al-Abbās and his family who quickly dispatched the last Umayyad Caliph and established the Abbāsid Caliphate in 750. In a fury of slaughter he proceeded to kill all who might be pretender to an Umayyad claim to the Caliphate, missing only one, Abd al-Rahmān, who ran as far as he could, finally settling in Spain 3,000 land miles to the west and founded the Spanish Umayyad Caliphate in 756. Meanwhile, al-Abbās was so satisfied with his handiwork that he added the epithet *al-Saffāh* to his name. It means "the Bloodletter."[20] Four years later he was dead of natural causes and succeeded by his half brother, al-Mansūr. Al-Mansūr further consolidated the family grip on the

Caliphate, by the usual means, but also felt free enough to truly begin the process of Muslim refinement that would reach its zenith under his grandson, Hārūn al-Rashīd (786 - 809). Among the more significant achievements of al-Mansūr was the removal the Caliphate from Damascus in Syria to Madīnat al-Salām (City of Peace) on the west bank of the Tigris River in Iraq, which he began building in 762. It is interesting to note that in spite of the pretentious effort of al-Mansūr in naming the city the rest of humanity insisted on calling it after the nearby ancient village, Baghdad.

The Abbāsid destruction of the Umayyads marked not only a change in dynasty but a fundamental change in focus for Islām. The Umayyads were primarily Arab with a tribal Bedouin outlook. Their capital was in Damascus with a corresponding interest westward to Byzantium and the Mediterranean. The Abbāsid capital was in Baghdad where the Persian influence with all of its customs and world view to the east was just short of overwhelming. Islām became universal, and before long left its Bedouin originators to return to their backwater in the Arabian peninsula where they would disappear from world history for a millennium.

Had a Muslim official followed the command of his Caliph and moved to the newly completed city of Madīnat al-Salām in 766, what might he have observed of the tide that was sweeping him along? Perhaps the first thing he would have noticed, even as he was approaching the city, was its design. As an official in the entourage of the Caliph he might easily have been a relatively well traveled Persian. The towns of Arabia and elsewhere in the frontier regions he may have visited were laid out with winding main streets from which branched many blind ways leading to the center of 'blocks' or quarters. They reflected the Bedouin heritage of free spirited disregard of urban life and structure, and never showed evidence of the rational urban planning that more sophisticated cultures developed. Yet Baghdad (Madīnat al-Salām) was different. As a Persian he would have found the wagon wheel like circular design with its four straight avenues radiating from the center very familiar and in no way like previous Arab cities. Indeed, the city was designed by a Persian.

27

Chapter 2

He would also have found a marked decline in Arab influence, beginning of course with the very location of the city only a few miles from the old Persian capital of Ctesiphon. Many of the administrators, like himself, were Persian. This trend, begun during the Umayyad Caliphate, became almost the rule in the Abbāsid Caliphate. The official demands of Empire simply exceeded an Arab's taste and lifestyle. And though Arabic remained the language of the Empire, the culture was quickly taking on Persian refinements.[21] The Caliph was no longer a man of the desert, easily accessible, with simple tastes and simple pleasures. The Caliph and his court began to live and rule with a Persian splendor that would dazzle the most sophisticated courtier on earth. With each passing decade he became more remote until, by the ninth century, only the highest officers of state had access to him. The Grand Vizier, always it seemed, a Persian, became more than his deputy; he became the effective head of state, sometimes ruling the Caliph himself. This of course was not without its dangers to the vizier; Hārūn al-Rashīd had his executed for becoming too powerful.

Our official would also have found that the Caliphs very quickly rejected a major element that brought them to power; there was to be no reestablishment of Shī'ī power. Shī'ī unrest had helped overthrow the Umayyads, but it was Sunnī orthodoxy that the rulers valued. In the second decade of the ninth century, al-Ma'mūn, son of Hārūn al-Rashīd, did try to end the Sunnī/Shī'ī schism by designating as his successor the 6th Imām (Shī'a) instead of his own son, but extremist elements were still not satisfied, and the traditional green flag of Alī's descendants flew over Baghdad only a short time before the return of the black flag of al-Abbās.

Baghdad is a name that invokes a flood of images of oriental splendor and the romance of the *Arabian Nights*. Ninth-century Baghdad was briefly not only the most splendid capital in the world but the cultural and trade center as well. Its highly literate aristocracy accounted for many public and private libraries. Some individual ninth-century, private libraries held more books than existed at the time in all of Europe combined. We hear, for example, of the vizier, Ibn Abbād, declining an invitation to visit

28

another capital because of the excessive effort of loading the 400 camels required to transport his library.[22]

With links to China, India, and ancient Greece through Persia, Syria, Palestine, and Egypt, the cultural resources of Islām focusing on Baghdad were breathtaking. Al-Mansūr (754 - 775) and many of his successors through Al-Mamūn (813 - 833) had collectively created the "House of Wisdom"(*bayt al-hikma*) by 830[23] where classical Roman and Greek texts from across the empire and beyond were gathered and translated. Requests for texts were even sent to Islām's perennial western enemy in Constantinople.[24] Plato, Aristotle, Euclid, Archimedes, Hippocrates, Ptolemy, and Galen were only a few of the authors of antiquity that eventually became available in Arabic.

The West is deeply indebted to Islām as one of the most important intellectual bridges linking classical Roman and Greek culture to the European Renaissance. Many of the texts we have today are known only through their Arabic translations. However, the products of the maturing Muslim civilization were not limited to transmission of the these classics; other contributions included paper making brought from China, and from India the "Arabic" numbers, the concept of zero, and the place value in counting by tens.

Over the next few centuries Muslims themselves made important and lasting contributions to the world's culture. Architectural examples range from the still standing, seventh-century Dome of the Rock in Jerusalem, and the 13th-century Alhambra palace fortress in Granada to the 17th-century tomb memorial, the Taj Mahal in Agra, India.[25] The architectural and calligraphic potential of the seductively flowing Arabic script has been sounded to amazing depths. To this day chemistry, anatomy, and optics retain elements developed during the Muslim flowering. In mathematics al-Khwārizmī's book on equations gave us the word "algebra" while al-Battānī extended and developed the trigonometric functions. These two are among the most important mathematicians of the Middle Ages and established algebra and trigonometry as we know them today. And in history modern historians stand in awe of Ibn Khaldūn's *Muqaddimah*. As geographers they measured the circumference of the earth at 20,000 miles, a figure considerably more accurate than the value known to Columbus several hundred years later, and they described India, Ceylon, the East Indies, and Africa, as well as China more than 400 years before Marco Polo.

With imperial culture and comforts the Abbāsids began the all too familiar slide into decay and ruin. The two external instruments of this ruin came in successive waves from the steppes of Asia. The first started as a trickle, individual slaves taken in the campaigns against the restless Turkomen tribes up on the northeast frontier. These slaves were excellent soldiers, and many eventually became palace guards. With the passing generations the Abbāsids became accustomed to them to the degree that many became officers. About 970 a more coherent tide began to move out of Turkistan and into the Muslim lands of Transoxania where they soon accepted Sunnī Islām. By the middle of the 11th century the internal Turkish influence as well as the successful invasion out of Turkistan rendered the Abbāsid Caliphate politically powerless. The Seljuk Turks asserted political and military power under a leader called the Sultan. However, the Seljuk Sultanate retained the Caliphs as convenient instruments to control the population through religion.

The influence of the Seljuk Sultan extended from Transoxania in the east to Syria, Palestine, and eastern Anatolia in the west. The Spanish Umayyads and their Moorish successors continued to ignore Baghdad and indeed had proclaimed their own Caliph. The political fragmentation of Islām scarcely stopped there however, for in Egypt and other parts of coastal North Africa the Shī'ī Fātimid Caliphate was established which would stand for almost 300 years before being destroyed by Saladin in 1171.

The Fātimids originated directly out of the Shī'ī schismatic Sevener Imamate. With the death of the forth Caliph, Alī, Shī'ī leadership rejected the authority of the Sunnī Caliphs in favor of Alī's descendants, the Imāms. For the Shī'ī minority the Imām was far more than the Caliph, the Imām was the divinely inspired, infallible interpreter of Islāmic Law. Moreover, unlike the custom of the Sunnī majority where every Muslim could look directly to the Qur'ān for guidance, the Imām stood between the believer and his God. Because of his divine appointment he alone determined religious truth, and by Islāmic extension, secular truth as well. For a Shī'a the Qur'ān was no longer the direct guide for behavior, it was the Imām's interpretation of it. With such a fundamentally different view, conflict with the Sunnī majority was inevitable.

Normally the Shī'ī community coexisted with and within the Sunnī community, but they recognized the Imām, not the Caliph, as their leader. In most cases survival required that they avoid overt expression of this altered allegiance, and on occasion they became almost a secret society. Accordingly, for the Shī'a there existed a kind of shadow government awaiting its chance to overthrow the orthodox rulers. For a moment when the Abbāsids were coming to power it looked like their time had come, but the needs of political stability prevailed, and the Shī'as were either suppressed or ignored as they returned to their practice of *taqīyah*, dissimulation.

The Shī'ī Imamate led by descendants of Alī survived for more than 200 years ending with the death of the Twelfth Imām in 874. Its most significant schism occurred with the death of Ismā'īl, the Seventh Imām, in 760. Some refused to believe that he had died. They insisted that he had gone into hiding to become a "Hidden Imām" who would return as "Mahdī" to bring the message of salvation to true believers just before the end of the world. With the passing of time the Ismā'īlīs became the most radical element of Shī'ism spawning not only the Fātimid caliphate but the Ismā'īlī (Nizārī) Assassins.

The Fātimids behaved just as one might expect and attacked their Sunnī brethren in exporting their brand of Islām. (The scenario, inspiration, and methods are familiar in our time beginning with the 1979 Islāmic Revolution in Iran.) For a time they controlled not only Egypt, where they founded al-Kahira (Cairo) in 969, but North Africa, Syria, Palestine, Yemen, and the Red Sea coasts including the holy cities of Mecca and Medīna. But all things end; by the end of the 11th century they had been fatally weakened by their continuous conflict with other Muslims, particularly the Seljuk Turks who were expanding at the expense of the Byzantine Empire and precipitating the Crusades. Then with the inadvertent assistance from the Crusaders the Shī'ī challenge to orthodox Sunnī hegemony over Islām ended with Saladin's destruction of the Fātimid Caliphate in 1171.

However, neither Shī'ism nor Ismā'īlism were dead,. The Persian Shī'ī community remained viable, if not prominent, in the continuing Imāmate. When the Twelfth Imām died in 874 the era of Imāms descended from Alī ended, and thereafter the Imām would be represented from generation to generation by his agents until his reappearance. The Twelfth Imām, like the Seventh Imām, was believed not to be dead, but "hidden" until his reappearance as *mahdī*. It is from this Twelver "Hidden Imām" that the present leaders in Iran derive their spiritual and temporal authority 1,100 years later (Figure 1).

In an almost bewildering array of successive fractures reminiscent of Christianity's development, Islām split between Sunnī and Shī'a; the Shī'as split into Seveners and Twelvers; Twelvers split into the majority Shi'as we now see in Iran and Iraq, and the Bahā'ī; Seveners split into Druze (whom we've seen fighting in Lebanon in the 1980s), Musta'līs, and Ismā'īlī Nazārīs (Figure 6 in Appendix D).

The fracture of the Seveners into the Ismā'īlīs leads us to the Assassins. In a dispute over the secession of a Fātimid Caliph in 1094, the Nizārīs faction took their own extremist path. They secured a number of fortresses in Syria and Persia where they exercised their influence throughout the Middle East by political intimidation and assassination. Some believe they acquired the name "Assassins" because it was thought that their agents were recruited and sent on suicidal missions by being put in a compliant euphoria through the use of hashish, hence, hashish eaters, hence *hashshsāhīn,* hence assassin. However, at the time they were known as *fidā'ī* (devotee)[26] and their organization, *da'wa.* Lewis reflects the opinion that the term 'assassin' and the accompanying stories of its origin began about 1177, some time after the sect was formed, and was used pejoratively much as we would condemn an "acid head" today.[27] After 150 years of

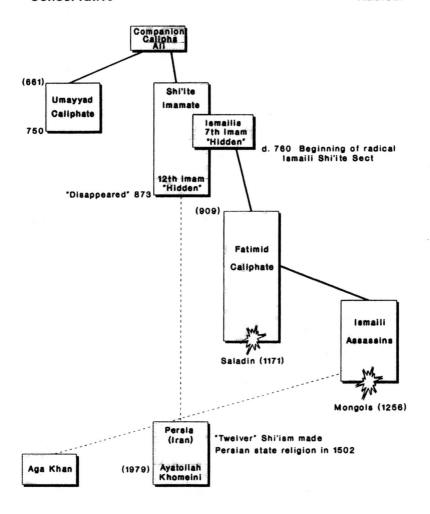

Conservative

Radical

Companion
Caliph
Ali

(661)

Umayyad
Caliphate

750

Shi'ite
Imamate

Ismailis
7th Imam
"Hidden"

d. 760 Beginning of radical
Ismaili Shi'ite Sect

"Disappeared" 873

12th Imam
"Hidden"

(909)

Fatimid
Caliphate

Ismaili
Assassins

Saladin (1171)

Mongols (1256)

Persia
(Iran)

"Twelver" Shi'ism made
Persian state religion in 1502

Aga Khan

(1979) Ayatollah
Khomeini

Figure 1
Shi'ite Family Tree

33

political terrorism their existence became an unacceptable threat to the occupying Mongols. In 1256 the Mongols invested and utterly destroyed their "impregnable" fortresses at Alamūt and elsewhere thus ending the long reign of political terror in the Middle East.

In one of the fascinating turns of history the Ismā'īlī sect benignly survives, mostly in India and Pakistan, under the current leadership of the Aga Khan. Some today may be familiar with the 1940s image of the portly Aga Khan III sitting on one side of a scale while receiving a birthday gift from his followers of his weight in diamonds (which he promptly contributed to charity). One of his sons, the "playboy" Ali Khan, was better known in this country for his wife, the film actress of the 1940s and 1950s, Rita Hayworth.[28] (See Appendix D)

Four hundred years after Muhammad's death the theoretical unity of Islām, the unity of life and the will of Allāh, as well as the unity of politics and religion, was in complete shambles. Indeed, almost all the major tenants of Islām were being ignored throughout the empire. Muslims were killing Muslims. Politics went its way ignoring religion, except where it was useful. Usury and idolatry were common. And wine, Qur'ānic prohibition notwithstanding, was not only enjoyed, but celebrated, as in the later, *Rubaiyat of Omar Khayyam*: "A Book of Verses underneath the Bough, a Jug of Wine, a Loaf of Bread - and Thou Beside me singing in the Wilderness - Oh, Wilderness were Paradise Enow!"[29]

Where then was the unity? Was there, or is there, a "Muslim World"? Yes, just like there was (is) a "Christian World." There was the common ideal manifest in the Qur'ān. There was a common script, and to a very important extent a common language. And notwithstanding the elastic treatment of religious principle, there remained many outward forms of religious practice, the daily anchor to a bedrock belief that helps individuals survive the random turbulence of history pounding in upon all sides. Nevertheless, the unity was, and is, often rather thin. Globally, the variety of belief and practice pitted Muslim against Muslim as often as Muslim against Christian. Indeed, 20th-century Muslim reformers have been particularly severe with their wayward coreligionists.

Of special note because of its current importance has been the role of language[30] for Arab/Muslim unity. There are relatively few loanwords from other languages in classical Arabic.[31] This is all the more unexpected given Arabic's vast exposure to other cultures during the conquests and more recently to the modern dominance of western culture. There is clearly some resistance here, and it is not difficult to see what and why. Arabic is the language in which Allāh, through His archangel Gabriel, revealed the Qur'ān, and thus change has overtones of sacrilege. One does not trifle with God's own words.[32] In addition, the oral literary tradition of the Arabs is their earliest and most cherished art form. The construction of new words from a rich storehouse of root words easily modified through the application of logical and systematic rules has rarely needed recourse to foreign terms for the expression of new ideas. The language is rich in rolling sonority, rhythms, assonances, and rhymes thoroughly appreciated by its speakers who value elegance of expression and brilliance of metaphor as well. For an Arab, language is not only an instrument of communication and an art form, it is a play thing, an occasion to enjoy the possibilities of wit. This pleasure in the use of the language has been manifest historically in his literature as well as currently in diplomacy. The Western style of communication sometimes misunderstands what is going on in the face of Arab loquacity, often taking it for stalling during international negotiations, as in the peace talks with Israel. In another recent instance the West understood Iraq's Saddam Hussein in the now famous "mother of all battles" statement as taunting and warning. That it may have been, but it was also for the Arab a natural exercise in the use of language to its fullest possibilities. On another occasion he said that he would, "Turn the skies into lava" if American aircraft tried to bomb Iraq. Putting aside the threat issue one cannot help but marvel at the wonderful verbal image. These examples show that the Arabic language is a profound manifestation of Arab identity and as such has been protected from adulteration with the same motivation one occasionally sees in threatened interfaith or interracial marriages.

35

Chapter 2

These examples also illustrate common and frequently misunderstood characteristics of Arab speakers as well. Exaggeration is part of the warp and woof of Arab communication. And exaggeration is often accompanied by emotionalism at the expense of the coldly analytical. Things are said that every Arab knows are not, and could not be true; it's just the way of talking. Saying something is often a substitute for doing it. On the other hand, repetition is a method of emphasis and a signal that the speaker is dealing with something important. In modern times these are important characteristics to remember as we listen to the dialog between the West and the Middle East.[33]

We saw earlier the growing dominance of the Seljuks as an external source of Abbāsid ruin. The second external source of ruin was considerably more draconian than the Seljuk. Of all the great nomadic invasions in the world's history, none was more sweeping or more terrifying to their victims than the apocalyptic Mongols (Map 3). The prospect for survival of civilizations in the path of the inexorable Mongol catastrophe seemed as slim to the peoples of that era as we have viewed our chances for survival in a Superpower nuclear war in this era. And for millions in the 13th century it truly was the end of history. Urgench, the ancient capital of Khwārezmia, was literally wiped off the face of the earth when the Mongols slaughtered or enslaved every last inhabitant, burned the buildings to the ground and diverted the course of the Oxus River through the ruins. The fabled cities of Bukhara, Samarkand, and Herat, as well as dozens of lesser cities were plundered and destroyed. We are told that of Herat's estimated 1,600,000 civil and military inhabitants, only 40 survived. More than 1,700,000 were slaughtered in Nishapur, and fewer than 100 of the 700,000 people of Merv survived. Though the numbers are undoubtedly high, the magnitude of the disaster remains inescapable.[34] A century later the renowned Muslim traveler Ibn Battuta[35] found many of these cities still in ruins, and Toynbee suggests that the historic decline of the Muslim world began in part because of the final destruction by the Mongols of the irrigation infrastructure in Iraq and its subsequent impact on

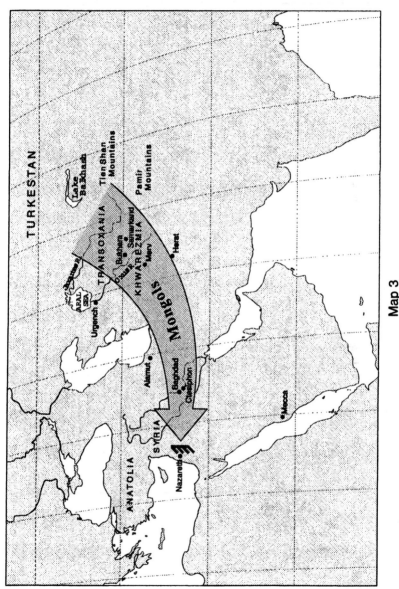

Map 3
Mongol Sweep into the Muslim World

agriculture which never recovered.[36] A thousand miles west, Baghdad with all that it represented and contained, was doomed.

The suicidal trigger was arrogance. In 1218, Jenghis Khan, busy directing his Mongol armies against north China, wished to secure stable and peaceful relations with the empires on his western flank. To that end he sent a trade delegation to the Sultan of Khwārezmia. One of the Sultan's provincial governors detained and executed the members of the delegation claiming that they were spies. When the Khan learned of this he sent an emissary to the Sultan demanding that the governor be surrendered to the Mongols. The Sultan had the emissary beheaded; after all, who were these nomadic savages in some vague place far beyond Lake Balkhash and the Tien Shan mountains to demand anything from a splendid and anointed leader of the world of Islām.

The Sultan made a bad call. When Jenghis Khan heard of the fate of his second mission he promptly wheeled his armies westward, and commenced an onslaught without precedent in human history, an onslaught that would change the history of the entire eastern Muslim world, and Russia as well; and, according to some historians, so weaken the Muslims that Western Europe could begin its 700 year ascendant over the Middle East.

The first major Mongol assault began in 1219, and affected mainly the eastern marches of the Muslim empire with the results just noted. The second assault came 37 years later when Hulagu, grandson of Jenghis, attacked and occupied much of Persia, Iraq, Anatolia, and Syria. Baghdad and 800,000 of its inhabitants were destroyed in 1258, not only ending the long impotent Abbāsid Caliphate, but terminating the institution of the caliphate as well.[37] The Seljuk Sultanate survived in slow contraction and disintegration as vassals of the Mongols for another half century then disappeared from history.

Mongol expansion westward through the Muslim world to the Atlantic appeared to be unstoppable. The Mamlūks who had replaced Saladin's dynasty in Egypt were the only military force of consequence remaining before them. In what was clearly one of the decisive battles of world history, they defeated the Mongol army in Palestine, near Nazareth, at the battle of Ayn Jālūt in September 3, 1260. Had the Mongols not been stopped the

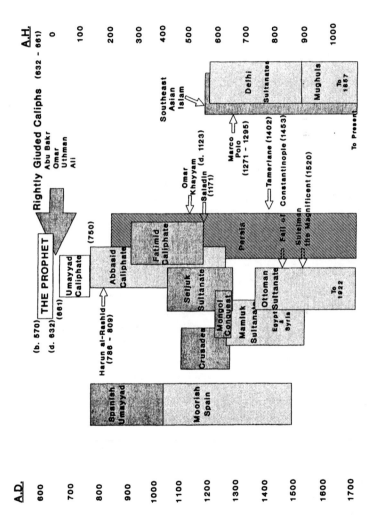

Figure 2
Simplified History of Islamic Power

39

political history of Islām might have ended with the 13th century, and the Ottoman rise to power over the next 200 years replaced with who knows what.

A moment's reflection is necessary before proceeding. Our chosen focus is the Islāmic tide of history. The view is of the breadth of events. Breadth is the emphasis. Nevertheless, beyond this focus immense turbulence existed in the affairs told of here, and our story should not imply otherwise. I, like many others, have chosen to identify and speak of nominal eras such as the several Caliphates and Sultanates (Figure 2). For our purpose this is acceptable, but know that the hegemony of the Caliphs and Sultans was uniform neither in time nor in space. At any moment in any part of the empire the influence of the Caliph or Sultan could be accepted, ignored, or challenged, as indeed was virtually always the case. So, for example, even during the era of al-Mamūm's culturally wonderful Caliphate serious local challenges to his authority existed in both the east and the west. The same is true of the history of the Imāmate. Shī'ī allegiance to the Imām was as variable and fractured as that of the Sunnī to his Caliph or Sultan. The history of the Nizārī Ismāīlīs touched on in Appendix D is typical in this matter and not at all exceptional. With this caveat in mind we can now more comfortably proceed with observing the great sweep of events, all the while knowing that the citizen of those times, just as today, was caught up in local matters that very likely masked the truly historically important events.

Chapter 3

Transition and Decline
The Ottomans

Muslim culture at the beginning of the 14th century had yet to peak in Cairo, Constantinople, India, and elsewhere. Yet Muslim political power was already passing. The first signs of this appeared as the Abbāsid Caliphate propelled the Umayyad fragment into Spain after 750. The Fātimid manifestation of the Sunnī/Shī'ī schism followed in 909 reaching Egypt in 969. The Turkish Seljuk dominance in Anatolia and Mesopotamia came a century and a half after that. By mid 12th century the Muslim world was so politically and religiously fragmented that it never again presented a unified threat to anybody, albeit from time to time even a fragment would get the attention of a sizable part of the civilized world. Baghdad and its cultural offerings of the ninth century were long past. That the centers of cultural glory at Cordoba, Granada, and Cairo remained to bloom only define the regionalism that Islām had acquired.

In this transition era we find the world of Islām represented by six largely independent political centers; Moorish Spain, Mamlūk Egypt, Ottoman Anatolia, the Arabs of central Arabia, Safavid Persia, and Mughul India. Only the Ottomans would reach the 20th century with any significant political influence, and by then even they were known as "The Sick Man of Europe."[38]

Moorish Spain was sufficiently far from the Muslim center of gravity in the Middle East that events as momentous as the Mongol invasions had no effect on it at all. In the meantime, its political history took the usual course of numerous petty wars among local Muslim power centers.[39] Eventually they were so

41

fragmented and weakened that the persistent, centuries long external pressure from Christian Spain prevailed with the expulsion of the last Muslims in 1492. It is somehow quite poignant that the slow political decline of Muslim Spain coincided with such wonderful cultural gifts to the future as the art and architecture of the Alhambra Palace in Granada. It is not possible to travel in southern California today without being immersed in the architectural echoes of this gift.

The Mamlūks of Egypt had their day expanding and contracting westward along the North African coast, eastward into Syria and Mesopotamia, and south along the Red Sea coast of Arabia. Cairo took its turn as a brilliant center of Muslim learning and culture in the early 14th century, but eventually Mamlūk decay and Ottoman power ended the Mamlūk Sultanate in 1517. Largely ignored, except as a source of tax revenues, Egypt rapidly declined under Ottoman rule into what some have called the "Egyptian Dark Age" where a neglected infrastructure precipitated famine and pestilence. Egypt recovered somewhat, but for almost two centuries it was to remain virtually anonymous until the arrival of Napoleon Bonaparte with his soldiers and scholars in 1798.

The Bedouin Arabs of the Nejd in Arabia had completely withdrawn from the center of what they had created. When Persian cultural influence overwhelmed the Arabs at the beginning of the Abbāsid Caliphate they returned to the desert and their old ways as abruptly as they had appeared. They left behind a world they had changed forever. In their desert anonymity, which was to last a thousand years, they would create relatively little of importance for our times except for the religious reform movement begun by Muhammad ibn Abd al-Wahhāb in the 18th century.

Ibn Abd al-Wahhāb was troubled by the inevitable evolution of belief away from the original practices of early Islām, and especially troubled by the liberal interpretations of the Qur'ān and the *hadīth* made by the Sūfī mystics. His essentially conservative teachings attracted one of the desert princes, Ibn Sa'ūd, who converted in the mid 1700s bringing with him most of central Arabia. As we shall see later, events unfolded after World War

Transition and Decline: The Ottomans

I where Ibn Sa'ūd's descendants formed the nation of Saudi Arabia, and where the conservatism of Wahhābī Islām is still very much in evidence.

Persia has from the beginning been the great problem for Islām and the Arabs. Though its Sasanid rulers were weakened by internal power struggles and internecine conflict with Byzantium at the time of first contact with its Arab conquerors, and the Zoroastrian state religion was becoming more oppressive, Persian culture and its traditions in art, literature, technology, commerce, and government were nevertheless exceedingly robust and vital. Of all the monarchial traditions dating from the world's earliest history, only the Persian has survived, albeit not continuously, into modern times. It is a tradition of profound import testified to by its tenacious persistence in the face of immense historical change over the millennia. Even after the Arab conquest it took centuries for Sunnī Islām to be thoroughly integrated into the culture, and several centuries more before its Shī'ī tradition was solidly established. Once achieved, Persian Islām was virtually indestructible. Its strength against foreign cultural forces was no doubt due in part to its robust millennia-old traditions. Its ability to survive internal stresses must be attributed in part to the time honored *taqīyah,* the Shī'ī ability to dissemble in the face of contrary power. The efficacy of the "Hidden Imām," the Twelfth Imām described in Chapter 2, was that even as secular or Sunnī rulers controlled their subject's bodies, their souls were in the hands of the Imām. Eleven-hundred years after his 'withdrawal' the 1979 revolution in Iran saw the secular ruler Shāh Muhammad Rezā Pahlavī abruptly overthrown and superseded by the Hidden Imām's deputy the Ayatollah Ruholla Khomeini.

After the devastation and occupation of the Mongols in the 13th century, Persia recovered to become a local power of significance under the Safavids during the 16th and 17th centuries. The transformation of the population from Sunnī to Shī'a Islām is an instructive example of the power of people's needs. At the outset Sūfīs were tolerated by the early Ottomans; the Shī'a were not. Since the masters of most Sūfī orders , whether Sunnī or Shī'a, traced their spiritual linage directly back to Alī, it was natural that Shī'ī believers would gravitate to Sūfī

43

orders, in this case often to the Safawī and Bektāshī, exercising *taqīyah* dissimulation for survival. Shī'ī Sūfīs successfully preached a more satisfying faith than that of the more austere Sunnīs, and with the special circumstances existing in Persia eventually (1501) freed themselves of Sunnī Ottoman influence.[40]

After a relatively brief existence of barely 200 years the Safavid were no more , and thereafter Persia would be more or less a pawn in the struggle between the growing power and imperial ambitions of Russia, and Great Britain. The Ottomans, too, were a player of consequence in the beginning, but their control in the east began declining even before it did in the west. The Persian state settled into its approximate current boarders in the 17th century. As it withdrew it left behind a large Shī'ī population in the south of Iraq which we have seen assaulted in 1991 by Saddam Hussein's secular/Sunnī regime, and now after Saddam's fall become politically dominant.

Nevertheless, however independent the Persians, Arabs, and other Muslim states, they as well as the West often, if not always, continued to acknowledge the Islāmic suzerainty of the Ottoman Sultanate. Though Islām was in retreat in the Iberian Peninsula it continued to expand at the other end of the Mediterranean, where, indeed, even Constantinople finally fell to the Ottomans. Ottoman hegemony continued to spread in advancing and receding waves not only up into the Balkans, but through Palestine, Syria and Iraq, and down into western Arabia, as well as around the Black Sea. Yet with all this expansion it is interesting that very few new Ottoman conquests in Christendom resulted in new conversions to Islām. In fact, apart from Bosnia and Albania conversions to Islām have been uniformly unsuccessful in Europe, even in the part of Spain where Muslim occupation lasted 800 years notwithstanding the many Spanish Muslims that were expelled or forced to convert. The contrast of failure and success between the lands north and south of the Mediterranean is striking. So it appears that the political power and inspiration of Islām remained effective, but the spiritual power was not generally capable of supplanting Christianity, at least where it was very robust, and thus left few marks on Europe.[41] By 1700 the great age of the expansion of the Muslim faith was over. Further gains over the next three centuries would be very gradual, evolutionary, and quite insignificant.[42]

The rise of the Ottoman Turks was the natural result of the power vacuum created by the Mongol subjugation of the Seljuks after 1258. Mongol control of Anatolia was gradually weakened as the remains of the Seljuk Sultanate disappeared toward the end of the 13th century leaving a dozen local amirs fighting among themselves. The Ottomans came from this group. Osman, who by 1356 had prevailed over his competitors in northwestern Anatolia, established a line that would reach the 20th century. In 1396 a descendant, Bayezid I, was so successful against the Christian Balkans that he was declared Sultan, thus cementing the legitimacy of Ottoman authority in the Muslim world. Then Mehmed II achieved in 1453 what Muslim armies had been trying to do for almost 800 years; Constantinople fell, and the Byzantine Empire was no more. Thereafter, the Ottoman Empire would be ascendant for another century.

Almost immediately Osman's initial success at unifying the Turks and his clear interest in the Balkans began to get the attention of Europe. In less than 50 years they were more than attentive, they were scared.

In the beginning the Ottomans considered attacking the fortified city of Constantinople, but like their predecessors they found it too strong. Accordingly, they bypassed it and began the envelopment of Greece and the Balkan states. Serbia, Bulgaria, and Wallachia (part of modern Romania) were either directly occupied or persuaded to become vassals of the Ottoman Sultan.[43]

The Ottoman conquest of the Balkans began in the mid 14th century leaving the Serbians with the bitter taste of defeat at Kosovo in 1389. Because of this defeat the Orthodox Serbs still resent Muslims, and by extension, Bosnians, even though in 1389 the Bosnians were not Muslim. The heathen Bosnians along with the Croats were converted to Catholicism somewhat before the tenth-century Serb conversion to Eastern Orthodoxy.[44] But Bosnian conversion was not as effective as that of the Croats and eventually evolved into a weak popular practice that was easily breached by the strength and advantages of Islām. Over the next few centuries a majority of Bosnians (and Albanians) became

Muslim. By 1600 we see a trio of religious interests, the Catholic Croats, the Muslim Bosnians and Albanians, and the Eastern Orthodox Serbs, still clearly visible as the irrational hatred underlying the war and 'ethnic cleansing' in the 1990s.'[45]

Other vassals included the Crimean Tatars, the decaying remnants of the Golden Horde and Jenghis Khan's Mongols.[46] Though they accepted Islām as early as the 14th century they were not brought under Ottoman control until 1475.[47]

When Suleiman the Magnificent became Sultan in 1520 the real world was entirely different from the Euro-centered one most of us learned about in high school history. We learned that the early 16th century was the age of discovery; the globe was being mapped, conquistadors were marching through the Americas subduing hostile natives and sending their golden booty back to Europe on hundreds of galleons braving storms, pirates, and privateers. Pope Alexander VI had divided the world in 1494, West for the Spanish and East for the Portuguese[48]. Henry VIII swaggered in England, and Titian painted an equally satisfied Francis I in France. The Renaissance ebbed, and the Reformation gained momentum. Petty scheming for advantage among western European monarchs was magnified for us into life and death struggles of global import. Meanwhile, in central and eastern Europe the Hapsburgs, ruling from Vienna, often seemed to be a kind of buffer between Europe and a vaguely acknowledged Muslim world.

They were a buffer indeed and twice almost became the property of the Ottomans. Arguably the most powerful state in the world, Suleiman's Ottoman Empire had within living memory finished off forever the eternal and venerable Byzantine Empire. His rule completely embraced the countries of the Mediterranean basin except for Italy, France, and Spain. With his navy in the eastern Mediterranean, and mastery of the Middle East, he controlled commerce to the Orient, a matter which played no small part in Western Europe's decision to go a'sailing elsewhere and thus make all those profitable discoveries. Suleiman's dominions also extended far south into Egypt, to the holy cities in Arabia, to Yemen, Syria, and Iraq, and to all of Anatolia; he virtually owned the Black Sea (to the chagrin of Russia), and of course, the Balkans.

Suleiman's struggle against the Hapsburgs for control of Hungary was successful enough to cause Europe to consider aiding the Hapsburgs, a strange situation since most of the time Europe was resisting them. It was a classic situation, one we have recently seen again in the Persian Gulf where United States aid alternated between Iran and Iraq. The problem was, and is, a matter of balance, to aid one enemy just enough to distract the other enemy without making either uncomfortably powerful. In the 1530s France was playing the same game with the Hapsburgs and the Ottomans as the United States played in the 1980s with Iran and Iraq. In both cases the balancing act led to unexpected results. The Ottomans in trying to get French help inadvertently set themselves up for immense future grief by granting the French, a nation they considered rather insignificant, certain commercial and legal rights within the Empire in what is known as the Capitulations of 1535 (about which more later.) Moreover, in the early part of the sixteenth century Ottoman pressure on the Hapsburg Empire may have saved the rest of Europe from Charles V.[49] And later through support of the Protestants, the Ottomans materially furthered the Reformation.[50]

The court of Suleiman the Magnificent was the most splendid of its time, indeed, it was Europe that gave him the sobriquet, "The Magnificent," for he was known in the Muslim world as "The Lawgiver." Through his vigorous building program he transformed Byzantine Constantinople into the Turkish city familiar to us as Istanbul (and though it wasn't officially renamed "Istanbul" until 1930 it was called such by Muslims from the 13th century. The word derives from a corruption of the Greek, *is tin polin,* meaning "to the city.") He was known and highly regarded for the exceptional competence of the administrators, lawyers, architects, and writers brought to his court or otherwise supported. Suleiman's treasury was fat with plunder and well sustained with revenues from his vast empire. His army was exceptionally good and included elite units of Janissaries, the soldier slaves taken in their youth from conquered Christian lands, educated as Muslims, and trained as the most highly professional soldiers in the world. Nevertheless, they weren't invincible.

Twice Ottoman armies stood at the gates of Vienna, but Vienna was saved, in 1529 by circumstances totally beyond its control, and in 1683 by an early sign of change developing deep in the tide of history. The salvation of 1529 lay in that old bugaboo of military operations, logistics. Unlike the highly mobile Mongols who were adept at living off the land and hearty enough to easily withstand European winters, Ottoman armies required a substantial supply base, which for reasons of efficient distribution elsewhere in the Empire had to be 800 miles away in Constantinople. This supply line was just too long to sustain, and their siege had to be lifted as winter approached.

The second siege of Vienna in the summer of 1683 failed because Ottoman resources were overextended, their military technology was now significantly behind Europe's, and their leadership, with few exceptions, had degenerated into habitual incompetence. Also, the Powers in Europe were individually stronger than ever before, and they were beginning to act in concert against the Muslim threat. The forced Ottoman withdrawal in the autumn by combined German and Polish armies unambiguously signaled the slow decline from which they would never recover.[51]

The decline began in fits and starts and was largely unrecognized at the time. Twelve years before the failure of the second siege of Vienna the Ottoman fleet of Selim II suffered its first defeat at the Gulf of Lepanto losing 230 of 273 galleys in one of the largest naval battles in history.[52] The Battle of Lepanto easily ranks among the ten most important naval battles of all time, since it essentially neutralized the Ottomans at sea and left the Mediterranean a European highway. There were still sea and land victories after that, but the signs of decay were there: in 1622 an English traveler described the Sultan as old and crazed with vice.

An attempt was made to reform the government and the military with the appointment of Mehmed Köprülü as Grand Vizier. A sense of the scale of corruption and incompetence at the time comes from the fact that in five years he had 35,000 officials executed. Upon his own death from old age his son Ahmed became Grand Vizier and continued the reforms, though without the bloodshed of his father. Nevertheless, the troubles with the Ottomans were so deep that no reform short of a cultural revolution was likely to succeed for long. The sickness of the culture was manifest in their overwhelming conservatism, their inflated self-image, and their supercilious ignorance of the political realities evolving around them. Nothing better captures these features than the Grand Vizier Ahmed Köprülü's 1666 remark to Louis XIV's ambassador, "Do I not know that you are an infidel, that you are a hog, a dog, a turd eater?"[53]

And yet this disdain was not completely impervious to the wiles of European culture. Unfortunately for the Ottomans, the imports were pitifully superficial. Thus we have the Tulip Period during the Sultanate of Ahmed III (1703 - 1730) where tulips brought from Holland and elsewhere became something of an obsession as the wealthy vied with one another for the best garden. For a few days each April the gardens of the Grand Seraglio erupted in exquisitely planned flower displays. At night all was illuminated with thousands of candles flickering among the tulips and made the more captivating and dynamic as turtles crawled randomly about with other candles fastened on their back.[54] In the meantime, education, politics, military science, industry, and commerce remained ossified in the conservatism of Islām and Ottoman degeneracy.

Why do the mighty fall? When a State is at the pinnacle of power and influence it seems inconceivable to its people that it could ever be otherwise. Nevertheless, it can happen, and did happen to the Ottomans beginning in the 16th and 17th centuries. As the 18th century developed the decline became apparent to all but the Turks. It wasn't until the 19th century that the Ottomans admitted their own weakness, but by then it was too late. Several attempts were made to recover, but events of the 20th century and particularly the storm of World War I swept them away forever. One could say that the Ottomans fell from a combination of political, economic, and cultural failures, or more generally, from the degenerating influence of high civilization as Ibn Khaldūn's analysis might suggest.

Chapter 3

Politically, the focus of all power on the Sultan worked as long as the Sultans were competent. However, many were not. As with any group of humans, the corrupting influences of absolute power and unrestrained comfort had their inevitable impact. Bad leaders made for bad policy which made for imperial decline. The Sultans also distrusted everyone around them; not only was the execution of officials frequent, but even the brothers of a new Sultan were strangled to eliminate possible competition. In such a milieu it is scarcely surprising that the interests of the Empire were not always foremost on the minds of the bureaucracy. As time passed the Sultans began to delegate more power to their Grand Viziers. An independent bureaucracy developed that further divided authority between the Sultan, and the Grand Vizier and his staff.[55] Corruption and intrigue flourished. Political adroitness instead of administrative ability determined success, and as the central government weakened, power dispersed to the elites in the provinces. The bottom line was a fatal lowering of the quality of government.

Economically, the Ottoman Empire was essentially a military State. The focus on the military led naturally to a certain contempt for all that was otherwise, thereby leading to a gradual neglect of agriculture, commerce, and industry. It became an exporter of raw materials and an importer of manufactured goods. This led to inflation exacerbated by the dilution and debasement of Ottoman silver currency by the enormous influx of gold and silver from the Americas. At the same time trade was bypassing the traditional routes to the Orient through Ottoman lands and following the Portuguese passage south around Africa.

Demographically, the population swelled beyond what the economy could support. This led to all sorts of problems including a serious increase of banditry by army veterans unable to find work.

Culturally, the Ottomans were trapped in the subtle and profound prison of Islām's natural conservatism.[56] As their Sultanate aged into comfortable power they no longer looked outward for ideas; Islām and their own importance was all that was of any value. The West and its technology passed them by, and they would not change or even acknowledge the need for change. Printing in Arabic and Turkish, for example, was forbidden in the Empire until the early 18th century[57]. The Sultans were almost totally ignorant of the West until Napoleon stepped ashore in Egypt in 1798.

We shall now pass over 200 years of mutual jostling by the states of the Middle East, of the ebb and flow of events pushing borders one way then another, of the conflicts between the Sunnī Ottomans and Shī'ī Persians, between Muslim states and Russia including the ten wars between the Ottomans and Russia between 1677 and 1877 (only one of which the Ottomans won), and between Muslim states and the increasingly dominant French and British Empires. We pass on, merely acknowledging that though French troops left Egypt after only three years, the seductive impression left by French (Western) culture would remain to confuse and haunt Muslims in Egypt into the 20th century. We must pass over most of this because the detail of events would too easily obscure the already identified tides of Muslim decline that have pushed events in our era. But before picking up our story on the eve of the 20th century in Chapter 5, let us examine the great expansion of Islām into South and Southeast Asia.

Chapter 4

Islām into South and Southeast Asia

We have spoken of the transition and decline of the western Islāmic world in the 14th through 19th centuries, but the history of Islāmic cultures is not that simple. There is an interesting irony here, for as Islām was losing its vigor west of the Fertile Crescent[58] it was expanding into South and Southeast Asia creating a polity and culture that would surpass in almost every way that of the Arab/Persian motherland. Simultaneously, however, it was creating a Muslim culture constituting a majority of the world's Muslims that would irritate and infuriate modern reformers who demanded a return to the purity of early Islām. What happened, and why?

The great wave of Muslim conquest swept out of Arabia and split three ways, west to the coast of Africa, north to Syria, and east through Iraq and Persia into Afghanistan and to the very threshold of India stopping only at the valley of the Indus river in 711. There it stalled.

It took 80 years to go the first thousand miles from Arabia to the Indus valley. However, it took three centuries to conquer the next 200 miles to the Punjab and its capital Lahore in northwest India. Another two centuries passed before a Delhi Sultanate[59] was established and one more to finally complete the conquest south of the Deccan. Arithmetic tells us that Muslim armies took about 600 years to conquer India, but history tells us that they never Islāmized it, for at no time have Muslims ever constituted more than one quarter of the population.[60]

53

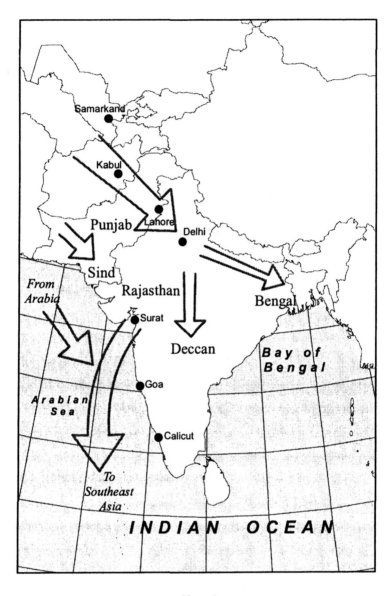

Map 4
Islām in South Asia

Why was this so? Even sophisticated Persia had become largely Muslim after 300 years. The answer has to do with the unusual indigenous religion encountered by the invaders. The land southeast of Afghanistan, beyond the Khyber Pass and onto the great subcontinent of South Asia comprising today Pakistan, India, and Bangladesh is home to arguably the oldest of the world's great religions.[61] Unlike the founded religions of Judaism, Christianity, Islam, and Buddhism, Hinduism is a traditional religion with no attributable founder. Its existence can be traced back to the Vedic beliefs of Aryan invaders of the subcontinent around 1500 B.C. and possibly also to indigenous cultures a thousand years older. Although Hindu beliefs and customs have evolved more or less continuously throughout its history, certain beliefs existed at the time of the Muslim conquest, as they do today, that are particularly relevant to our story.

The first of these is called, *adhikāra*, meaning spiritual competence. It is the notion that one believes and worships in accordance with one's natural spiritual development, for example it is alright for a simple farmer to believe in all sorts of spirits, gods, miracles, etc.. At the same time it is equally natural and acceptable for a highly sophisticated holy man or Brāhman to see the world entirely differently and view all of existence as mere illusion.

Next is *ista-devatā*, chosen deity. Thus it is perfectly acceptable for a believer to choose to focus his worship on one particular god of the very many that may be out there. This recognizes the devotee's need to be comfortable and satisfied with his religious choice. It in no way reflects superiority or inferiority of another's choice; all are acceptable.

The concept of *māyā*, the illusion of the existence of self,[62] indeed, the illusion of perceived reality, is one of the cornerstones of the Hindu religion. It is the goal of the believer, through however many reincarnations it takes, to attain a full understanding of this illusion and finally escape individuality and reunite with the universal All.[63]

As we shall see, these concepts made it relatively easy for Hindus to accept Islam, and at the same time for Hinduism to survive. As with so much of Hinduism, these characteristics make it an immensely flexible religion with great assimilative power and culturally almost bullet proof. Accordingly, it is not surprising that notwithstanding Islām's success in the Subcontinent and its six century political dominance, Muslims were always in the minority.

Arab traders, even from pre-Islāmic times, were found on India's western coast all the way to Calicut near the southern tip. The later conversion to Islām of these traders, however, had little effect on the populations they were in contact with. It was via the overland route that Islām would truly penetrate India.

The Subcontinent's history from the first moment of significant Muslim hegemony in 1206 to the present can be divided into four eras: the Delhi Sultanates, the Mughul Empire, the British colonial era, and the time of independence and fragmentation.

It is, however, a bit misleading to present the Muslim conquest of South Asia as some sort of planned, organized, relentless, and rapid assault by Arab armies out of the Fertile Crescent. In fact, as mentioned above, it was quite slow. Moreover, it was neither Arab nor organized. After the Abbāsid caliphate ran out of energy it was largely up to the loosely affiliated Muslims in Afghanistan to carry the torch. And their movement into India was more in the nature of coalesced raiding, that is, petty Turkic/Persian leaders punching away at largely disorganized kingdoms in northern India until one day they found themselves permanently resident in Lahore, then Delhi.

They were of Turkish stock, like the Seljuks and Ottomans, but their culture was Persian. Though warfare was their occupation, they also had ambition to high culture which was facilitated by scholar and artisan refugees from Persian lands devastated by Jenghis Khan's Mongols. Coming out of Afghanistan these Muslim warriors eventually settled in Delhi and successively established five sultanates from 1206 to 1526 known together as the Delhi Sultanates. They would begin the creation of a unique Hindu Persian culture in India.

The Deli Sultans began with an Islāmicaly self-conscious rule, but by the mid 14th century the siren chorus of Hindu culture was working its magic. Sūfī political influence became manifest and ironically helped to inculcate Hindu views in the ruling Muslim class. Hindu temples, previously destroyed on sight, were now permitted, and Hindu functionaries served in an official capacity for their Muslim masters. Islām itself was taking on a new form in the Subcontinent. Not only was there a Persian and Hindu overlay, there was also a clear artifact of native culture beyond religion as well. We see this in the writings of the two best known travelers of the time, Marco Polo and Ibn Battuta who tell us of bare-breasted women, of divorcees who scandalously decline to leave the homes of their former spouses, of *satī* (the practice of a widow voluntarily burning herself to death on her husband's funeral pyre), and judicial suicide where the condemned may choose to kill himself.[64] Muslims by no means accepted all of these practices, yet they coexisted with Islām and for the most part were resistant to Muslim pressures. Battuta in the role of *qadī* metes out beatings to ex-husbands for their errant behavior as well as to those who do not promptly go to prayer when called by the muezzin, and he remarks with apparent exasperation upon the hopelessness of getting the ladies to modestly cover themselves.

At this point one may be wondering how Sūfīs could "inculcate Hindu values'. From Appendix C we see examples of Sūfī beliefs and an acceptance of the many approaches to the one true God. Thus it is natural that Sūfīs in India would find something congenial in such Hindu concepts as *adhikāra* and *ista-devatā*,[65] and indeed, that Hindus would find such receptiveness seductive. The line between beliefs was at times almost invisible, and it was common for subsequent popular religious practices to combine the two religions, even to the point of worshiping each other's gods and saints.

Sūfīs appeared on the scene quite early. The Chishti order was the first in India, and in fact may have originated there in the early 13th century in Ajmīr, Rajisthan.[66] Shortly thereafter the Suhrawardis came from Iraq where they had been founded in the 12th century.

The Chishtīs were the most popular of the Sūfī orders in India and were notable in the beginning for their distaste of worldly power and wealth, their pacifism, their breathing exercises with repetitive chanting (*dhikr*) of the names of Allāh, and the use of music (*sama*) as a spiritually elevating device.[67] Their notion of the oneness and unity with God has Hindu echoes that made Islām seem more familiar to the locals than might otherwise have been expected. However, even with their early distaste of power, they were nevertheless politically influential at least as early as the reign of the Delhi Sultan Iltutmish (r. 1211 - 1236) and became more so as the centuries passed. This naturally made them more competitive with the Suhrawardi order.

The Suhrawardīs were in many ways a contrast to the Chishtīs. Originating in Iraq in the 12th century they appeared in India only a few years after the Chishtīs. They were more actively engaged in political affairs, particularly in providing a connection between the natives and their Muslim overlords. Otherwise they were reluctant to have much to do with the poorer Hindu. They disapproved of 'musical performances', *samā*, but did use the *dhikr* repetitive chant. Although both claimed to live by the *sharī'a*, the Suhrawardīs were clearly more committed to its strict and narrow interpretation.

Of the many other Sūfī orders that found their way to India, or originated there, we merely note here the Shattāri, the Qādira, and the most conservative of all and last to arrive in the mid 16th century, the Naqshbandī. Each accepted or rejected music, dance, repetitive chant, reverence for saints and holy men, breathing and body exercises not unlike Hindu yoga, and miracles and magic. Each had its style in the Indian Muslim society, particularly with respect to ritual, and connection to the native Hindus. They also varied considerably in their religio/political involvement and like the conservative Naqshbandi later become very reform minded. It is interesting to note that they all asserted their commitment to the Qur'ān, *hadīth*, and *sharī'a*, yet their beliefs and practices ranged from the extremely orthodox to extremely liberal. Politically, the orders existed in competition with the *ulamā* for getting the sultan's attention. As the case has always been, the sultan was largely preoccupied with political matters, and despite his natural commitment to Islām, used the *ulamā* and the orders as the moment required. Thus there was often considerable tension between the politics and religion. Nevertheless, the Sūfī orders in India were the major instrument for spreading Islām

because of their example of holiness and good works, while direct
and explicit missionary work was considerably less important.
Moreover, the example of holiness was itself influenced by
previous Sūfī traditions of flexibility (Appendix C) as well as by
the Hindu milieu, the latter greatly facilitating Sūfī influence

As a general rule conversions were made throughout Muslim
conquered lands by appeals to basic religious needs and the
attraction of Islām's simplicity. Social, commercial, and
matrimonial reasons were also important, as well as a sense of
snobbish superiority. Moreover, there were practical legal
advantages where, for example, a Muslim's word according to
sharī'a law carried more weight than that of a non-Muslim's
word.

Perhaps no better example illustrates the encounter and fusion
of Hindu and Muslim cultures than the appearance of the Urdu
language and script. The most prominent native language of India
was and is Hindi. It is derived from Sanskrit and shares with it
the characteristic Devanāgarī script written as English is, from
left to right. The Hindi mother language spawned Urdu giving it
Hindi grammar. But Muslim influence gave it an Arabic/Persian
vocabulary and script as well as the Arabic convention of writing
right to left. (See Figure 3.) Sūfīs in the subcontinent spoke
Hindi, but before long they began to blend it with the more
familiar and comfortable Arabic and Persian. The result was
Urdu[68] whose first recorded use was in a Sūfī work in 1308.
Today Urdu is the official language of Muslim Pakistan, though
only 8% speak it. English is also an official language, probably
about 2%; otherwise Punjabi is spoken by 48%. Hindi is one of
the official languages of India, spoken by 30% of Indians. Once
again, English is also an official language.

Some elements of Hindu culture even aided conversions to
Islām. Hinduism not only limited social mobility, but often

Hindi ⇨
(read l to r)

शुरू अल्लाह के नाम से जो बड़ा मेहरबान
बहुत बहुत रहम करनेवाला है।

Urdu ⇦
(read r to l)

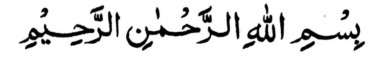

Arabic ⇦
(read r to l)

بِسْمِ اللهِ الرَّحْمٰنِ الرَّحِيْمِ

English ⇨
(read l to r)

In the name of Allāh, the Beneficent, the Merciful.

Figure 3

The Bismillah in the Languages of South Asian Islām
Note that though Urdu comes from Hindi, its script is closely related to Arabic

fostered contempt and hostility between the castes. On the other hand, Islām recognized no class - or caste. In principle the *umma* was a single community of believers where a Muslim could reasonably expect advancement to be based on merit alone and not on caste.[69] Accordingly, the attraction of Islām for low-caste Hindus was obvious, since it offered a way up usually reserved within Hinduism for another reincarnation.

Notwithstanding the expansion of Delhi Sultanate power throughout much of India, there remained considerable resistance, both by local Muslim governors to the Sultan's central authority and by surviving Hindu princes, particularly the Rajas of Rajasthan. This fractiousness and concomitant weakness was irresistible to a minor Muslim prince battling away in what is today Uzbekistan and Afghanistan.

Bābur (meaning "lion") was the first Mughul ruler. Born less than ten years before Columbus discovered America - and Islām's final loss of Spain - he came from a family of warrior leaders that traced its ancestry five generations to Timur (Tamerlane), and on his mother's side 13 generations to Jenghis Khan.[70] They were called Mughuls because of this Mongol connection.[71] Although an abstinent youth like any good Muslim, by his early twenties he transformed into a drinker of some note, though it never effected his military genius. There even exists an Indian miniature painting depicting him riding into camp stone drunk.[72] And his talents were not limited to the battlefield; he was an enlightened administrator, and a writer and poet of considerable skill. Indeed, his memoirs are ranked among the finest ever written.[73] As a very young man he had taken and lost Samarkand, twice, then taken Kabul. Then he crossed the Khyber pass and descended into the Subcontinent. There followed the usual battling, most notably the Battle of Pānīput where his force of 25,000 defeated 40,000 opponents, elephants and all, due to excellent generalship, good cavalry, and especially his artillery. Two years later he defeated the formidable Rājputs who never again would be a serious organized threat. When he died in 1530 a thousand mile swath across northern India was under his control. However, he was buried not in India, but in Kabul, where even today one can visit his remarkably modest tomb. Bābur's legacy was chiefly the foundation of the Mughul dynasty that ultimately united most of the Subcontinent. Apart from that we find little else was created geopolitically or culturally. It remained for his grandson, the celebrated Akbar the Great, to extend the empire to the Deccan and forever imprint "Mughul" on the history of India.

Akbar, born in 1542, was ruling his modest patrimony by the age of 18. After Bābur's time the family dominions had shrunk in the face of Hindu and Afghan ambitions. He quickly set about regaining these territories and eventually expanded them south to the Deccan before his death of natural causes in 1605. Of particular note, and entirely characteristic of his historically influential rule, was his method of dealing with the independent-minded Rājputs. Though he didn't hesitate to use military force when resisted, he clearly preferred to use diplomacy, and it was through diplomacy that he brought over most of the Rājput leaders by 1570. Vassalages and alliances were typically formed by bringing their leaders into his army, and by marrying Rājput princesses.

Akbar was easily the most religiously cosmopolitan of the Mughul emperors. Not only did one of his Rājput wives become the mother of Jahāngīr, his successor, but she and the other Rājput wives were allowed to continue to practice their Hindu religion. Akbar's chief tax collector was Hindu, as were many of his generals and provincial governors. Indeed, Hindus made up 20% of the Mughul aristocracy. Clearly he not only tolerated Hindus but accepted them with an open-minded interest in all religions. Nevertheless, he was, more or less, a Muslim (to the consternation of Jesuit missionaries who mistook his interest in Catholicism as a step towards conversion.) Sometimes his Islāmic credentials were questioned, especially by the *ulamā* when he disestablished Islām as the state religion, and in 1580 appeared to be toying with the idea of a new, modified Islām with the ultimate power of juridical interpretation of the *sharī'a* to be his alone. Though he was illiterate, he was highly intelligent and open minded. New ideas did not frighten him as they did with so many of the *ulamā*.

That the Mughuls were largely comfortable with Hindu culture is self-evident from the ease with which the classic

Mughul culture was synthesized from the Persian and the Hindu. Architecture (Humayun's Tomb and the Tāj Mahal), painting (distinctive and engaging miniatures and manuscript illuminations for example), language and literature (development of Urdu), and particularly for our story, religion itself (popular Islām) were transformed. However, religious interests aside, Akbar was first a politician. He used the *ulamā* and Sūfīs to his own ends in service of the power of the state - which meant his personal power.

Throughout the remainder of the Mughul Empire there was only a slight decline in the acceptance of other religions by the emperors until Aurangzīb's (r. 1658 - 1707) Islāmic orthodoxy prevailed over his family heritage of religious flexibility. He became quite hostile levying tax penalties on non-Muslims, and tearing down their temples. Meanwhile he was inflicting the usual purist prohibitions on drugs, alcohol, prostitution, and even music at court and the like. One may trace the rather rapid decline of the Mughul Empire from his reign.

At this time there emerged an interesting cycle in Muslim history that we see time and time again throughout its world, reaction! The Sūfīs had been flexible in their demands of converts. This inevitably lead to popular practices considerably distant from orthodox Islām. Ever present latent zealotry and religious conservatism eventually erupted into demands for reform and return to the pure Islām of the Companions. Reform began to get serious and sound modern with the protests of the Naqshbandī Shaykh Ahmad Sirhindī (1564 - 1624) and his later follower Shah Waliallah (1702-1763) both of whom lamented all the Sūfī/Hindu distortions of faith including the worship of Sūfī saints, and urged the return to pure Muslim values of early Islam. Not surprisingly, Sirhindī's position landed him in prison as he quarreled with Jahāngīr's liberalism.[74] Later, Shah Waliallah, living in a time more amenable to reform, placed the responsibility on the government to guide the people to proper belief, established the *sharī'a* as the basis of government, and created an Islamic state through and through. We will see similar thoughts from Mawlana Mawdūdī two centuries later. (See Appendix E)

Chapter 4

Meanwhile, Aurangzīb's son Bahādur Shāh I (r. 1707 - 1712) retreated somewhat from fundamentalist Islām just as new powers were entering the arena in force. They first appeared in 1498 when the Portuguese Vasco da Gama reached Calicut. In less than 200 years the Dutch, French and British came, either passing through to the Indies or to stay in the Subcontinent. At first they were innocent enough, but as was so often the case, the virulence of European colonialism became manifest. There was a sorting out of power and 'spheres of influence' resulting in an important British commercial and cultural presence. This presence became more irksome to both Hindu and Muslim Indians as time passed. The most significant reaction came with the eruption of the so called Sepoy Mutiny which rapidly transformed into a full-scale rebellion. The Sepoys were Indian soldiers employed by the British East India company. New rifles introduced in 1857 required the soldier to bite off the end of the paper cartridge to load it. Alas, the cartridges were greased with pork fat, an apparently offensive matter to Hindu and Muslim alike. They mutinied. However pork was only the trigger,[75] albeit a perfectly apt one. The military mutiny expanded into a general rebellion in northern India reflecting not simply the soldier's ethnic abhorrence of pork, but an already existing and widespread discontent with the British presence. Indians were being shamelessly exploited, corrupted, humiliated, proselytized, and disregarded by a thoroughly insulting British colonial arrogance. By 1859 the rebellion had been crushed. Reprisals of considerable savagery followed on demand of an 'offended' British public. In the end, the Mutiny[76] was more than the British East India Company could handle even with its highly competent company army. Thereafter, Her Majesty's Government took complete control of the company and all Indian colonial affairs. Shortly thereafter the last Mughul ruler, Bahādur Shāh II (r. 1837 - 1857) died exiled in Burma by the British. The Mughul dynasty was dead, and with it what was left of Indian independence, whether Hindu or Muslim.

The Mughul dynasty fell for a number of reasons. First, the Muslim invaders were too few to have an impact on the relatively large indigenous population, and Hinduism was just too resilient to be pushed aside by Islām no matter how attractive the Sūfī version. Thus, failure to convert the population made conquest superficial, and those who were converted were for the most part only half Muslim. The weakness was popular Islām. Second, the reform movement in this heterogenous Muslim culture for the most part merely generated discontent with resurgent, purist Islam and thereby weakened the whole religio-political structure. Third, though in the early centuries the Muslim fleet was the dominant maritime power in the area, the Mughuls were indifferent to a navy and thus their maritime trade was vulnerable to foreign interference. Fourth, the native commercial infrastructure was too weak to withstand the competition, intrusion and dominance of western colonial powers. Moreover, cheap labor discouraged the use of cost reducing machines, while a self-interested aristocracy was only interested in its own opulent lifestyle even as the cheap labor starved. What remained was a residue of bewilderment and discontent leading to a new episode of reformism which we shall encounter in the next chapter.

Now let us look at Muslim Southeast Asia, mainly today's Malaysia and Indonesia.[77] If one looks at a map of South and Southeast Asia one is immediately struck by the natural funnel formed by the Malay peninsula to the north and the island of Sumatra to the south. The Strait of Malacca between them is 500 miles long and eventually narrows to 25 miles from Malacca to Singapore. From Singapore it widens again but is so chocked with islands that one is always but a few miles from land before regaining the relatively open waters of the South China Sea. Here as in few other places on earth geography invites history.

Recall that at the very beginning Mecca was a trading center in pre-Islāmic Arabia and how goods were passed to Yemen for shipment to India and China. This trade, even as early as the seventh century found its way across the Arabian Sea to the western shores of India and beyond to China. Similarly, the Chinese were shipping goods the other way. The Strait of Malacca was the Southeast Asian highway linking the two worlds

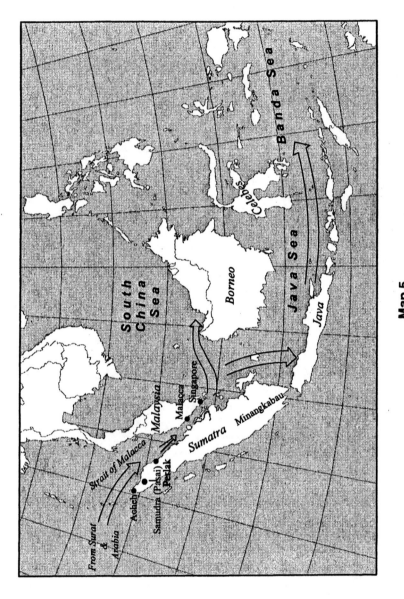

Map 5
Islām in Southeast Asia

and a natural area where traders would find profit in trans-shipping both ways. Thus Arab and Persian traders first appeared along the west coasts of India and in the Malacca Strait very early on. Interestingly enough, the coming of Islām changed very little with these business people. The traders were Muslims, yet they were relatively ineffective in spreading their beliefs in their coastal enclaves in India and Southeast Asia. Some scholars believe that this failure was because early Islām's austere message was not very appealing to the Hindus, Buddhists, and animists encountered. Indeed, it appears that Islām's real success did not begin till the arrival of the Sūfīs coming largely from the Subcontinent about 600 years later. It is thought that Sūfī traders and missionaries (though hard historical evidence is wanting for their timely appearance[78]) offered a version of Islām much more congenial and familiar to the region's masses and thus greatly facilitated conversion. Part of the evidence linking the source of Southeast Asian Islām to Muslim traders from coastal India and not to the Islāmization of the Subcontinent in general comes from their common legal school. Most Indian Muslims followed the Hanafī school, yet Southeast Asian Muslims were Shāfi'ī just like the west-coastal enclaves at the time of interest for us. (This followed from their more direct links to the Middle Eastern Shāfi'ī areas rather than Afghanistan.[79]) The earliest converts were local rulers hoping to cut into the mercantile wealth of the highly regarded Muslim merchants in their port cities. With their conversion they could more easily enlist their new Muslim friends in trade competition with their neighbors. Yet, even in these cases, beyond city limits Sūfī influence and religion for the most part remained inconsequential for several centuries. And here we begin to see a historic evolution that differs considerably from that which we have seen in India, for the driving engine here was trade by sea. In India it was conquest by land. However, the net consequences for 20th - 21st century Islām are very similar, about which more later.

The monsoon winds in the Indian Ocean and the seasonal trade winds in the South China Sea brought Muslim traders east and Chinese west to the Malacca Strait and Sumatra. Here the first Islāmic trading kingdom of Acheh developed on the island's northwest coast during the 13th century. Here also, and later in other ports in the area, goods were brought in not only from China and the Middle East but from local sources, i.e., 'the Indies'. They were then exchanged for transshipment - silk, damask, satin, brocade, incense, ceramics and all sorts of pottery, sandalwood, pepper, spices (nutmeg, mace, cloves) west to India, Persia, and Yemen, while glass objects, precious stones, fine woods, spices, and Indian cotton textiles went to China in what one early Portuguese adventurer described as virtually a vast fair. "Goods from all over the east are found here; goods from all over the west are sold here."[80] In return the Malacca Strait states received much needed food stuffs and the wealth and influence that commerce always brings.

Marco Polo in 1292 and Ibn Batutta in 1345 both testify to Islām's presence, at least in nearby Perlak and Samudra. Their accounts are the earliest reliable mention of Islām in Southeast Asia. Though a healthy commerce existed there before Muslim traders arrived, it is clear that their appearance accelerated matters and added greatly to the regions prosperity. Trade, political power, and the spread of Islām cycled from Acheh and Samudra (Pasai) on Sumatra, to Malacca across the Strait on the Malay peninsula, then back to Acheh over the two hundred fifty years from 1300 to 1550. The considerable commercial and military activity in the area also included other city states and their rulers, yet no ruler, secular or religious, stands out the way Bābur and Akbar do for the Subcontinent. This may be accounted for because the hegemony of each of these states was relatively limited in time and space no matter the appellation of "Empire" or "Kingdom" frequently applied to some of them. Indeed, individually and collectively they remind one more of the tribal milieu of the early 19th century North American Indians than any coherent empire such as that which existed on the Subcontinent. This individuality and competition was also taking place among Muslim states regardless of the theoretical unity of the *umma*.

How did the area become Muslim and why did the *umma* fail to fully develop, or at least fail to prevail? The ruling elite in Southeast Asia were usually the first to be converted and become the seed for future Muslim dominance in the community. The masses were later brought around and more or less converted, first in the port cities, then along the coasts, then into the interior. However, the more remote from the ports the more pre-Islāmic Hindu, Buddhist, and animistic religious beliefs were encountered, and the longer it took for Islām to penetrate. Indeed, it is clear that traditional Islām has never dominated the Muslim societies of Southeast Asia. The practice of Islām has always been in its popular form existing in comfortable company with its predecessors. Social authority in the villages, particularly in Sumatra, was often divided between the political, secular, and religious interests with the village headman exercising as much influence as the mullah or sultan. The headman represented the local, pre-Islamic social/political tradition (*adat*) that was incorporated into popular Islam.[81] However, even with the harmony usually found in such an arrangement some tension did exist with the Muslim traditionalists that from time to time erupted into open conflict with the ruling power, Muslim or otherwise. Today these eruptions are viewed through the grossly distorting lens of a globally emergent, militant Islām.

Why the absence of a strong and cohering *umma*? Because Islām was not so orthodox as elsewhere in the Muslim world. This was because of the elasticity of Sūfī demands for conversion which led to the retention of considerable portions of the old faith, all of which tended to dilute any sense of a unified community in the archipelago. That they were Muslim they would passionately assert; yet in the same moment they would pilgrimage to the tombs of non-Muslim saints even to the point of equating it to the *hajj*, believe in spirits and the most outlandish magic, conduct marriages in the old way,[82] and considerably bend sharī'a inheritance law. Accordingly, almost from the very beginning, the more traditional Muslims were scandalized and forever trying to enforce 'true' Islāmic practices. They have never succeeded, though the struggle has been virtually continuous for 600 years.

There was a second reason that Southeast Asian Muslims remained 'tribalized' and that was because their leaders were as much interested in the material benefits of conversion as the spiritual. Thus commercial and political motives more or less

Chapter 4

equaled Muslim missionary zeal in spreading Islām slowly but surely even into the 20th century.

A seminal event for Southeast Asian Islām was the arrival of the Portuguese in the Indian Ocean. Vasco da Gama rounded the Cape of Good Hope in 1497 and reached Calicut in May of 1498 where he was treated with the barest civility before his return to Portugal. Next, Pedro Alvarez Cabral arrived in 1500 and was greeted more aggressively than da Gama and returned the favor by bombarding the town. Da Gama returned in 1502-3 and decisively defeated Calicut's Muslim defenders as Portugal continued its ambitious and brutal economic and religious penetration of the Indies. Diogo Lopes de Sequeira was the first to sail beyond India arriving at Malacca in 1509. The local Muslim leaders had heard of the Portuguese and wanted no part of their trade competition nor religious proselytizing. After a failed attempt on de Sequeira's life, his fleet departed, but not for long. In 1510 Afonso d'Albuquerque destroyed Calicut, conquered Goa on the west coast of India, crossed the Bay of Bengal and took Malacca in July of 1511. This drumbeat of a seemingly endless stream of Portuguese warriors announced a new era; Portugal and the West had indeed arrived. And with this arrival came a new source of Muslim discontent in the area. *Hajjs* had been returning from the pilgrimage disturbed by the lax and foreign Islāmic practices of the natives, but now they were also faced with a very aggressive Christian confrontation as well. This set the stage for more than 400 years of conflict leading to the emergence of national identities and independence while leaving behind bitter memories of Western imperialism.

Petty kings and sultans continued their thousand-year-old struggle for power in the stew of the Southeast Asian archipelago as the 16th century opened and the first Europeans appeared.[83] The Portuguese introduced a whole new political/social/religious dynamic when they sailed in and took possession of Malacca in 1511. Ironically, when the Portuguese took Malacca they at once created a reaction that forced Muslim power into new areas and actually helped spread Islām further throughout the region.[84] Acheh regained influence as well as Johore near modern day Singapore and the Mataram state controlling much of the island

70

of Java. While the Portuguese were exploiting the Indies Islām spread afield reaching parts of Borneo, the Celebes, and the Philippines by the 17th century.

Portugal's European monopoly in the spice trade eventually provoked the Dutch to enter the Indies about a century later. Between 1605 and 1640 they increased their presence, often in alliance with local Muslim powers until they took Malacca from the Portugese in 1641 and thereafter became dominant in the "Dutch East Indies" until the mid 20th century. However, local political ambition remained as rulers seeking advantage over their neighbors, sometimes even within their own kingdom, continued to make alliances with the Dutch for control of home-grown trouble makers.

The trouble-makers would be familiar to us today; they were Muslim purists expressing a host of objections to the way Islām was being practiced, and as time passed, to the presence of foreign domination. The Dutch East India Company founded in 1602 exercised enormous control over the Indies much as the British East India Company would in India. And like the British they were mainly interested in commercial exploitation with everything else secondary, though military, political, and religious issues could not be separated. European competition in the area eventually eliminated all players but the Dutch and British who agreed by treaty in 1824 upon spheres of interest, a matter portending the British and French Sykes-Picot agreement almost a century later in the Middle East. And as in the Middle East, no one bothered to ask the local population what they wanted.

In Minangkabau in central Sumatra the growing oppression of foreign dominance was exacerbated by the economic turmoil that followed changing market demands for pepper, gold, and coffee. Three *hajjis* returning from the Meccan pilgrimage in 1803 and inspired by the Wahhābīs started the Padri reform movement appealing to those displaced by the turmoil. Not entirely unexpectedly this reformist/fundamentalist movement broke into factions. Meanwhile, the village headmen refused the reformer's exhortations and called for Dutch help. Eventually the movement expanded from religious reform to include anti-imperialism, and went from preaching to violence. The violence was justified by declaration of *jihād* and was directed to uncooperative and apostate Muslims as well as to the Dutch. The heretofore influential Shattārī Sūfīs were particular targets because of what the zealots believed to be their religious laxness.[85] The Padri War was not suppressed until 1838. Elsewhere in Sumatra the Achehnese would rebel and fight the Dutch in there own war from 1873 to 1910.[86] Additional conflicts took place in Java, only with local twists. There were more than a dozen rebellions between 1820 and 1888. Frequently local elites looked to the Dutch for support in maintaining the status quo, i.e., retaining popular Islāmic practices and what little political power they had.

Thus, the dynamic in Southeast Asia was an exceedingly complex mixture of Islāmic revivalism, anti-imperialism, and civil war. Though for the most part these conflicts were internal Islāmic affairs, they did coincide with the rise of the West and could not escape being related, particularly as a Muslim reaction to political impotence. The net result by mid 20th century was the further spread of Islām, the ejection of European colonialists, and all the while the retention, for the most part, of popular Islāmic practice.

Chapter 5

The Twentieth Century

"Rule, Britannia! Britannia, rule the waves." This 1740 verse by James Thomson could have been the epitaph of the Ottoman Empire, and indeed, of the independence of every Muslim state on earth. By 1890 Britannia ruled the waves, and effectively, much of the Middle East as well, with a little help from the French, and an occasional distraction from Russia.

The growing economic power of Europe, especially in England and France, coupled with rapid advances in technology, fueled imperial ambition in the 18th and 19th centuries that swamped a Muslim world too conservative to keep up. The lands of the Middle East were becoming objects to be manipulated or pushed aside if insufficiently accommodating to the particular European power appearing at their doorstep; they were pawns in someone else's chess game.

In 1798 Napoleon landed in Egypt hoping to strangle England's lifeline to her empire in India. An unsuccessful expedition from Egypt into Syria and Lord Nelson's appearance off Alexandria persuaded him of the futility of his design, and he withdrew to France. This episode was the first clear strike of the death knell of the Ottoman Empire and Muslim influence in the world. It focused European interest on an area largely overlooked up to that time; scholars discovered the antiquities of ancient Egypt at the same time politicians and merchants started considering a canal at Suez and acquiring bases and treaties in the Persian Gulf area. All of this was taking place through a century that saw three wars between the Ottomans and Russia, while increased pressure in the Balkans gradually forced Ottoman withdrawal from Greece, Wallachia, Bosnia, Herzegovina, Serbia, and Bulgaria. In 1875 the Ottomans went bankrupt followed seven months later by Egypt. A weak economy and second rate technology could not support the inflated Empire; it shrank and was kept from collapsing only because England and France wanted it as a buffer to the ambitious Russians.

The exploitation of Egypt and other Middle Eastern countries by England and France was greatly facilitated by what at the time appeared to be harmless concessions to European business interests. The Venetians, Portuguese, Russians, French, and English had at one time or another, beginning in 1453 with the Genoese, obtained commercial concessions, called Capitulations, from the Ottomans that gave extraterritorial privileges to their nationals living and working within the Empire. These privileges included exemption from Ottoman laws and taxes. The eventual problem was that ambitious Europeans could exploit Ottoman resources and yet keep the created wealth for themselves. Over time this led to effective foreign control of the Ottoman economy and the bankruptcy we have noted. This humiliating control by foreigners was also an important element in inspiring nationalistic elements in Egypt and Turkey.

As if things weren't going bad enough for the Muslims of the Middle East, a new current was added to the tide. Zionism was a movement working for the establishment of a national homeland in Palestine for the Jewish people. It originated in the 16th and 17th centuries, but became significant only at the end of the 19th century when a combination of growing anti-Semitism, especially in Russia, Ottoman weakness, and European strength and imperial ambition made the concept potentially viable. The time was right.

Theodore Herzl, an Austrian journalist, had been thinking for years about a homeland for the Jews. He originally believed that Jews would be best served by assimilation, but when he saw that this wasn't going to happen he organized the first Zionist Congress in 1897 to discuss a homeland. It was about this time that the movement became political and was beginning to be called "Zionism." The West looked favorably upon Herzl's ideas even if the Ottoman Sultan did not.

A small Jewish immigration into Palestine was beginning with the financial assistance of the Rothschild family. The immigration rate picked up with the continuing encouragement of the succeeding Zionist Congresses and another pogrom in Russia in 1905, but the opening of World War I momentarily stopped it.

However, eventually the war turned out to be more of an impetus than barrier to the Zionist cause. Three war related factors pushed this tide, the final collapse of Ottoman Empire thus removing any organized political resistance to Zionist plans, the full maturation of British and French imperial power where they felt complete freedom to dispose of the Middle East as they saw fit and without much appeal to the wishes of indigenous populations (as nicely exemplified by the Sykes-Picot Agreement, about which more in a moment), and the need of the Allied Powers to bring as much force against the Central Powers as possible.

The British Cabinet was working very hard to get both the United States and Russia into the war. Russia had been in, but the trauma of the first years of combat and its own political disarray had greatly weakened its effort. It was thought that the population of influential Jews in both countries might move their respective governments to join the war effort if the British government supported creation of a Jewish homeland. Accordingly, on November 2, 1917, the British foreign secretary Arthur Balfour sent a letter containing what has ever since been known as the Balfour Declaration to Lord Rothschild, a leader of the British Jewish community, saying, "His Majesty's Government view with favour the establishment in Palestine of a national home for the Jewish people, and will use their best endeavours to facilitate the achievement of this object, it being clearly understood that nothing shall be done which may prejudice the civil and religious rights of existing non-Jewish communities in Palestine ..." The proviso for protection of the "rights of... non-Jewish communities" seems naive at best, and the Palestinian population was anxious from the start.

It is not difficult to understand why Arab and Middle Eastern nations today look at the West with a very cautious eye at best. The Balfour Declaration was an arbitrary action taken unilaterally

Chapter 5

by Great Britain and supported by her allies. It was clearly motivated by self interest, albeit a self interest with some altruistic intent and which seems to have been rather a cut or two above the usual dealings in international affairs of the time. Nevertheless, the Arabs saw this Declaration and its subsequent execution as a betrayal of their rights by the Allied Powers, as indeed it was. But the Balfour Declaration was only half of a double barrel blast at the Middle East, and there was no mitigating element in the other shot.

Earlier, while Britain and France were trying to coordinate their Middle Eastern war efforts without unduly upsetting each other, they came to an agreement in 1916 through their ministers Messrs. Sykes and Picot identifying their mutually acceptable 'spheres of influence.' This is a polite diplomatic term for dividing up the pie. The pie was the Middle East, the French slice was Lebanon and Syria, and the British slice was Iraq and Transjordan. Palestine was to be nominally under international control, but the British were to have the Mandate. Since no one could see a use for the interior of Arabia, it was left to the Arabians, who, unbeknownst to all, were sitting atop a large part of the world's oil reserves. While enlisting the Arabian leader Sharif Hussein to help fight the Turks the English and French encouraged the misconception that after the war the Middle East north of Arabia would be his to rule. The details of the Sykes-Picot Agreement were kept secret. When they later became known the Arabs felt that once again they had been betrayed by the West. This double dealing is depicted in the very entertaining 1962 film, "Lawrence of Arabia."

Wars have often been the signal of historic change, but rarely in history has a war marked so pervasive and deep a change in the world as World War I and its organic sequel, World War II. The end of World War I marked the end of one age and the inchoate beginning of another. The tragic slaughter and profound disillusionment of the West in World War I, and the awesome and horrendous technologies produced by World War II are important but not key to the issues we are following here. In our focus we find that shortly after World War I the Ottoman Empire is no more, and that the "Young Turk" faction is coming to power and fundamentally changing the political and social structure of the nation now called "Turkey." We find that out of the geopolitical machinations of France and Britain a swarm of nations have been created in the Middle East. We find that not only are the seeds of the nation of Israel well planted, but thoroughly nourished by the Balfour Declaration and the subsequent League of Nations Mandate. And we also find that a new mineral treasure has been discovered that will become the most significant determinant of Middle Eastern history for at least a century to come.

Oil. The full fruition of the industrial revolution would be unthinkable without it, and without it the dominance of the West might be problematic. It is literally and figuratively the essential fuel for the engine of commerce and industry. Its impact has been felt by everyone from the common man in his daily affairs to heads of state planning the destiny of empires. Oil changed the world beginning with its first commercial production in Romania in 1857 and in the United States in 1859. Petroleum energy, with a respectful nod to coal, transformed transportation, heating, and lighting that otherwise hadn't changed significantly in thousands of years. It was and is the energy bridge to the future. Oil will drive the planet's civilization until nuclear or solar take over.

Of all the avenues of influence of oil one may argue that it was with the military that oil's potential was first fully appreciated.[87] Wisely anticipating the inevitable, the British navy at the end of the 19th century decided to convert from coal fired steam propulsion to petroleum and thereby double the efficiency of its warships. However, the British Admiralty was not keen on relying for its lifeblood on the United States or Russia who between them accounted for 90% of the world's production at the time. Fortunately, there was an alternative. (Indeed, without this alternative one might argue that the British navy's supremacy through the next half century might never have occurred. Think of what that would have meant in the two world wars!) The British had been sniffing around the Middle East for possible sources of petroleum that they could control. A 1901 oil concession with Persia finally paid off in 1908 when oil was discovered in the southwestern part of the country. Oil has since been discovered in Iraq in 1927, in Saudi Arabia in 1936, in

Kuwait in 1938, and in the several minor countries of the Gulf region so that by the last decade of the 20th century more than 20% of the worlds petroleum production and 66% of its reserves are located there.

The Middle Eastern oil discoveries of the 1930s didn't become fully developed until after World War II in the 1950s and 1960s. The immense wealth and political leverage that came with the development of this resource were synergistically coupled to the fall of Western imperialism and the rise of Muslim nationalism.

Turkey, representing the core of the old Ottoman Empire, was the first of the Muslim states to break free of the West. Paradoxically, it managed to do this by becoming the most western-like of any Muslim country. It also had the advantage of half a millennium of imperial tradition; it was accustomed to ruling itself, not in being ruled by others as was the case in much of the rest of the Muslim world. Moreover, it was preparing for independence well before the Ottoman collapse. In the late 19th century an educated middle class of professionals developed that was dissatisfied with Ottoman incompetence and corruption, and eventually forced the Sultan to institute reforms. The organizational force, as has so often been the case in modern times, was the young military officer corps. This active revolutionary group, known as the Young Turks, had among its members Mustafa Kemal who later was responsible for the transformation of the wreckage of the Ottoman Empire into the modern Turkish state we know today. His program, carried out in the 1920s and 1930s, was breathtaking in its scope, and amazing in its success; he replaced the Arabic script with a modified Roman alphabet and script, abolished the Sultanate and Caliphate, closed traditional religious schools, abolished polygamy, instituted secular Western legal codes, abolished or discouraged Muslim forms of dress including the fez and veiling of women, introduced the Gregorian calendar, and ordered all families to have family names as in the West. In accordance with this last act he took the family name of Atatürk, meaning "Chief Turk" or "Father of Turks," and has since been known as Kemal Atatürk.

In the process of building a new nation he managed to keep the West, and Russia, from partitioning Turkey, to keep Greece from biting off a big chunk after World War I, and later to make peace with Greece. Thereafter, Turkey continued to modernize and provide a modest prosperity for its people even without the benefit of the prodigious oil revenues accruing to many of its Muslim neighbors. Of particular note is the fact that Turkey has remained Muslim and more or less politically stable, apparently in spite of its substantial Westernization. And thereby lies a very interesting tale, especially with the apparent re-emergence of Islāmic political influence.

Atatürk's problem was how to save a virtually helpless post-World War I Turkey from the voracity of its neighbors and recent enemies. Russia had for centuries hungered after Turkey and its control of the exit from the Black Sea, but fortunately Russia was preoccupied at the time with her Communist revolution. Greece was not so preoccupied and saw a real possibility for the reestablishment of at least some of her classical empire across the 'wine dark sea' in Anatolia. Britain and France had their own imperial interests that would not be good for the prostrate Ottomans but did leave some slack for an independent Turkey under the right circumstances. Thus the hunger of its neighbors and enemies could be managed - if Turkey were to put up a sufficiently stiff resistence. This is what Atatürk did, and he furthered guaranteed Turkey's independence by forcing his people to adopt the Western ways that had so obviously been successful with Turkey's enemies. His method was to break the grip of conservative Islām on Turkish society and arouse the people to a strong sense of nationalism.

The reforms noted earlier were carried out between 1922 and 1935. Superficially it appeared that Islām had been socially neutralized and reduced to private practice in the home. Nothing, however, could have been further from the truth. What was really going on was a spotty control of religion affecting different parts of the society differently. First there was Turkey's religious heterogeneity; up to 30% of the population was Alevi Shī'a, second there was a large minority of Kurds, possibly 20%, professing both Sunnī and Shī'ī Islām, and third and most importantly, the population at the time was more than 80% rural living in small remote villages and practicing a popular Islām only loosely connected with the orthodox faith of the Caliph and the *ulamā*. Thus when decrees were handed down, the remote majority merely nodded ascent and continued on largely unnoticed and unhindered.

Sūfism was the popular Islām being practiced in the Turkish hinterland, and for the most part it was of the Nakshibendi order. As so often happens in Islām, the peasants bearing the burdens of a tough life looked for religious comfort not to the cold formalities of submission to Allāh but to the more personal ministering of Sūfī masters and their followers. The Nakshibendi were neither mystical nor theatrical nor radical, they were, however, notably realistic in assessing the social and political environment and flexible in adapting to it. Thus they laid low, and even with their official abolition by the Kemalists after they supported a Kurdish rebellion in 1925, they were carriers of the spirit of Islām in the hinterland.

Islām was also alive among the Kurds in Eastern Turkey even if they were severely manhandled after their 1925 revolt. The same was true among the Alevi Shīa who supported the government in suppressing the Sunnī Kurds, because they feared them.

Matters remained relatively stable between the Turkish state and Islām for the remainder of Atatürk's life, but when he died in 1938 pressure began building for a release from the prevailing one-party rule. In 1950 other parties were permitted to seek power. This political liberalization inspired politicians to seek new votes in the villages thus tapping the reservoir of latent Islāmic culture in the countryside. Though Turkey has remained a secular state for the succeeding half century, a very interesting political phenomenon has taken place; Islām has reemerged but not in the self-absorbed, self-righteous, West-hating form frequently seen in Muslim extremism elsewhere. The moderate positions taken by the several Turkish Islāmic parties has worked its way past several military coups and bypassed and neutralized the Islāmic radicals. The Turks are now more comfortable with their fusion of faith and nationality and may well provide a successful model for other Muslim states.

The period between the World Wars saw Western influence dissolve and nationalist movements arise in many of the Muslim proto-states of the Middle East. The League of Nations legitimized the Balfour Declaration and the Sykes-Picot Agreement by substituting Mandate responsibility for the *fait accompli*. From the legal point of view this meant that Britain and France could do what they pleased with the Middle East, but neither the League of Nations, nor Britain, nor France had bothered much to consult with the Middle Eastern peoples. Moreover, it seemed that nothing could control the tide of Jewish immigration into Palestine, especially after 1933 when Adolph Hitler came to power in Germany. This situation was a constant problem for Great Britain, because the Palestinians were becoming increasingly unhappy with the virtual invasion of their land by the Jews, and the Jews were reacting to Palestinian resistance.

The British with their hands full trying to keep control of events in Palestine finally concluded in 1937 that their Mandate was unworkable, and accordingly proposed the partition of Palestine. No one liked this idea, neither the Palestinians nor the Jews who both objected to the proposed boundaries. The hiatus of World War II only made matters more acute, and the British eventually turned the whole mess over to the United Nations which also recommended partition in 1947. The State of Israel was proclaimed in 1948 when the British left.

The independence of Transjordan went relatively smoothly given its physical linkage to Palestine. Transjordan annexed the West Bank (territory extending 15 to 30 miles west from the Jordan River and the Dead Sea) including half of Jerusalem, and changed its name in 1949 to the Hashemite Kingdom of Jordan, or less formally, simply Jordan. During this time national identities developed in Jordan and the other new states of the Middle East contributing to the isolation of the Palestinians from their Arab brothers. After the United Nations permitted the State of Israel to come into existence in 1948 a brief war ratified the fact, and the Palestinians were more or less left adrift without consistent, long term support for their cause in the international community. Whatever was done by the other Arab states was rather episodic and often motivated by interests other than Palestinian welfare.

Elsewhere Muslims had had enough of European control and began fighting for their independence. Although clearly outgunned, they were troublesome enough to eventually succeed. Sometimes complete independence came in stages with an initial period of rule by a monarch appointed by the British, as in Iraq and Egypt. Sometimes there was a long, relatively trouble free incubation before independence, as in Transjordan. Sometimes there was a long drawn out guerilla war as in Algeria. In any case, independence came, even if only nominally at first, to Egypt in 1922, Iraq and Saudi Arabia in 1932, Lebanon in 1943, Syria and Transjordan in 1946, Libya in 1951, Morocco and Tunisia in 1956, and Algeria in 1962.

Meanwhile, Persia hadn't escaped the attention of Britain, or Russia either. Disastrous dynastic conflicts had virtually destroyed the Persian infrastructure and greatly facilitated the growth of foreign influence. Throughout the 19th century British and Russian commercial and geopolitical interests manipulated Persia with the same disregard for its people as the British and French were to do later with the rest of the Middle East through the instruments of the Balfour Declaration and the Sykes-Picot Agreement. Britain viewed Persia as a very important communications link with its Indian Empire, and later as a vital source of oil. Russia, always interested in expanding its Empire, especially where there was potential for access to warm water ports, looked longingly at Persia (and not for the last time) at the same time that it forced its commercial interests. Persia's savage and corrupt Qājār dynasty was overthrown by a military coup in 1921 bringing Rezā Khān to power. Rezā Khān was supported by the Majles (National Consultative Assembly, i.e., Parliament) and the mullahs (religious leaders) who, fearing Persia might be transformed into a secular state with the rejection of many Muslim customs as was happening in Turkey under Kamel Atatürk, eagerly supported his assumption of the crown in 1925 and he became Shāh Rezā Pahlavī.

In the process of making the country more independent and

competitive with the West, the Shāh eventually brought about many of the reforms that the mullahs feared; Iran (for so it had been officially renamed in 1935) became a secular state with education and law largely taken out of the hands of the mullahs, Western style higher education was greatly encouraged, and traditional Muslim dress codes for women were abolished. The seeds of the 1979 revolution were sown. There remained only the nourishment of tyranny and poverty to bring them to fruition.

The 20th century evolution of Muslim societies in South and Southeast Asia has been in response to at least three problems: first, freeing themselves from European domination; second, securely establishing themselves in the modern world; and third, dealing with the ongoing internal struggle of finding an acceptable form of Islām. The first two are for the most part external affairs in politics and economics. The third reflects the deeper and more universal historic problem for Islām of finding its identity, especially in the context of a rapidly changing world. This search for identity, for acceptable norms, has been a constant struggle from the beginning. What Christianity worked out in a few centuries, principally in the Reformation, has continued for 1400 years in Islām. Because at its core it is so naturally conservative, it has struggled with change and novelty from the seventh century Khārijites to the twentieth century Al-Qaeda. Nowhere has this struggle been more characteristic than with the novelty of South and Southeast Asian Islām and its popular solutions.

We pick up the story in the Indian Subcontinent with the Sepoy Mutiny. Hindus and Muslims alike were increasingly intolerant of the colonial yoke. After the putdown of the Mutiny in 1859 some Muslims began to plan for a long struggle correctly assessing that a direct confrontation with the British was fruitless. One very important result was the establishment of the Deobandi madrasa to train *ulamā* in the teachings of orthodox Islām.

The word "madrasa" has had almost as much attention in the West in recent years as *"jihād"* and *"sharī'a"*, and is equally misunderstood. Madrasas are not "jihād factories"[88] any more than Catholic schools in Northern Ireland are training terrorists. Though some graduates in each case have gone on to become terrorists, only in very rare instances has a madrasa been hijacked for villainous purposes. "Madrasa" is a general term with a meaning too broad in time and place to be meaningfully painted with a single stroke.[89] "Madrasa" is Arabic for a place of study, a school, and more particularly, a religious school. It first appeared at least as early as the 11th century as a kind of college for advanced religious learning that prepared individuals to be imāms, jurists of the *sharī'a,* judges *(qadīs),* and the like. It was similar to today's Christian Bible college or theological seminary. It was intended to produce members of the religious establishment, the *ulamā.* Its inspiration was to preserve the learning and values of pure Islām untainted by innovation *(bid'a).*This role continues today, but it has expanded to include elementary education of children as young as six. Nevertheless, the object is to teach the student about his religion; all else is secondary.

Madrasas have traditionally been privately financed, though there are occasional exceptions. They charge no tuition and offer free room and board. School supplies, clothing, and 'spending money' are also sometimes provided. With these inducements to a free education it is not surprising that madrasas attract those who are seeking an education but are too poor to afford government or public schools. Madrasas are found throughout the Muslim world from Morocco and Mali to Turkey, Afghanistan, Pakistan, India, Indonesia, the USA, and Europe. However, notwithstanding their free tuition, only a fraction of Muslim youths attend them: less than 3 % in Egypt,[90] and 10 to 20 % in Indonesia.[91]

Naturally enough the curriculum has always largely focused on religious subjects. The Qur'ān was memorized, the *hadīth* studied, and the jurisprudence of the various religious legal schools analyzed. Sometimes other studies were offered like medicine and later a few trades. Often, particularly beyond the Middle East, classical Arabic, Persian, and one of the local vernacular languages such as Urdu were studied. This language fluency imparted an important sense of community to the students and 'graduates.' It also facilitated the deeper understanding of the original Arabic texts. For the first several hundred years of madrasa history curricula were informally structured and presented, and 'graduation' might consist merely of a license from a particular scholar under whom the student studied.

Rather striking changes occurred in the late 19th century as some madrasas began to acquire a formal institutional structure and experiment with broadening the curriculum. The most important of these new schools was the Deoband madrasa founded in 1867 in the town of Deoband northeast of Delhi.[92] It had its own buildings, including a good library, and it was not affiliated with any mosque. Deoband education was noted for its emphasis on the study of the *hadīth* and its loose association with several Sūfī orders, particularly the Chistīs. Its curriculum lasted six years (ten years when first organized) and was carefully structured including periodic examinations and a formal graduation with a diploma. Non-religious curricula varied from school to school and could include computer science, general science, and history.[93] Deobandis took a reformist but non-confrontational position to resist British and Hindu influences on Islāmic beliefs and practices. Deobandi madrasas were so successful that by 1900 there were more than three dozen in northern India. There were 8934 Deobandi madrasas by 1967.[94] This number, incidently, clearly reflects the expanded admission policy to include children.

Deobandis have always been conservative, and this conservatism, clearly in reaction to Hindu influences, was thought necessary to protect the faith and restore the believer to God's favor. At the same time it ran counter to Muslim popular practices cherished in the Subcontinent and to modernistic trends beginning to dominate the world's cultures. On the whole one cannot escape the conclusion that appeals to conservative Islāmic purity have been largely a failure even if a considerable source of angst in the West. Simultaneously, however, conservatism has not served the Muslim community well. Instead of opting for the more modern Western education espoused by the British, Muslim focus on religious education in the Deobandi madrases and elsewhere eventually left them without the means of integrating into the modern world. On the other hand, Hindus readily accepted British education, and it was not long before Hindus dominated in holding commercial, professional, and administrative posts and businesses. The tables had been completely turned from the days of the high Mughul period. The situation was worse in the relative backwater of Bengal in the most easterly part of the Subcontinent. The net result was that Muslims often became second class citizens, again particularly in Bengal. One Muslim observer noted, "In Bengal, the landlord is Hindu, the peasant Muslim. The money lender is Hindu, the client is Muslim. The jailor is Hindu, the prisoner is Muslim. The magistrate is Hindu, the accused is Muslim."[95]

Throughout India hostile opposition was widespread and frequent but more or less manageable. With the passage of time it became less manageable and more burdensome. At first the British resisted, then tried to compromise, then under the impact of the two World Wars resigned themselves to Indian independence. Mahatma Gandhi represented the aspirations of the majority Hindus while Mohammad Ali Jinnah led the Muslim minority. Throughout this time it was growing obvious that Indian independence would also entail partition of the Subcontinent into Hindu and Muslim nations. This was made explicit in March 1940 when Jinnah and the Muslim League[96] called for creation of a separate Muslim state to be named "Pakistan."[97] Matters got worse as the Indian National Congress and the Muslim League failed to reconcile their differences. Mutual suspicion and recriminations escalated, and a state of virtual civil war existed from 1945 to 1947. Independence from Britain occurred on August 15, 1947. Partition immediately followed with a staggering transfer of population, perhaps 12 million in all, Hindus leaving the northwest and Bengal, and Muslims coming from elsewhere in the Subcontinent to the two Pakistan states, east and west. Some estimate that as many as 500,000 to 1,000,000 were also killed in the accompanying rioting before things were sorted out. Though East and West Pakistan became overwhelmingly Muslim, India remained heterogenous with those staying behind constituting the world's third largest Muslim population. Although freedom of religion is part of the Indian constitution, agitators on both sides have continued to assault and kill each other; and tension with Pakistan remains perennial.

Pakistan's 97% Muslim population might lead one to think that religious strife would be a thing of the past, but this has not turned out to be the case. First there was political instability as secular and sectarian issues were dealt with. Fundamentalists wanted an Islāmic state under the *sharī'a*, others opted for a Muslim country under a more secular law. The classic struggle of Islām's theoretical belief in the identity of religion and politics and the historical reality of their separation was once again being worked out. Several regime changes and three constitutions have not yet solved the problem. And now we have the recent involvement of Al Qaeda and the Taliban from across the boarder in Afghanistan that has increased pressure on the president, General Pervez Musharraf, to denounce his Western (American) ties. Furthermore, from the very beginning there was a natural political/social instability with a nation formed of two desperate parts, East and West Pakistan.

It was inevitable that Muslims in East Pakistan (the old Indian Bengal and now Bangladesh) would come to a parting of the ways from their brothers in West Pakistan, since they differed in so many ways from geographic isolation, to culture, to practice of Islām. First came the problem at Independence and Partition in 1947. East and West Pakistan were separated by a thousand miles of intervening Indian territory, every foot of which was hostile to the Muslim separatists. Maintaining national coherence in a situation of such dispersal would be a challenge in the best of circumstances. But the circumstances were rather the poorest, not the best. Recall that in the 12th century many conversions, especially in the Bengal area were of low caste Hindus seeking the egalitarianism of Islām; thus the motivation was as much social/economic as religious. And the resultant popular Islāmic practices allowed by the Sūfī missionaries were often very Hindu-like. Particularly striking yet typical was the widespread Muslim worship of the Hindu god Oladevi, called by Muslims, Olabibi, the deity for protection from cholera. Such practices conflicted with the more conventional Islām in the northwest of the Subcontinent and contributed to the eventual schism. In Bengal there was also a very strong attachment to Bangla, the local language they jealously guarded and valued,[98] whereas in the

87

northwest, Persian/Arabic fused with Hindi to give Urdu, a language spiritedly rejected by the Bengalese even as it was forced on them. When the two Pakistans were formed, lack of skilled and trained professionals in East Pakistan required their importation from West Pakistan. Thus, Bengalis once again experienced being governed by 'foreigners' and were made second class citizens in their own land - this time by their own co-religionists. Affairs worsened as economic development in the east lagged that experienced in West Pakistan in the 1960s. The situation was impossible to maintain, and in March 1971 after years of tension and conflict East Pakistan (Bangladesh) declared its independence. By the end of the civil war perhaps as many as one million East Pakistanis had been killed by West Pakistanis attempting to suppress the rebellion. Success came only with the intervention of India the following December.

The new country, now the world's fourth most populous Muslim land, has turned out to be something of a surprise. Bangladesh is a very densely populated, very poor country. Its population is about 7/8s Muslim and 1/8 Hindu. It has had a politically rocky time since independence with governments alternating between the military and the non-military. All, however, have at least pretended to respect the constitution. The constitution is interesting for its rejection of extremist Islām, indeed, the original 1972 document described Bangladesh as a "secular" state. In 1977 religious feelings caused the word "secular" to be changed to, "absolute trust and faith in the Almighty Allah",[99] and in 1988 the Eighth Amendment to the Constitution was passed declaring an "Islāmic Way of Life."[100] Otherwise, the country has steadfastly resisted attempts to make the land a *sharī'a*-based Islāmic state. These attempts have become increasingly violent in recent years, possibly reflecting fundamentalism's frustration with its failure to get *sharī'a* courts installed, and the continued practice of popular Islām by the people.

Southeast Asia (for our purposes modern Malaysia and Indonesia) may be the most interesting part of our 20th century survey. Today (2007) about two-thirds of Malaysia's 25 million people are Muslim. As with so many Muslim countries in the 20th century, they do not seem to know quite where they fit. Fundamentalists have been pushing to make Malaysia an Islāmic state under *sharī'a* law, while the majority are content to retain the status quo as a secular state with Islām merely designated the official religion. Since Malay ethnic identity is closely bound to Islām, all native Malays are by law Muslim. The remaining third of the population is religiously distributed among Buddhists, Hindus, Christians, and Traditional believers. A certain success has been achieved in assimilating these minorities as reflected in the numerous religious holidays that are also official holidays, for example, the Buddhist Wesak Day, the Hindu Deepavali, Christian Christmas, and the Traditional Spring Festival. However, these religions and their practitioners sit uneasily in the state that only reluctantly accepts them. There are two parallel legal systems, the secular based on English law, and the *sharī'a*. The *sharī'a* applies only to Muslim citizens, and only in matters of family and religious law. Secular law applies elsewhere, but secular law cannot overrule *sharī'a* law.

Indonesia has been relatively permissive in its commitment to Islām, a matter of no small consequence given that one out of every six Muslims in the world today lives there.[101] Some of this permissiveness may be traced to the positive reaction to an unusually enlightened Dutch colonial policy in the early 20th century that included not only a tolerance for Islām instead of support for Christian proselytization, but a recognition that Islām was neither monolithic nor highly organized, and that fanatics were not representative of the local Muslim masses.[102] Alas, all this ended in the late 1920s when Dutch conservatives began to fear Indonesian stirrings for independence. When independence did come after World War II the Constitution's Preamble was specifically purged of the words,"...with the obligation for adherents of Islām to follow the *sharī'a*..." thus putting Muslim formalists, i.e., the sharī'a-minded, and their fundamentalists allies, aside. The path chosen by Indonesia has consistently been one of moderation rejecting the extremes of being either a secular state or an Islāmic state. Article 29 of the Constitution states that, " The State shall be based upon the belief in the One and Only God." Clearly Islām has not been rejected, it has been embraced in spirit, or as Hosen has put it, "Indonesian Islām follows the substantive approach of syari'ah (*sharī'a*), not the formal one."[103] Needless to say, the formalists/fundamentalists have been pressing since 1945 to get Article 29 changed and have failed, the last attempt being in 2002. In the 2004 National Legislative elections 90% of Indonesian voters rejected those Islāmic parties that supported changing Article 29.[104]

Islāmic schools in Indonesia have played a role similar to that in other Muslim countries in South and Southeast Asia. Only a small fraction of students attend them, and overwhelmingly they teach Islāmic values, not hate of the West. The religious schools in Indonesia have taken a slightly different turn with the majority being the so-called 'pesantren', boarding schools that however are rarely free as madrasas are elsewhere. Their faculty tend to be more politically involved than that of madrasas, but on the whole moderate in their outlook with a very few of the extremist ilk. The extremism is largely an export from the Middle East, particularly Saudi Arabia and is more a reaction to popular Islām than to the West. The so-called 'madrasas' of Indonesia are more recent institutions that are trying to be more modern with the inclusion of secular subjects. With one exception the Muslim attitude towards the West and America is surprisingly benign. That exception is a reaction to the excessively unilateral policies of America vis-a-vis Islāmic terrorism. This has transformed their view of America from largely favorable to overwhelming unfavorable in a mere two or three years since 2000.

Apart from the matters already mentioned, that is, the dissolution of Western imperialism, the emergence of independent Muslim states in the Middle East, and the final precipitation of the State of Israel, World War II (and its precursor World War I) had one more effect of interest in our story, the emergence of the two Super Powers, the United States and the Soviet Union. The Soviet Union, and Russia before it, had long been interested in Persia and the Ottoman Empire. At first Russia feared the Ottomans, then as the power balance changed, she coveted parts of its territories. At one time or another Russia aspired to control of the Bosporus and other lands in Turkey and around the Black

Sea. She wanted the Caucasus between the Black and Caspian Seas and even fancied making Iran one of her Soviet Socialist Republics after World War I. As history has shown, it never got the Bosporus, nor an Iranian Soviet Socialist Republic, though it did get the Caucasus and the northern side of the Black Sea.

By the 1950s the Cold War between the Super Powers had provided a wonderful tool for the Middle Eastern states where they effectively sold their 'friendship' to the side that would pay the most. Egypt is easily the best example of this, switching sides twice. Unfortunately, most of the 'payment' was more often than not in the form of military rather than economic aid. This led to numerous dictatorships that have had very little indigenous support, and as these dictatorships were almost invariably secular, they have led to some interesting balancing acts. The Muslim clergy was unhappy with the sellout to evil, non-Muslim powers, and the people in their poverty were unhappier still. To control this, Middle Eastern leaders professed Islām while building their armies. Money better spent in relieving poverty instead flooded into a military armed to the teeth and never quite sated with a quantity of arms far beyond any reasonable defense need.

We can identify at least three major currents in the tide of Middle Eastern history for the last half of the 20th century; the overwhelming influence of oil, the turbulence of secular Arab nationalism and Islāmic fundamentalism, and the growing presence of the state of Israel in Palestine.

The political leverage accruing to the producers of Middle Eastern oil became apparent in 1974 when they embargoed shipments to countries that supported Israel in the 1973 Yom Kippur War. The impact on the West, and necessarily on the rest of the world, was as shocking as it was dreadful. Gasoline prices tripled and quadrupled triggering an inflation that soon demonstrated to the Arab oil producers that such embargoes were two edge swords that drove their costs up as rapidly as their income. Moreover, Western energy conservation and competition from non-Arab oil producers eventually weakened this source of political leverage. Nevertheless, both the Middle East and the West discovered a new power balance in the world.

In 1960 in the first coordinated effort to control their destinies four Middle Eastern oil producers joined with Venezuela to form the Organization of Petroleum Exporting Countries (OPEC). Since then six other states, all Arab except Indonesia and Nigeria have joined. Of the eleven members in 2003 only Venezuela has a non-Muslim majority population.[105] OPEC's intent is to co-ordinate and unify their petroleum policies to ensure the stabilization of oil prices with "...due regard being given at all times to the interests of oil-producing nations."[106] Although OPEC worked for awhile, and generally works well today, there was a time when independent market forces eventually took charge and left many extravagantly spending Middle Eastern states deeply in debt. Nevertheless, oil revenues gave formerly backward and vulnerable countries such as Saudi Arabia, Iraq, and Iran prodigious sums of money. By 1975, Saudi Arabia, the richest of the oil states, had financial reserves exceeding those of the United States and Japan combined. Some countries used this new wealth to buy weapons, some to improve their infrastructure, and some to invest in the West. In most cases, however, the new national wealth did not relieve the common man of his misery. This fostered a profound discontent in the masses and contributed to a hate of the West that was viewed at once as their exploiter and seducer. Since the United States was the West's quintessential materialist state it often became the special target of Muslim rage.

Nowhere is this better illustrated than in Iran. The United States in its Super Power struggle with the Soviet Union encouraged the Shāh to develop his armed forces, a plan the Shāh was pleased to pursue for his own ends as well. The Shāh's reinstallation of the imperial throne with its accompanying splendor and extravagance left the Iranian masses very much as they had been before the discovery of oil, only this time their misery was easily contrasted with the crown's comfort. And this time there was also the alternate promise of Islāmic fundamentalism. The Ayatollah Ruhollah Khomeini successfully returned from exile in Paris by promising to abolish the monarchy, restore the jurisdiction of the *sharī'a,* and lift the oppression of the common folk. He persuaded all groups and classes in Iran to support the revolution by avoiding mention for the time being of his most radical plans. Even the middle and upper classes, often with only a nominal interest in their Muslim heritage, detested the Shāh's regime, especially because of his hated and feared secret police, the SAVAK.[107] The net result was a quick revolution in 1979 that largely rejected the West and established the new Islāmic Republic of Iran. Once in power Khomeini no longer needed the support of the "moderates" and proceeded to dump them as his extreme programs were enacted. The whole process is reminiscent of the Abbāsid overthrow of the Umayyads 12 centuries earlier where the essentially Sunnī Abbāsids used the Shī'as and *mawālī* to come to power, then rejected them when no longer needed (also, this is exactly what Hitler did when he came to power.)

The essence of our story, and the final focus of events, is the Middle East's reassertion of its independence with its more or less successful escape from Western domination through its development of secular Arab nationalism, and almost simultaneously, Islāmic fundamentalism.

The 20th-century Muslim world has been seriously experimenting with secular, nationalistic government, most notably in Turkey, Egypt, Syria, Iran, and Iraq. As we have seen, Turkey appears to have been the most successful in this experiment, Iran, an utter failure. For the others, the jury is still out.

The most important Arab figure in secular nationalism was Gamal Abdul Nasser, born in 1918, undisputed leader of Egypt in 1954 two years after a group of army officers ousted King Farouk, and president of Egypt until his death from a heart attack in 1970. Nasser's promise was to restore dignity to the Arab people who had so often been humiliated by the West. His success and failure was directly tied to the degree that he could accomplish this. In the beginning he was very successful. He nationalized the Suez Canal and succeeded in thwarting a combined British, French, and Israeli invasion to regain control of it.[108] He demonstrated that his own technicians were well capable of operating and maintaining the Canal in the face of Western assertions that Egypt was incapable of such a feat. He charted an independent course for Egypt in the Super Power struggle choosing on his own who he would befriend. When the

West wasn't forthcoming with aid to build the High Dam across the Nile at Aswan he turned to the Soviet Union with better results. He inspired other secular Arab nationalists in Libya, Syria and Iraq, and briefly formed the United Arab Republic in union with Syria. Generally speaking, he was very highly regarded by the peoples of the Middle East. However, this was not the case with other Arab rulers, most of whom either distrusted his ambition, or were unsympathetic with his governmental secularism.

Nasser's success turned to failure as he coped with the growing hostility of other Arab leaders and with the dissolution of the United Arab Republic in 1961, but the most serious blow to his image came with the humiliating defeat in the 1967 Six Day War with Israel. Israel's attack destroyed Egypt's air force even before it could get off the ground, while Egypt's army was man-handled and ejected from the Gaza Strip and the Sinai. Israel achieved all this while simultaneously dealing with Syria and Jordan.

Egypt's economy began to deteriorate, partly because it was unable to support the cost of Nasser's military establishment. The combination of humiliation and hard times seriously reduced his popular appeal and eventually brought into question the efficacy, if not the very legitimacy, of secular Arab nationalism. King Feisal in Saudi Arabia was constantly raising this question and assumed more influence in the Arab world as Nasser's influence declined. To compromise the concept further, other Arab nationalist states such as Iraq, Syria,[109] and Libya were becoming one man dictatorships, more or less secular, that were highly oppressive and exploitive of their peoples. The time was ripe for the reemergence of a force that had lain largely dormant for several centuries, a force that called to the very soul and being of Arabs and Iranians alike, Islām. However, the political force of Islām needed an extra boost to be effective in this milieu, and that came from fundamentalism.

"Islāmic fundamentalism" is not a well defined term. Rather like "Christian fundamentalism" it embraces many sects and points of view. Its one common meaning and point of view is the notion that the true Islāmic life and government is attainable only through a return to the basics of Islām and the rule of *sharī'a* law. Islāmic fundamentalism is manifest by Sunnī and Shī'a alike, and it would be a profound mistake to identify it only with the vocal Shī'as of revolutionary Iran. On the other hand one Muslim's notion of fundamentalism can be another's idea of apostasy or conservative corruption (witness Iran's hostile view of the traditionally conservative and Islāmicly pure Wahhābī Saudi Arabia.) Again we can turn to the more familiar Christian milieu to understand this variety in what constitutes the true faith. Christians are all over the place, even in interpreting the meaning of the Bible, and so it is with Muslims in interpreting the meaning of the Qur'ān and *hadīth*.[110] (See Appendix E)

Islāmic fundamentalists are chiefly concerned with the corrupting effect the West has had on Muslim culture. While some elements of Western culture such as science and economic power have impressed them, they completely reject the seamier parts that have weakened what they believe is their historically superior civilization. They are particularly troubled by alcoholism, bars, theaters, night clubs, movies, drugs, the unrestricted public mixing of sexes, women's Western dress, pornography, materialism, secularism, and the absence of compassion that has permeated their culture from the West. Muslims feel the threat of Western ideas even in their own homes where emancipation of women and the growing disrespect of their children for their elders has had no precedent. But the essence of the inspiration for 20th-century Islāmic fundamentalism is the profound sense of humiliation felt by virtually all Muslims at the hands of the West. Arab and Iranian Muslims have very long memories. The absence of the glorious hegemony of Islām and the decline of its brilliant cultural centers in Baghdad, Cairo, Damascus, Constantinople, Cordoba, and Granada are difficult to accept, especially with the belief that it is somehow unnatural and sinful for unbelievers to rule believers.

"Fundamentalism" is a denial and rejection of history. This is perhaps its one common characteristic across all religions. It not only refuses to recognize changes with time, it rejects all views of history except that to which it is committed, the fictitious modifications used to serve its needs of certitude. Thus, fundamentalists are pseudo-literalists in the sense that their interpretations of founding events and texts are more self-serving than rationally and historically supportable. This is the sense in which I use the term 'fundamentalism' here.

Islāmic fundamentalism is not a new phenomenon. It was manifest in the very earliest days of Islām with the Sunnī/Shī'ī schism, the Khārijites, and notably later with the birth of the Fātimid Caliphate. It has periodically reoccurred numerous times in Muslim history driven by the moment's dissatisfaction with the status quo. In recent times the tide of Western domination and humiliation has been the latest source of the dissatisfaction (along with the ever present irritation of popular religious practices.)

Although there were calls for a return to basics in the 19th century, the first important manifestation of Islāmic fundamentalism in modern times came in 1928 with the founding of the Muslim Brotherhood in Egypt. It and its offshoots remain today arguably the most important, though by no means the only, fundamentalist movement in the Middle East. At its founding it stressed moral and social reforms in response to a deep feeling that the reason the West was so successful in dominating the Muslim world was because Muslims had corrupted their practice of Islām, and God was punishing them for it. Islām had to rid itself of Western secularist ideas and decadence. The West was at once God's cause and effect of Muslim decline. However, the call for moral and social reforms was found to be insufficient, so in 1939 the Muslim Brotherhood became political declaring that, "Islām is a comprehensive, self evolving system; it is the ultimate path of life in all spheres. Islām emanates from, and is based on, two fundamental sources, the Qur'ān and the *hadīth*. Islām is applicable to all times and all places."[111] By 1946 the Egyptian Muslim Brotherhood had grown to a million members and sympathizers. They found inspiration to resist British influence and control in the Brotherhood slogan, "The Qur'ān is our constitution, the Prophet is our guide; death for the glory of Allāh is our greatest ambition."[112] (It is worth noting, however, that though, "... death for the glory of Allāh is our greatest ambition," extremely few of the million chose to exercise that ambition.

Clearly, this slogan is a characteristically Arab utterance with its completely predictable exaggeration, passion, and verbal substitution for the act.)

The Muslim Brotherhood now exists in all Arab states, either under its own name or another name assumed for political reasons; in Algeria it's The People of the Call (*Ahl al Daawa*), in Tunisia it's The Islāmic Party (*Hizb al Islāmi*), in the Gulf States it's The Society of Social Reform, and in Syria it's the Young Men of Muhammad (*Shabab Muhammad*). In addition to these Sunnī groups we find numerous others, some Sunnī and some Shī'a such as the Party of God in Lebanon (*Hezbollāh*), Algeria's Islāmic Salvation Front, the Islāmic Resistance Movement (*Hamas*), and the Islāmic Jīhad, both in the occupied territories in Palestine, and the Shī'a Amal. Scholars estimate that there are perhaps several hundred fundamentalist organizations across the Muslim world with most in the Middle East. Analysis, however, suggests that total membership is less than two or three million representing less than 0.3 percent of Muslims globally and less than one per hundred in the Middle East.

Fundamentalist or sectarian viewpoints are very rarely asserted when confronted with political expediency. In 1980 the Islāmic Republic of Iran put aside its fundamentalist principles (to the consternation of the fundamentalist Syrian Islāmic Front) and made alliance with secularist Syria against secularist Iraq. At the same time, elements of the fundamentalist Muslim Brotherhood chose to support secularist Iraq. There is a principle operative here that should not be forgotten: In a confrontation between religion and politics within a given religion, politics always prevails. Sometimes it takes awhile, but in the long run it does prevail.[113]

The variety of fundamentalist movements suggests the wide appeal of fundamentalism among the Arabs and other Middle Eastern Muslims.[114] That fundamentalism has not swept the day may only be due to the disorganization and fragmentation of the phenomenon, for contrary to some Western fears, it is largely local with local peculiarities often at odds with similar movements elsewhere. Islāmic fundamentalism is nowhere near being a coherent, universal Muslim movement. The appearance of Al-

Qaeda, contrary to popular opinion,[115] does not change this, notwithstanding the enormous impact of 9-11. In those countries where the secularist governments are oppressive and have failed to cope with the problems of poverty, Islāmic fundamentalism is finding ample opportunity for expansion. The impoverishment and humiliation of Nasser's Egypt by the 1967 Arab/Israeli War nicely illustrates a secular Arab nationalist failure and the subsequent opportunities provided to the fundamentalists. Probably only the very strong repressive measures by Nasser kept the country from turning into an Islāmic State. A similar dynamic existed in Hafez al-Assad's Syria (and continues under his son Bashar al-Assad) and Saddam Hussein's Iraq. These secular states have been maintained through their oppressive Ba'th Parties and secret police. How long Syria can survive is an open question. Iraq's Ba'th is now outlawed and the Iraqi people are choosing their political/religious future for themselves, no doubt with considerable pressure from the Shī'ī majority.

Where economic and political conditions have been less stressful for Muslim peoples there seems to be less inclination to support fundamentalist movements. Turkey and Saudi Arabia come immediately to mind.[116] However, perhaps the best example was the occasion of Anwar Sadat's assassination in Egypt by members of the Al-Jīhad movement in 1981. The plotters had expected the assassination to trigger a general uprising and demand for the installation of an Islāmic State to be ruled under the *sharī'a*. No uprising took place, probably because the country's prosperity had improved from the low of the late 1960s.

As the last decade of the 20th century opened, a continuing confusion of historically minor storms distracted one from a sense of the tide upon which these events are riding. Sunnī secularist Iraq and Shī'ī fundamentalist Iran concluded a decade-long war in 1988 that exhausted both and left neither a winner. United States involvement here and with the never ending Palestine/Israel crises continued to provoke Muslim rage and provide significant inspiration for Islāmic fundamentalist movements. Iraq had no sooner freed itself from its war with Iran than it invaded Kuwait in the summer of 1990. World intervention through the United Nations with largely United States and European military forces ejected the Iraqis, but there was substantial ambivalence in the Muslim community about involving the West to settle what many saw as an essentially Arab problem, oil interests notwithstanding. As the immediate threat from Iraq to other Arab states subsided after the Gulf War their support of the UN (the United States) in this matter palpably cooled, and Arabs once again began experiencing the feeling of humiliation at the hands of the West. Even Kuwait became cautious of American influence. Moreover, the continued presence of United States forces in Saudi Arabia after the war infuriated some Muslims as an infidel violation of Islām's holy land. The consequences of this became staggering on 9-11-01.

For the past several years Al-Qaeda has drawn the attention of the United States more than any other militant Islāmic fundamentalist organization. This is so because it has focused its terrorist efforts directly against the United States and its citizens including the attack on the USS Cole and the 9-11 attacks. There is relatively little reliable information available on Al-Qaeda though a great deal has been written.[117] Al-Qaeda was formally organized in 1988 from an existing group of Arab volunteers fighting the Soviets in Afghanistan. Apparently these volunteers were informally organized in 1979 by Abdullah Azzam, a Palestinian member of the Muslim Brotherhood, with Osama bin Laden playing a somewhat subordinate role at first. Nevertheless, bin Laden's zeal and money quickly brought him to its leadership, especially after the mysterious assassination of Azzam.[118] Thereafter bin Laden appears to have been most influenced by Ayman al-Zawahiri, an Egyptian and former leader of the Egyptian Islamic Jihad, the organization that assassinated Anwar Sadat. Success in Afghanistan against the Soviets, and the subsequent fall of the Soviet Union, emboldened and deceived bin Laden and Al-Qaeda into believing that they could successfully take on the United States and the rest of the non-Muslim world. Bin Laden's dream was to use Al-Qaeda as an organizing force to bring about the rectification and unification of the Muslim world against fallen away Muslim leaders and the infidel West. It did not take long for him to develop a special dislike for the United States as the American military became resident in Saudi

Chapter 5

Arabia, the land of the holy cities, during the Gulf War of 1991. Although Al-Qaeda is often described as an umbrella or financial enabler and coordinator for other militant organizations it seems that it has been most effective on its own. The threat from Al-Qaeda has assumed epic proportions including assertions that it has trained up to 110,000[119] terrorists, exists in 60 countries around the world with sleeper cells in many awaiting the command to strike, and has well equipped laboratories for the development of weapons of mass destruction, and indeed already possesses them.[120] Apart from the patent hysteria of it all, one is perplexed by the absence of terrorist activity in the United States in the years since 9-11.[121] A reasonable assumption on the face of it would be that the threat was overblown and the United States response in Afghanistan and elsewhere substantially disarmed what was real. Perhaps only time will sort out the truth.

A historic social experiment is taking place in the Middle East. The experimental question is, can one of the world's great religions become an effective social instrument in the 21st century in the face of a contrary secular world culture of immense vitality and historic success? No question of greater historic scope has ever been asked. The dynamics before us involve Western culture that is rational, scientific, and successful beyond the wildest dreams of any person born before the 18th century. Its success is so seductive because it not only promises everything, it delivers; but there's a price. For all the material wonders obtained, the West has had to surrender a certain spiritual strength. An accommodation was reached with religion where 'spheres of interest' were recognized that effectively pushed aside religion and transformed the public West into a largely secular culture. The physical benefits from this deal have been wonderful, but the spiritual and social consequences have left a void acknowledged even by the West. Because we have lived with this evolving transformation for several centuries we have had some opportunity to adjust, however incompletely. Moreover, this is a product of our own heritage. On the other hand, the Islāmic culture of the Middle East has had no such comforting buffer. For 1,400 years they have immersed themselves in a way of life that submits to the harmonious needs of the inner man, that introspectively accommodates its world with no need to conquer the enveloping physical environment. The supremacy of religion and its complete identity with the political (at least in principle) and social milieu answered all questions with a reverent bow to the past. The Qur'ān and *hadīth* provided all that was necessary and sufficient. A comforting situation indeed, but materially it led nowhere, at least in the long run. With the passage of time Western material advances superseded the splendid cultural achievements of Islām. The Muslim world ignored this until it was forced on them. The cultural shock was devastating. All at once Muslims were second class citizens in their own lands. Even their glory was second class. What was worse still was that the Muslims themselves wanted the Western material well being, but they had neither the heritage nor the leisure to facilitate the change. By the mid 20th century the Muslim Middle East had found that the material benefits of the West's culture were not worth the spiritual price they were paying, so they began a search for something more acceptable. Different styles of nationalism, socialism, secularism, and most recently, Islāmic fundamentalism, and Islāmism have been, and are being tried. Some attempts have failed dismally, others have had some limited success, and others have yet to bear fruit.

If one word were to be used to describe the modern inspiration for Islāmic fundamentalism it would be "humiliation." To the degree that secular Middle Eastern nationalists and non-militant Muslim states fail to deal with the humiliation experienced by their peoples at the hands of the West, to that

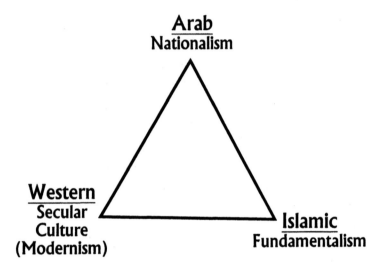

Figure 4

**Twentieth-Century Search for Identity & Rule
In the Muslim Middle East**

degree will Muslims turn to fundamentalism and Islāmism, especially if they are economically depressed as well. Where some pride and economic well-being or hope exists, as for example in Turkey, and in Nasser's Egypt before the 1967 war, there one will find less interest in Islāmic fundamentalist revival. Accordingly, whatever the West does, however inadvertent or well meaning, to humiliate and take the pride of the people, who incidently are not necessarily synonymous with the government, that will increase the success of Islāmic fundamentalism and Islāmism. Unfortunately, the breathtaking American ineptitude in Iraq after defeating Saddam Hussein in 2003 is not reassuring. The torture, and the treatment specifically designed to humiliate, and the detention and killing of innocent persons at Abu Ghraid prison in Iraq and Guantanamo Bay in Cuba, as well as the publication of photographs of Saddam Hussein in his underwear in his cell, all exacerbate Muslim anger with the West.

Of course other factors are operative here as well. After all, Saudi Arabia can scarcely be viewed as a state humiliated at the hands of the West, and yet it too has been struggling with militant fundamentalists. Specialists frequently cite the rapid urbanization in many Muslim countries along with an oversupply of highly educated citizens for which there are no jobs. Clearly economic discontent and simple political ambition are also operating. Indeed, the symbiosis of economic discontent, political ambition, and militant fundamentalism often mix cause and effect into an indistinguishable mess.

The main contest in recent years has been between secular nationalism, a Western import, and Islāmic fundamentalism with fundamentalism clearly in the ascendent. Algeria and Egypt were the principal nations under varying degrees of siege in the 1990s. In Algeria the legacy of French culture has left an influential secular residue which allowed the country to experiment with socialism. After more than a decade of peace and relative prosperity, partly based on oil revenues, the experiment failed as economic problems fueled popular discontent. With the legalization of the Islāmic Salvation Front in 1989 the fundamentalists got 55% of the vote in local elections and later gathered 49% of the vote in the first round of national elections in 1991. The military seized power and canceled the second round of elections when it was evident that the fundamentalists would win and carry out their stated plan to transform the country into an Islāmic state under *sharī'a* rule. The Islāmic Salvation Front (FIS) was resuppressed as rioting and assassination followed, including the assassination of Muhammad Boudiaf, the popular president of the ruling council. Throughout the 90s the suppressed Muslim fundamentalists terrorized the population until elections were held in 1999 that brought Abdelaziz Bouteflika to the presidency. He appears to have popular support as well as army backing. His 2005 sponsorship of the Charter for Peace and National Reconciliation which offered amnesty to many insurgents was supported by a large majority of voters further strengthening his position. Meanwhile, the FIS was forcefully dissolved, though within a year a new terrorist organization emerged, the Groupe Islamique Arme. The economy has improved slightly, but is highly vulnerable to oil prices, though the sharp increases in 2005 have been beneficial.

Egypt has been on an economic roller coaster for decades, and accordingly has experienced several episodes of zealous fundamentalist activity. As in many other Muslim states when the economy is good the fundamentalists have had only marginal success at best. However, the opportunities during a failing economy are another matter, and become so attractive and unique that the militants have taken to attacking the sources of whatever prosperity Egypt can muster. Their rationale effectively says 'if you will not support fundamentalism because you are comfortable, we will remove the comfort, and then you can reconsider.' With an acute sense of Egyptian economic vulnerability the fundamentalists began attacks on foreign tourists and businesses in 1992 hoping to deprive the country of this very important revenue source. The plan succeeded admirably causing a substantial decline in tourism. The government responded with increased security for tourists and a very aggressive assault on the fundamentalist infrastructure. Although tourism has recovered how this will eventually turn out remains in question. It is worth noting that in recent centuries Egypt has often felt rather closer to the West than many Arab countries except possibly Algeria and

Lebanon. Accordingly, appeals to throw off the humiliation of Western dominance have been less effective. The fact that the fundamentalists have had to resort to attacking the economy and thereby appeal to the material interests of the populace rather than their Islāmic heritage supports this view, although the militants maintain that the attacks are to drive out the corrupting Western travelers and businesses. No doubt this is partially true, but the argument is otherwise unpersuasive, albeit typical of radical groups fanatically committed to maintaining ideological purity.

For many years Iraq and Syria had things pretty much under control, principally because of the strength of their individual dictatorships. Control and repression were so thorough that no significant organized alternatives to their secular governments were possible. However, because their regimes were largely personal, the absence of Hafez al-Assad in Syria or Saddam Hussein in Iraq might have opened unique opportunities for the fundamentalists. Interestingly, there was no fundamentalist uprising with the death of al-Assad and the take over by his son Bashar in 2000. An even more interesting situation is evolving in Iraq after the ouster of Saddam Hussein by American forces in 2003. It is the American intention to let the Iraqi people decide the nature of their government. Whether it shall be secular or Shī'ī Muslim remains to be seen, but Iraq's Shī'ī majority and its proximity to Iran cannot help but have a significant influence on the outcome. The stability of Syria seems for the moment to be assured, but Arab Syria and Iraq remain heir to the discontents with the West we have previously mentioned. Accordingly, the pressure of arguments to reject the West and return to the original purity of early Islām remains in the background always ready to erupt.

United States foreign policy in the face of Iran/Iraq interactions was driven in part by a wish to prevent any fusion of interests, and especially any political fusion. The possibility of a unification of Iran and Iraq with their immense oil resources and consequent geopolitical leverage was more than the United States could accept. Accordingly, the Sunnī/Shī'ī and secular/fundamentalist divisions between them suited the U.S. just fine. American foreign policy during the Iran/Iraq War of the

1980s illustrates this. We wanted neither side to win.

Another American anxiety was that a unified state under Islāmic fundamentalist rule would exert a powerful force in the Muslim world toward a further expansion of fundamentalism and its anti-Western and especially anti-American attitude. However, the fear of a local or general pan-Islāmic union seems unrealistic in light of the history we have summarized in the past four chapters. Not only is there little in the one-and-a-half millennia history of Islām to suggest any potential success in such an undertaking, but the very character of the Arab militates against it. Their tendency to fratricidal conflict is of legendary proportions with intergroup animosities inversely proportional to the distance between them. The success of the seventh-century Arabs can only be partly attributed to the cohesion of the *umma* defined by Muhammad. The attraction of plunder for these nomads must have been equally as powerful. Today, the only plundering probable would be of each other.[122]

A successful long term union of Iran and Iraq, of Persians and Arabs, seems equally problematic given not only their character differences but their deep religious differences as well. Recall that in this context the forces of union are the various fundamentalist movements, and that by their very nature they are extreme and essentially inflexible. We have seen for example how fundamentalist groups will fight each other, even siding with secular forces to prevail. This rigidity guarantees an unstable union.

Nevertheless, there are attractive forces at work as well. For example, the irritation of the state of Israel in their midst is an exquisitely painful reminder of Arab and Muslim humiliation at the hands of the West. And there are memories of the glorious Muslim civilization which existed while the infidel Europeans were barely more than a bunch of forest savages to the northwest. Moreover, there is the shared wealth of oil revenues that in spite of the disproportionate distribution to the rich, still helps the poor majority if only by providing jobs now and then. The *zakāt* is after all one of the five pillars of Islām and becomes as efficacious now with oil revenues as it was in the seventh century with booty from Persia and Byzantium.

The Twentieth Century

As we look at the Middle East today we see a storm of local interests carried upon the tide of emerging self- assertion. This self-assertion first became prominent in the half century following World War I with the political independence of Muslim states from Algeria to Iran. Economic independence, to the degree that any state can have it, came largely with the growing global importance of oil, especially after the oil embargo and OPEC increases in 1973 and 1974. But the deepest and most profound self-assertion is occurring now as Middle Eastern countries battle to achieve cultural independence. Some countries feel the need for it more than others; Turkey's self-image seems to have been secure enough that they have unabashedly taken Western cultural elements to themselves ranging from the Roman alphabet to Western style clothing, names, and laws. And they have accomplished this without renouncing their Muslim faith. At the other extreme Iran, through the vehicle of Islāmic fundamentalism, has tried to reject many elements of Western culture. Yet, as the years pass after 1979 there seems to be an almost inevitable release of tension and a return to a more moderate world view as seen in everything from the easing of women's dress code to democratization to gestures of rapprochement with the United States. Other Islāmic fundamentalist movements, rarely connected to the Iranians, have been pressing their programs elsewhere, all in service of breaking the Western cultural influence in their lands.[123]

It is natural for a people to want to be free. For the Muslim peoples of the Middle East the Western cultural, political, and economic bondage that remains is like a fine scarf; in some ways it is comfortable and pleasing to wear, but restricting and humiliating, because its long tag is held elsewhere, and it could be fatal if tightened like a noose. The task and challenge is how to slip the noose. Some, like the fundamentalists, say destroy it. Others say transform it; keep the comfortable, stylish qualities and dispose of the dangerous, restricting, and humiliating elements. Each approach has its promise and problems.

The central problem for Middle Eastern Muslims is to reconcile the rigid and archaic practices of early Islām with the exigencies of today, for if one accepts the view of the Iranian scholar, Dr. Husain Nasar, as many Muslims do, that, "For Muslims, Islām is not one of the elements of life; Islām is life itself" they are faced with a paradox. The genuinely Islāmic life advocated by fundamentalists is incompatible with the modern world. It reflects an unrealistically nostalgic view of the past as well as a mischievously naive view of the present. This incompatibility has been demonstrated time and time again, and perhaps most persuasively by the evolution of Mawlana Mawdudi's thought.[124]

In Muslim countries political expediency always prevails when confronting religious principle, a behavior of course not unique to Muslim countries, but unique in the size of the gap between practice and principle. Islām has always faced the conflicting imperatives of religious doctrine and political reality, notwithstanding its claim of universal jurisdiction in life. From the viewpoint of a religious purest, it has been an utter failure, more striking because of its claim on life. Of course Muslim scholars deny this (a common Shī'ī rational cites the Qur'ān's permission to use dissemblance in response to overwhelming political repression) but their arguments are unpersuasive and smack of sophistry. Christianity has faced this conflict too, but it has been notably more successful in the accommodation with the ready rationale of, "Render unto Caesar..."

Islāmic fundamentalism is proposing a path that cannot succeed, neither locally nor globally. Given the absolutist characteristics of the various sects there is little cohesion or potential for cohesion among them. Local in nature and spiritually isolated from one another because of their absolutism, these inward looking communities will simply be washed away by the tide of history as incidentally as a sand castle on the beach vanishes with the passing tide. If they choose to be flexible and compromise, they become what they have condemned. So it appears from the broadest perspective that Islāmic fundamentalism has little long term potential for success, albeit even in its failure the short term (a few decades) could be a very trying time for the West.

The short term indeed has its perils; the 'oil card,' nuclear weapons and other weapons of mass destruction, and the appearance of a *mahdī*, to name some obvious possibilities.

What the Muslim Middle East does with the economic gain and political leverage of oil is a short term issue that will have the greatest long term impact. Thus far this immense windfall has been largely squandered in the purchase of weapons used mostly for show in an exhibition of machismo unparalleled in history. The world's proven oil reserves are about one trillion barrels, or about a 50 year supply at current consumption rates.[125] Since the Middle East currently has virtually no other asset for generating wealth, it must look to these oil revenues as the sole source of leverage to develop the capability of competitively sustaining itself in the late 21st century. It has less than the lifetime of one human being to make the transformation. Muslim children of today can expect to see their world without significant oil resources as they pass into old age. To the degree that we see the Muslim countries of the Middle East use their oil revenues to develop infrastructure like roads, railroads, airports, communications, seaports where applicable, power plants, and desalination or other water supplies, as well as education and a suitable industrial potential, to that degree we will be seeing a historically significant tide. Otherwise, Islāmic fundamentalism, secular nationalism, or any other 'ism', will be nothing more than a passing historical storm, and the Islāmic Middle East will fail to completely reemerge and establish its full potential in history.

Oil has influence far beyond the mere revenue it brings. Ever since the formation of OPEC and the oil embargo the West has been much more accommodating to the wishes of the oil nations than it might have been otherwise. The challenge for the Muslim oil states is to use this leverage just enough to get what it wants politically without making the West fear that its vital interests are threatened and thus provoking the West to military intervention. The two Iraqi wars are only a hint at what could happen if these larger interests are disregarded or miscalculated by future Saddam Husseins.

The issue of nuclear weapons and other weapons of mass destruction has recently emerged from the background as one considers the future of the Middle East. Not only have there been demonstrably active indigenous programs to develop weapons of mass destruction in Iraq and Iran, as well as in nearby Pakistan, but the collapse of the Soviet Union may well have made available some of their weapons as well. The early organizational and economic chaos in the constituent states of the old Soviet Union certainly created fertile ground for individuals and institutions to want to sell nuclear materials. With their fractured lines of command and control and neutralized government authority only the most wishful thinker could believe that items as valuable, marketable, and portable as tactical nuclear weapons were not available to those with the money and connections. Few in the world have more money and better connections than the Muslim Middle East. Indeed, it was said that Iran had purchased two to four nuclear warheads from the Republic of Kazakhstan, and as of 1993 was merely awaiting delivery.[126] If Iran ever declares that it has nuclear weapons the geopolitics of the area would change forever. The restraint of a "mutual assured destruction" (MAD) policy would probably work given Israel's certain possession of a nuclear counterforce. Nuclear blackmail among Muslim states seems more likely in the region. This could draw the nuclear powers into alliance with the nuclear have-nots which could either ease the threat or exacerbate it. The threat to the West itself would also be real, albeit not on the same scale as that to the Middle East. The advantage of the West in facing any nuclear threat from the Middle East is one of vastly superior supporting military technology without which a nuclear capability is severely limited. It takes rockets and very sophisticated electronics to effectively deliver nuclear weapons any distance. Of course, terrorist, clandestine delivery is also possible, but the risk of premature discovery is also higher. Of course terrorist use is not inhibited by MAD since the terrorists are for the most part anonymous. As for the other weapons of mass destruction (WMD) commonly feared, chemical and biological agents, it is clear that no chemical weapon used in this context would have a meaningful impact beyond a momentary hysteria. This is so because they are of very limited scope, notwithstanding the unfortunate and misleading WMD classification. Biological weapons are another matter. The technology to produce and distribute them is relatively modest, the cost is low, and they are

110

easy to surreptitiously transport and distribute. This leads to the new and complicating dimension that has appeared in recent years, the non-state possession and use of WMDs. In this case they need only a successful attack to 'win,' for even a faulty detonation would create such havoc that the United States would be irrevocably transformed, if not by the event, then surely by the reaction. Accordingly, the threat is to the Middle Eastern Muslim world and the West alike. The history of international relations in the area is not comforting. This is especially discouraging to consider, given the highly emotional nature of the Arab, and at times even the Iranians, and the absence of that quality of diplomatic savoir-faire that tempers and adds wisdom in judgement. The former Iraqi president Saddam Hussein could be the archetype of this kind of leadership. Cunning is not wisdom, and unlike wisdom, it is the slave of passion. And in the added case of terrorism, passion clearly prevails.

The concept of the *mahdī* has some interesting potential for mischief. The first notion of the *mahdī* originated with the death of Husayn, one of Alī's sons, at Karbala in 680, and evolved into its present form with the disappearance or "occultation" of the Twelfth Imām, the "Hidden Imām" in 874. The messianic idea of the *mahdī*, which means, "rightly guided one," expresses the belief that the Twelfth Imām will reappear to restore proper Islāmic belief to the world and bring on a short era of several years duration where truth, justice, and virtue will prevail before the end of the world and the Last Judgement. This is clearly of Shī'ī origin, although some Sunnī Muslims, even without Qur'ānic or reliable *hadīth* support, have from time to time accepted the concept as well. These millennial prophets tend to appear when times are difficult for Muslims, a phenomenon also familiar to Christians. Individuals calling themselves the *Mahdī* have appeared regularly throughout Muslim history. Perhaps the best known in the West was Shakyh Muhammad Ahmed who led an uprising in the Sudan in the 1880s against the Egyptians. Ahmed finally occupied Khartoum and killed General Charles "Chinese" Gordon in 1885. The Mahdī died under mysterious circumstances five months later. His successor ruled till 1898 when a British force under the command of General Kitchener reoccupied the Sudan and killed him.

The mischievous element in the mahdī belief springs not only from the blatant political agenda invariably espoused by the claimant and similar to that of the Islāmists today, but by its eschatology. Key is the triumph of Islām (and of course it is the *Mahdī's* version of Islām) as a preparation for the end of the world. Before the nuclear and biowarfare age such millennial expectations were harmless. It is, alas, no longer so. It takes no great imagination to foresee a passionate Muslim leader saturated with ambition and zeal for the final triumph of his religion, a leader who finds one or more weapons of mass destruction in his hands, who would plan to use them as a natural, indeed inevitable, fulfillment of God's will. And lest one believes that this is too wild to ever be possible, we should remember that the deeply religious President Reagan once publicly speculated[127] on the millennial role of the United States nuclear arsenal. In any event, the mahdī tradition is an ideal instrument for the would-be demagogue, and it would be surprising if none appeared in the next few decades.

In the United States there is a repeat of recent history vis-a-vis a perceived threat to national security. In the days of the Red hunting Senator Joseph McCarthy everyone was afraid of the 'international Communist conspiracy.' Today there is a virtually exact copy in the fear of the 'international Islamic terrorist conspiracy.' In the 1950s and 1960s no distinction was made between the Communism of Soviet Russia, Communist China, North Vietnam, or Yugoslavia notwithstanding their substantial differences and frequent disagreements. They were not the monolithic block or menace perceived by fearful America. Similarly, Muslim terrorism scattered about the world today is not monolithic. The Muslims in the Philippines, Palestine, Saudi Arabia, Iran, etc. have remarkably little in common least of all a grand notion of reestablishing the caliphate, no matter the intrusive opportunism of Al-Qaeda.

It is disappointing that orientalists like Bernard Lewis and some of the contributors to the Encyclopaedia of Islam see Islām as static, monolithic, threatening, and ignoble, when in fact it is dynamic,, variegated, struggling for truth and peace, and noble.

The West has been and remains deceived by its own prejudices and too often ignores these differences. Western media in particular, and many influential writers persist in the fable of a clash of civilizations, where a more insightful position would be to recognize the essential worth of Islām and the natural unity we have with it.

As for Muslims themselves, a good case is often made today that classical jurists centuries ago condemned the modern fundamentalist's *jihād*. The jihādist replies, 'All these juridical pronouncements are superfluous and un-Islāmic, for they are distortions of the pure Islām of Muhammad's time which is what we believe in.' The fundamentalist position is very similar to the orientalist, both of whom refuse to recognize context and the evolution of thought and belief. On the other hand, though this theological debate is satisfying to the intellectually inclined, it largely misses the point, to wit, Muslim fundamentalists are not driven by theology, Qur'ānic quotations notwithstanding; they are driven by a discontent whose only religious connection is through specious rationalization. Thus their message may be momentarily attractive to the Muslim masses, especially as these masses are also upset by Western exploitation, but deep down it has little religious staying power. That is why fundamentalist movements have always failed; they do not speak to the heart of belief.

Finally, let us summarize a few erroneous beliefs about Islām rampant in the United States that we have exposed in this survey.[128] 1./ There is an exceedingly deep feeling in America that Islām is very far removed from Christianity. Yet, as we have shown, Islām is an organic part of the Abrahamic tradition, Jews, Christians, and Muslims. Though for Muslims the Qur'ān supercedes the Old Testament, it is closely connected to it, and is full of Old Testament references. Muslims respect the Old Testament and its prophets, and Jesus is second only to Muhammad in the long line of prophets going back to Adam and Abraham. Thus we are indeed all 'People of the Book'.

2./ The early Muslim conquests were neither rapid nor unusually savage for the time. It took centuries for the military/political expansion to reach its zenith and centuries longer for the majority of the subject peoples to become Muslim, if ever. At times the religious pressure to convert was almost nonexistent; recall that it was in fact profitable for the conquerors to allow pre-conquest religious practices to continue, because a special tax was levied on these practitioners. Moreover, perhaps half of today's Muslim world got that way not by conquest and military occupation, but by peaceful conversion. That is how the world's most populous Muslim nation, Indonesia, got that way.

3./ Throughout much of Islāmic history there was little hatred of Europeans, the West, Jews, or Christians as such. In fact, Muslim hegemony was often accompanied by an unusual degree of religious and ethnic tolerance. Typical and telling was the reaction of the resident Christian minority in the Holy Land when the Crusaders descended upon them, where for good reason they eagerly awaited the reappearance of their old Muslim masters. In another even more instructive example we see the Muslim treatment of Christians and Jews in Spain for the most part to have been quite civil. But when the Muslims were finally evicted in 1492 there occurred terrible persecutions of the Muslims left behind and of the resident Jews. The intense anti-American, anti-Jewish feelings that is so widespread at present among Muslims has been well earned by colonialist, imperialist behaviors nicely exemplified by, but not by any means limited to, the Balfour Declaration and the Sykes-Picot Agreement. However, these feelings are not a natural part of Muslim tradition as any reading of the Qur'ān will verify.

4./ *Jihād!*[129] There are few bugaboos more unnerving to the West than this complicated but oversimplified Muslim concept. The meanings of *jihād* are many and as often good as bad or threatening. Classically, *jihād* meant special effort, usually in service of Islām and Allāh. Things begin to get complicated as one tries to define what kind of effort. There can be no doubt that this effort is first and foremost an internal effort at self purification (Greater *jihād*), and only secondarily the external effort in war (lesser *jihād*), and defensive war at that. That said, yes it is true that *jihād* has historically meant physical war against an enemy, notwithstanding considerable limitations in Muslim holy literature about it being permissible only in defensive war and never against other Muslims. Its self-serving use as holy war by Muslim extremists and concerned Westerners should not deaden us to its richer meaning.

5./ It is often said that Muslims make no distinction between religion and politics, 'church' and state are seamlessly fused into one ruling entity. We know that the founding of the Muslim community in Medīna suggested such a fusion, and that from time to time in one place or another such was the case. Indeed, this is often the goal of modern fundamentalists. Nevertheless, in practice it has been quite rare. Political behavior has run independently of religious power, except indeed where it has so often cynically used and manipulated it. Even in today's religious fervor there are few 'Islāmic Republics', and fewer still bowing in fact to the complete authority of the *sharī'a*. Secular sensibilities have run consistently throughout Muslim history that fly in the face of religious zealotry, witness for example the frequency of alcohol consumption and the very widespread depiction of human and animal figures in Muslim art, Allāh's prohibitions notwithstanding.[130]

6./ The Qur'ān is for the most part <u>not</u> a straightforward message to be literally understood. Its message is often deep and subtle and requires a significant commitment to understand for Muslim and non-Muslim alike, especially in the modern world so far removed from Muhammad's time. Muslim fundamentalists and prejudiced Westerners share a will to disregard these subtleties and in the process wrongfully vilify most of Islām's practitioners.

7./ The world of Islām is uniform in neither time nor space. Throughout its history there has been a huge variety of beliefs and practices from Sunnī to Shī'a to Sūfī to popular Islām. The changing political milieu around them has brought to fore first one Islāmic belief then another. The history of the Nizaris (Assassins) illustrates this probably better than most. And remember that Shī'ī Iran was originally Sunnī. And Sunnī Egypt was originally Shī'ī Fatimid. Geographically, there has never been one Muslim world since the time of the Umyyads, and today there are a billion Muslims in seemingly as many interest groups; *Clash of (which) Civilizations?*

Chapter 6

Tides of History

My object in telling this story of fourteen centuries of Islāmic culture has been to establish a sense of scope, importance, and context for the present. I have chosen to pass over the waves and storms of detail in order to view the whole sea of history. I hope that in so doing the view will more easily reveal the tides that otherwise would be lost in the splash of momentary events. This is relatively easy to do for eras past, but not so easy as we approach our own time. That is the challenge, not only for the writer, but for the reader as you try to interpret the events before your eyes, what is significant and relevant to the tide and what is not.

Part of the challenge is in putting aside the personally convenient units of time, the days, weeks, months, and years so appropriate in our everyday lives, and adjust to the longer perspective of history. Our personal perspective inevitably leads to a distortion of perceived time. Just as visual perspective presents objects at a distance as foreshortened, so too events and processes centuries and millennia distant appear to span but an instant. Yet an historical "instant" is often a decade, a lifetime, or more. For example, the Arab conquests after Muhammad's death are invariably described as "rapid," "explosive," "amazingly speedy," "in an astonishingly short time," etc., yet the military conquest of some countries took decades and the conquest of the future Muslim world took centuries. Conversion to Islām of the conquered territories took two to five centuries more.[131] From our perspective it happened in a flash; from the perspective of an Arab merchant in the year 650 it encompassed his lifetime, and those of his children, grandchildren, and several generations thereafter. Clearly, the time unit of history's clock exceeds a lifetime. One says of historic changes that they happened in the past or will happen in the distant future. The beat is often subtle and difficult to identify for historic change of the present. We feel that our world, at least the world close to us, is more or less permanent. And so it has been for all men; imagine for a moment how permanent one's world must have appeared to the citizen of Hārūn al-Rashīd's Baghdad in 800, or of Suleiman the Magnificent's Constantinople in 1530 (or indeed, of George Bush's Washington, D.C. in the early 2000s). Yet the tides of history measured in decades and centuries reveal them as passing affairs sometimes leaving no trace whatsoever. Even the original site of Hārūn al-Rashīd's Baghdad, its glories only 11 centuries distant, but the victim of neglect and sack, is problematic since the modern city has been rebuilt many times and in slightly different places from the original. So we must take the longer view. Somewhat paradoxically, however, we are often powerfully persuaded that the event of the moment is the decisive hinge upon which all the rest of history will swing. This is rarely so.

The longer view, alas, is not facilitated by modern news media. The media, and especially the electronic news media, necessarily seek the sensation of the moment for their own natural, commercial ends and contribute little to an understanding of the true import of events. They are shackled by their very efficiency at presenting events of the moment; they are, after all, instruments of immediacy projecting momentary images. Their ephemeral presentations lack the permanence of a book, and lacking this permanence give us no sustained occasion to reflect and question their substance. There can be no dialog with the TV. On the other hand, one is reminded of the possibilities of leisurely contemplation in Gibbon's farewell after his epic consideration of the decline and fall of the Roman Empire; "It was among the ruins of the Capitol that I first conceived the idea of a work which has amused and exercised near twenty years of my life, and which, however inadequate to my wishes, I finally deliver to the curiosity and candor of the public." Here we have the opportunity to converse with Gibbon for 2,000 pages, and for a lifetime if we wish. In the present work we share this taste in temporal sweep. Yet, I am anxious with my presentation here, for I dash casually through the decades and centuries as if they were but moments. Moments to summarize: centuries and millennia to live. Hopefully, however, these pages will give some perspective, and an occasion for reflection not found with electronic media.

What good is it to have a longer view of events; after all, what possible interest can we have in events that unfold over decades and centuries, especially as most often we will not have been witness to their beginning, nor will we be there for the denouement. Part of the answer is of course that there is no beginning or end. History is process. Given the turbulence of events on the personal scale, the historic significance of the moment is all but lost, and surely can be of no consolation to the victims of the moment. For those who are not the victims but the beneficiaries of the moment, most often the personal rewards accruing from the process consume our fullest attention. Victim or beneficiary, the reality in which we are immersed is usually not only primary but exclusive, or to quote a black friend of the author's remarking on reality in the inner city, "Reality is a brick on the side of the head." However, where circumstances permit for the less acutely involved observer, the long term perspective of history can be satisfying and fruitful. We can discriminate and discover the links between the moment and the tide. Then the long term view will lend meaning and understanding to events often seeming to be meaningless. Understanding leads to wisdom which leads to serenity and wise action. So we can observe, identify, and understand the process and tide of history in which we are afloat, and out of that perhaps even derive some pleasure.

Although the issue of what drives history is largely beyond the scope of this work it is perhaps worth a moment to look back over our story and see if it gives us any hints in the matter. Clearly some individuals can have truly historic impact; arguably, Muhammad was the single most influential individual in human

Chapter 6

history. Alī, Abu al-Abbās, Suleiman the Magnificent, and Gamal Abdul Nasser have had lesser impacts. On the other hand, it is difficult to separate cause and effect in distinguishing whether the individual affects history or history carries the individual. In his masterpiece, "War and Peace," Tolstoy asserts that the 'great man' theory of history is all wrong and that Napoleon, the Russian Emperor, and the several Field Marshals and Generals were merely riding the tide of events and were simply carrying out what history allowed and ordained for them. From this point of view Muhammad didn't do anything that wasn't already in the cards. The time was right; had Muhammad not come along, someone else would have. Remember the weakness and instability of the Byzantine and Sasanid worlds, remember the restless energy of the Bedouin tribes, and remember the prevalence of the *hanīfs*, the monotheistic and messianic prophets of the time. So who can say for certain which is cause and which is effect; perhaps each is both, and like the theory of chaos in modern science, extremely small differences in either can grow to profoundly influence everything, what the scientist calls sensitive dependence on initial conditions.

Human behavior is a rich and never ending source of 'initial conditions' to seed history. Greed and the thirst for power are important in our story. The Muslim surge out of Arabia in the seventh century was largely driven by the promise of plunder with religion probably nothing more than a organizing rationale. Had the potential for plunder not been there it is unthinkable that the Bedouin would have attacked anyone other than themselves. With the successes of Islām came an endless succession of power struggles. Mu'āwiyah against Alī to begin the Umayyad Caliphate, al-Abbās against Marwān II to begin the Abbāsid Caliphate, Shī'as against Sunnīs, Shī'as against Shī'as, and Kharijites and Assassins against everyone, all driven by a thirst for power only sometimes rationalized by the zeal of religion. The Ottoman Sultans often schemed to get power, and having achieved the sultanate, just as often murdered their brothers and other potential pretenders to keep it. Modern times have seen no change as we view the careers of Shāh Rezā Pahlavī in Iran, Khadafy in Libya, Assad in Syria, Saddam Hussein in Iraq, and any number of Islāmic fundamentalist leaders with specious claims of high moral purpose. Human ego should always be suspect when its bearer finds himself prominent. Idealism is also important, but it rapidly loses its soul as it attains power (and before we become too smug in pointing to the failings of our Muslim brothers we should humble ourselves by recalling that the West has produced at least as many examples of comparable human behavior).

The need for certitude appears to be a powerful force in history, and nowhere is that need more inflexibly manifest than in religion. With Muslims it has too often been believe or die, or sometimes, pay more taxes. Shi'as and fundamentalists are notably less inclined to grant the tax option. Spiritual certitude can sometimes be serenely directed inward as has occurred in Sufī mysticism, but then it can be aggressively directed outward as is often reflected in the Qu'rān. The world's great literature is full of this struggle between freedom and certitude; Dostoyevsky's episode of The Grand Inquisitor in *The Brothers Karamazov*, and the Bible's Genesis to name but two.

Certainly other factors appear to have an influence on history as well. Climate, geography, and geology to name a few. Climate seems to have conspired with geology to produce in the Arabs a hardy people hungry for expansion and plunder and capable of more sacrifice than their adversaries. Ibn Khaldūn recognizes this toughness as a necessary ingredient for the foundation of empire. He remarks that nomads are the source peoples for civilization, the renewing blood stock that rejuvenates a decayed civilization. The geographical inheritance of the Ottomans astride the outlet of the Black Sea and gateway to Asia contributed to their power for centuries and in the end prolonged their life because of the West's desire to have a buffer and blockade against the Russians. Similarly, the geography of the Malacca Strait focused Islāmic expansion in Southeast Asia. Of course the oil blessings of geology for the Middle East are too obvious and profound to need further remark.

Karl Marx's economic theory of history, though terribly one dimensional, receives partial support from the ebb and flow of Muslim fundamentalism. We have observed that material well being has frequently smoothed the highs of passionate advocacy and the lows of despair. No example of this principle better illustrates the matter than the secular-fundamentalist power duet in Turkey and Egypt during the last half of the 20th century. If the people are comfortable then the niceties of religious dogma are overlooked and the humiliations of foreign influence are grating but bearable. Accordingly, materialism is the Great Curse of fundamentalist Islām, and it is not difficult to see why given its seductive nature. Is it any wonder then that the mullahs of the Islāmic Republic of Iran call the most materialist of nations, the United States of America, the "Great Satan."

So now we consider the breadth of our vision and try to identify the tide of evolving Islām through the centuries and millennia into the present and beyond. The first matter that strikes us is that not only is there more than one current but that there is a hierarchy of currents at all historic scales pulling events this way and that, with lesser flows sometimes apparently overwhelming the deepest currents. A similar and illustrative situation exists in astronomy where we observe the motions of the Earth in space. The Earth's motion is affected by the gravitational force of the Sun even while it also circles with the Sun around the center of our galaxy. At the same time the Earth, the Sun, and our galaxy flow with other galaxies of the local galaxy group in a direction and speed determined by the overall gravitational force of a super cluster of galaxies in this part of the Universe. And finally, there is the dominant motion of the Earth in the Universe defined by the expansion of the Universe as a whole.

The ebb and flow of the deepest, most profound historic tide is perhaps reflected in the rise and fall of civilizations and cultures. This cycle has been repeated since the dawn of history; civilizations emerge, grow, prosper, become decadent, weaken, and are assaulted and overwhelmed by barbarian conquest. Thereafter, these simpler, more energetic conquerors evolve, become more sophisticated, are seduced by the comforts of what they have taken, prosper, become decadent, weaken, and themselves fall victim to new conquerors. In recent centuries the cycle has changed somewhat because of the impact of technology. The fall of the civilization is delayed because of the immense advantage given it by technology. However, eventually enough technology seeps through to the "barbarians" to catalyze their superior *esprit de corps* and energy, all while the civilization continues to weaken, so that the "barbarians" prevail after all. (Neither "civilization" nor "barbarian" should be literally restricted; "civilization" can mean almost any dominant political group, and "barbarian" any out group. For example, the Chinese word for barbarian also means foreigner.) Ibn Khaldūn says that this process is unstoppable, while both Thomas Jefferson and Mao Zedong have explicitly noted the benefits of periodic or continuous revolution to maintain a civilization and preclude its decadence.

We have seen this largest of cycles with the rise and decline of the Muslim world itself, especially in the Middle East. We have also seen it within the history of Islām with the rise and fall of the Umayyads, the Abbāsids, the Fatimids, the Seljuks, and the Ottomans. And we have seen it in an interplay of the strong and weak as interests grow powerful, faction develops, and unity is fractured; the Sunnī/Shī'ī schism, the multiple simultaneous caliphates, the simultaneous sultanate/caliphate, nationalism, and the secular/fundamentalist dynamic.

The tide of Islāmic revival is now before us. Is it a major or lesser current, or simply a minor turbulence? Is the question answerable? Perhaps the answer lies with understanding how the Islāmic revival in the Middle East articulates with the history just noted. Does it follow naturally from the great cycles of history or from the internal rhythms of Islām?

Muslim dominance in an area typically (but not always) began with military conquest followed immediately by political control. Later, sometimes in only a few years, sometimes taking as long as several centuries, followed religious conversion of the population and after that cultural integration. There are numerous exceptions to this, but generally speaking this was the order of things. Today the Islāmic Middle East is fearful of a reversal, of losing its religious and cultural integrity. Restated, the question is, is the Islāmic revival a tidelet or a principal tide of history? Will this revival, even if successful, have major and centuries-long lasting consequences for the world as did the first appearance of Islām in the seventh century? Will it significantly reverse the centuries-long

Chapter 6

decline of Middle Eastern influence in world affairs? If the answer is yes, then we are looking at a principal tide.

Clearly, with the integrated political-religious-social quality of Islām, Islāmic revival for many Muslims necessarily implies a simultaneous political, religious, and cultural recovery as well. Is this enough to reestablish the former glory of Islām? Many fundamentalists, and especially the Islāmists, believe this is enough.

Perhaps the four most important events contributing to the decline of Muslim power and the Middle East were the incredible devastation from Transoxania to Iraq caused by the Mongol conquest of the 13th century, the reawakening of the West beginning in the 15th century with its subsequent commercial bypass of the Middle East around Africa to the Orient, and the West's technological development. These essentially economic events were what started the ebb of the Muslim tide. The forth major contributor was the essential conservatism of Islām. However, this conservatism appears in Islāmic history as a matter of degree: among the early Sūfīs there were some very novel and liberal interpretations as we have seen in Appendix C. These were rejected leaving the range of choices from conservative to reactionary. Yet, even within this range there has been considerable stress and conflict. It is clear that Islām has not yet got its house in order. The struggle for proper belief and practice has continued for 1400 years; we are only chance witnesses to the latest chapter of that struggle. Unfortunately, as witnesses, we are caught in the spillover of their turmoil. Western, and especially US, societies have mistakenly confused the incidently spillover as a "clash of civilizations", when its essential quality is inner turmoil.

If economic destruction and social conservatism are the villains, is Islāmic revival the necessary and sufficient condition for recovery? Not if it is in the form of Islāmic fundamentalism, for by its very nature fundamentalism preaches a return to values and mind sets that have proved inadequate in the face of Western competition.

What about oil resources? Surely this can be the instrument of economic recovery for the Middle East. Unfortunately, the historic evidence suggests that the oil wealth currently being squandered by privileged and corrupt classes, as well as on culturally useless military hardware, is unlikely to ever significantly benefit the overall health of the region. Indeed, it has every characteristic of a cancer. Without other significant resources it is imperative that oil revenues go to establish a viable economic infrastructure that will sustain the region after the oil is gone. This is not happening, and there is no evidence that it will happen in the future. Saudi Arabia, Iran, and Iraq with their vast oil resources are pathetic examples of this historic mismanagement. The case of Iran is especially instructive since its major asset of oil, used largely in support of its sterile Islāmic revolutionary aims, is the lubricant of its slide to exhaustion. Ironically, here Islāmic revival very likely will not be the vehicle of resurgence but the vehicle of decline. Of course the religious leaders of the Middle Eastern Muslim world deny this, but the facts speak for themselves.

It is instructive to note that with all the fuss being made by the Muslim religious leadership there is remarkably less supporting popular zeal. We see the highly organized popular demonstrations from time to time with their ecstatic and angry shouts supporting whatever local cause, but for the millions upon millions of common people leading lives of simple faith in the ultimate goodness of God and struggling to capture a moment's succor here and there between birth and death there are few grand visions of empire for Islām.[132]

The Islām practiced by the masses has been called "popular" or "folk" Islām. (See Appendix F) It is often remote from the public Islām presented and encouraged by the shrill Muslim leadership. It provides the cannon fodder of war, the soil and soul of the economy, and the litmus test of historic movement.[133] And here the litmus test fails. From Turkey to Indonesia to the Sudan it reflects the majority culture. It is often hated by the mullahs and fundamentalist zealots for its flexibility as well as the difficulty to control it. The striking absence of specifically Islāmic inspiration and rationalization in the Palestinian drive for freedom from Israel may very likely reflect the true position of popular Islām in the Muslim revival. Clearly, political/economic matters are substantially more important to the average Palestinian Muslim than the purity of Islāmic practice or the supremacy of Islāmic law notwithstanding the religious motivations of Hamas and the like. Imperial Islām, West hating, activist, fundamentalist, is a product of relatively few Muslims invariably committed to a political agenda so aggressively pressed that the religious element is almost invisible. This suggests that the Islāmic revival of the late 20th century is barely more than a disconnected group of national political movements led by ambitious, angry men using the cloak of religion for their own ends. Historically, Islām was invariably used to legitimize claims to political power, the most recent of which was Saddam Hussein's public displays of piety during the Gulf War of 1990-91. But when the masses have been called upon to support such claims, especially in modern times where support of the masses has become more important, the masses have declined. We note the conspicuous absence of any will to fight for Saddam Hussein in 1991, or of a called for popular uprising with the assassination of Anwar Sadat in Egypt in 1981, as well as the failure of a popular revolt to materialize when the Grand Mosque in Mecca was taken over in November, 1979, and the absence of Iraqi Shī'ī interest in furthering Iran's struggle with Iraq in the 1980s. So there is a clear gap between militant Islām and popular Islām. This is not the sort of indicator one would expect were the Islāmic revival a manifestation of some deep current of history. (One might argue that Muslim anger with the West seems deep enough, but I believe so far it has not reached a stage where irrevocable damage has been done, and the possibility remains for a mutually satisfactory resolution.)

Indeed, the often heard wistful and angry call to return to its roots, to go back to basics may be a reaction to pure change more than anything else. Recall our own reaction when the familiar is taken away or destroyed while many new and unfamiliar things happen around us. Then consider for a moment the situation for a typical urban resident of the Middle East. At one time there were neighborhoods, quiet and familiar, into which he could retreat for comfort and respite from the world at large. The old urban design had streets based on pedestrian traffic and a hierarchy of scale from the quiet personal residential court connected to other courts by small passages leading off narrow streets that wound about finally making it to a main thoroughfare. Then the Western motor car arrived punching wide swaths of highway through the local 'quarters' invading and destroying the intimacy of the neighborhood with a flood of noise, air pollution, and congestion. And not only his neighborhood but his home is invaded as well. From a culture traditionally slow paced he is within a lifetime overwhelmed with images of change via radio then TV. His children mock the traditional authority of the father, his wife and his daughters behave in 'promiscuous' ways, his proud heritage of Muslim dominion is humiliatingly made subservient to the wills not only of non-believers but non-believers who he thinks are the source of all that is decadent in the modern world. Under such culture shock, if indeed not Alvin Toffler's "future shock"[134] who wouldn't react and reject it all and want to go back to the good old days? It is inconceivable that fundamentalist-revivalist Islām wouldn't have appeal under such circumstances. It doesn't have to be just; it doesn't have to be true; it doesn't even have to be realistically possible; it only has to give hope.

But the message of fundamentalist-revivalist Islām has a fatal flaw, for its claims to perfection through the Qur'ān, *hadīth,* and the *sharī'a* are insupportable when administered by imperfect men and in a world so different from the source world of these documents. The contradiction is that to adjust to modern circumstances the fundamentalists will have to deviate from their fundamentalism and thus destroy themselves. Such altruism is not seen in history. So the fundamentalists will continue with their vision, a vision poisoned by its unsuitability to the times, and by the inevitable corruption of imperfect men pretending to be perfect. This has happened several times before in Muslim history from local mahdist movements, to the rise and fall of the 10th-century Fātimids in Egypt, to the Nizārī Ismā'īlīs, to the 16th-century Safavids in Persia. Accordingly, it appears that the Islāmic revival is more consonant with the internal rhythms of Islām and thus not a major tide in global history or the beginning of a "clash of civilizations". It is possible, however, that the Middle Eastern Muslim's search for a satisfying and viable identity might be achieved by a synthesis of Western and Muslim values, perhaps facilitated by Sūfī flexibility and mysticism. Similar Sūfī syntheses have almost worked in the past.

On the other hand, the potential of oil and weapons of mass destruction, assertively used by the Muslims of the Middle East, could profoundly change the picture. If oil revenues were to be used to create an infrastructure and commercial base that could sustain these countries after the oil runs out, and moreover, if these revenues were to be used to acquire weapons of mass destruction, and especially nuclear weapons that may be on the clandestine weapons market, then the global political and economic leverage would have every possibility of having substantial lasting consequences. In which case we would be witnessing a major tide in history.

The future is not predictable; we merely choose between guesses. As we examine the currents of history we try to pick out of contemporary events those items that most likely could signal the presence of important tides. For the future of Muslim discontent perhaps the appearance of a successful pan-Islāmic *mahdī*, the uses to which oil revenues are put, and the success or failure to acquire nuclear weapons and other weapons of mass destruction may be important factors if not indicators of what is in store for us all. However, in the last analysis the sources of Muslim discontent are as much internal as external. It is something they will have to work out on their own, and in so doing, our best position may be one of noninterference and avoidance of confrontation informed by a sound understanding of the breadth and variety of Muslim history.

Appendix A

Jihād

Muslims have been urged to *jihād* by the Qur'ān and *hadīth* from the very beginning to protect themselves from external attack. At the same time these seminal sources have also commanded them to strive hard to master their inner weakness and to be a good person. The special effort, striving, or struggle in self defense on the one hand and inner growth on the other defines the word, *"jihād." Jihād* means struggle, particularly on behalf of Islām. But more particularly and meaningfully, it means struggle for victory of good over evil. Again, from the very beginning, two kinds of *jihād* were recognized, the lesser struggle *(al-jihād al-asrar)* that involves defensive war, and the greater struggle *(al-jihād al-akbar)* that involves individual internal striving *(jihād an-Nafs)*. The lesser *jihād* of defensive war is mentioned in the Qur'ān in many places: for example,, "Permission to fight is given to those on whom war is made" (22:39). Similarly, the lesser *jihād* is frequently the subject of *hadīth*: for example, "...Allāh guarantees that He will admit the Mujahid in His cause into Paradise if he is killed, otherwise He will return him to his home safely with rewards and war booty."[135]

However, the greater *jihād* of inner struggle and personal goodness is also treated in the Qur'ān, "...those who strive in Our Cause, We will certainly guide them to Our Paths (29:69), "Oh Prophet, strive hard against the disbelievers and hypocrites" (i.e., preach)(9:73), "Therefore, listen not to the unbelievers, but strive against them with the utmost strenuousness, with the (Qur'ān)."(25:52). Greater *jihād* is the subject of many *hadīth* as well:"The best jihād for you is the performance of the hajj." (Bukhari, Vol. 4, Book 52, Number 128.) "The most excellent Jihād is that for the conquest of self." (Unspecified *hadīth* in, Allama Sir Abdullah al-Mamun al-Suhrawardy's, *The Sayings of Muhammad,* Carol, Secaucus, 1999, p.63.)

There is no question that *jihād* is often used to mean war and that this definition has been consistently understood as such throughout Muslim history. Nevertheless, its dual meanings cannot be ignored either, and one is compelled to be careful with the word, like our use of 'crusade' as 'holy war' that has evolved over the centuries to mean any special effort, and is rarely used as holy war now. (Note how wilful some Muslims, especially extremists, are about insisting on only the original meaning of crusade, just as we insist on focusing on only part of *jihād's* early meaning.) Bernard Lewis tends to dismiss early interpretations of *jihād* as inner struggle in favor of external war and believes the Qur'ān to be quite clear on the matter.[136] Though on occasion the Qur'ānic context clearly supports the military meaning, there are, nevertheless, numerous occasions in the Qur'ān where the meaning is spiritual struggle. Lewis also tends to brush aside as revisionist any contrary interpretation by modern Muslims. This Western difficulty in understanding the meaning of *jihād* is reflected in numerous translations of the Qur'ān. For example, two popular translations by the Western scholars Rodwell and Dawood* overwhelmingly translate *jihād* as "fight", or "make war", whereas translations by native Arabic speakers or Muslims render it for the most part, "struggle hard" or "strive hard" and the like.[137] The Arabic word for "fight" is *qital* and is so used in one form or another in the Qur'ān when referring to armed struggle. Unfortunately, *jihād* and *qitāl* have become homogenized in the minds of too many Muslims and non-Muslims alike.

Interestingly, the commentary in the prestigious, *Encyclopaedia of Islam (New Edition)* is all muddled up about "*djihād*" (*jihād*).[138] Perhaps Edward Said is more right than I conceded in my preface. However, one does not have to be an anti-Orientalist to detect here a serious lapse in scholarly

---

* One may argue about Dawood's 'Westerness', a Jew born in Baghdad, he was educated and lived his life in England.

detachment when the article author dismisses out of hand "spiritual *djihād*" (greater *jihād*) as, "in opposition to the *djihād* which is our present concern..." Here the Encyclopaedia is explicitly indicating a selective concern with only part of the entire concept of *jihād*. Other, related confusions about use of the term occur when treating physical war, or lesser *jihād*, between Muslims. The Encyclopaedia author labels it, "...only an abuse of language..." when one Muslim group proclaims *jihād* against another. 'Abuse of language' or not, that is the term Muslims used, and usage ultimately determines meaning. On many occasions *jihād* was justified by one group of Muslims declaring another group with whom they disagreed as unbelievers. This illustrates how amorphous the terms "unbeliever" and "*jihād*" can be in the hands of the ideological and doctrinaire, and how they can be used to any purpose. We first saw this with the Khārijites in the seventh century, and we see it all the time today as Muslim fundamentalists are as savage with their fellow Muslims as they are with the satanic West. Some Christians have from time to time succumbed to similar temptations in their own religious zealotry. And finally, the wholesale rejection of a long defensive tradition of physical *jihād* (the lesser *jihād*) as, "at the present time a thesis, of wholly apologetic character..."[139] is breathtaking in its narrowness. A much better and more balanced exposition of the meaning and use of *jihād* can be found in Chapter 1, "The Myth of a Militant Islam" by David Dakake in the book cited below.[140]

Appendix B

The Sharī'a

Following Muhammad's death the Muslim community was uncertain how to individually and collectively carry out God's will. For guidance they naturally looked to the Qur'ān and the *hadīth* and its *sunna*,* the example of Muhammad and his companions. This more or less worked in the simple times and the limited locale of Arabia. Yet time passed, Islām expanded out of Arabia and was no longer local, the *Hadīth* was growing by leaps and bounds, often with suspicious authenticity, and the complexities of ordinary life quickly revealed the limits of the inspired sources. The general command was clear enough, command good and forbid evil, and follow God's direction. But the inspired sources, the Qur'ān and the sunna (*hadīth*), were not only woefully incomplete, but distressingly ambiguous. What to do when *hadīth* contradict the Qur'ān, or either in itself gives multiple or contradicting answers, or the real situation is grossly different from that of the Prophet's Medīna?

A century after the Prophet's death Muslim scholars were actively searching for answers to these exceedingly important and perplexing questions. By this time there were many and various local 'laws' on proper Islāmic practice that would become known as the sharī'a, the path to God. In the meantime, however, Muslim scholars were addressing the reliability of the *hadīth*, eventually reducing several hundred thousand to less than 10,000[141] of the most trustworthy. Others were bringing to bear their legal

---

* *The sunna* is the content of the *hadīth*, however, the terms are often used interchangeably.

expertise on matters of consistency, meaning, applicability, and the like to the source materials of the sharī'a. Their standards and intellectual tools for achieving this were varied, and sufficiently characteristic to uniquely identify the jurist and his school of legal thought. Originally numbering 130, many legal schools became extinct or coalesced for the most part into the four Sunnī and one Shī'ī schools dominant today. Figure 5 only hints at the richness and variety of legal thought that lends to the practice and application of the sharī'a an immense flexibility. This is particularly important to understand as Western commentators tremble at the thought of sharī'a-based governments gaining sway in the world.

Specialists are fully acquainted with the law's flexibility and the fact that the draconian punishments for theft (cutting off the hand) and adultery (stoning to death) have almost never been carried out until recently, even in the strict, Hanbalī countries. Like our "Blue Laws", especially common in the New England states, they are on the books, but largely ignored. Moreover, *hadīth* were available and readily used to avoid or mitigate these extreme penalties. Jurists of all schools recognized very early the unique circumstances of Muhammad's time and place and worked hard to find the humane essence of the Law. Indeed, it can be said that the history of the development and application of the sharī'a is one of humanity and attention to the special circumstances of each situation. Extremist regimes like those in Saudi Arabia and the Taliban in Afghanistan are not typical.

The sharī'a is the law of Islām. It is God's direction to man on the proper path to obey and worship Him in all things and thereby attain Paradise. The sharī'a covers all aspects of religious behavior, family life, personal hygiene, etiquette, and commercial and criminal law. Its spiritual source and authority come from God through the Qur'ān and the inspired life of Muhammad and his companions as reflected in the sunna. Because of its breath of application it transcends specific duties and becomes an ethical system. As law, it differs from the West where precedent is powerful and desirable for the predictability it gives; for Islāmic law, precedent is valuable but not allowed to shadow ethical correctness. The sharī'a is very discerning in its categories of

Authority & Method Used \ Legal School	Hanafi	Maliki	Shafi'i	Hanbali	Jafari
Where Most Influential	Europe Turkey Arab Middle East India, Pakistan & Bangladesh	Largely Africa and Kuwait	Indonesia South East Asia East Africa	Saudi Arabia	Iran Iraq
Quran	X	X	X	X	X
hadith Sunna	X	X	X	X	Hadith of Ali & Imams
Analogy (*qiyas*)	x	x	Limited	Very Limited	Very Limited
Consensus (*ijma*)	x	From Medinan Community Only	x	Rejects	Very Limited Relies on Imam Only
Public Interest (*istislah / maslahah*)	Limited	x	Largely Rejects	Rare	
Notes	* Most liberal * Most adherents * Relies most on independent reason	* More conservative than Hanafi		* Most conservative * Fewest adherents * More dogmatic and suspicious of reason	Shi'i only

Figure 5
Legal Schools Used in Interpreting the Shari'a

obligation on the believer: 1./ there is the lawful and obligatory, 2./ the lawful and recommended, 3./ the lawful and permitted, 4./ the not unlawful, but reprehensible, 5./ and the unlawful and forbidden. This is clearly not the black and white world of the fundamentalist or the Western Islāmophobe. Matters not expressly prohibited by the sharī'a are tolerated.

The five most important schools of legal thought about the sharī'a,[142] in order of their founding, are the four Sunnī schools, Hanafī, Malikī, Shāfi'ī, and Hanbalī, and the Shī'ī, Jafarī school. All appeared between the mid eighth and ninth centuries. Within the Sunnī group all Sunnī schools are generally accepted today, and it is customary in particular cases for the participants to voluntarily select the school under which the matter at hand will be adjudicated. As indicated in Figure 5, different schools tend to predominate in different areas. The Hanbalī, the most notorious and conservative, is for the most part limited to the Arabian peninsula. In Figure 5 we note the universally accepted and divinely inspired Qur'ān and sunna with large "X"s. Small "x"s elsewhere indicate a man-made role subordinate to these divinely inspired sources. There are more methods used to try and understand the application of the Qur'ān and sunna to the law than indicated in the figure, for example, "*ra'y*", personal, subjective opinion by the jurists in the absence of precedent is acceptable to the Hanafīs and Malikīs but rejected by the Shāfi'ī, Hanbali, and Shī'ī Jafarī, while *istihsan*, the freedom of jurists to decide on the basis of the common good, is acceptable to the Malikī and Jafarī, and Hanafī, but rejected by the Shāfi'ī and Hanbalī. Hopefully, Figure 5 will help make sense out of this stew of variety and give a feeling for the many and flexible ways Islāmic jurists have sought to make humane sense of divine sources of Islāmic law. However, alas, we cannot escape the arcane niceties of law by going to Islamic jurisprudence, for the boldness of my entries in Figure 5 in fact mask considerable variability within each entry[143]. The purpose of the figure is to succinctly show with reasonable accuracy the differences in the legal schools.

Figure 6 illustrates the way in which God's will gets put into practice. Note that the sharī'a does not translate directly into practice, notwithstanding its holy sources. Its interpretation in the

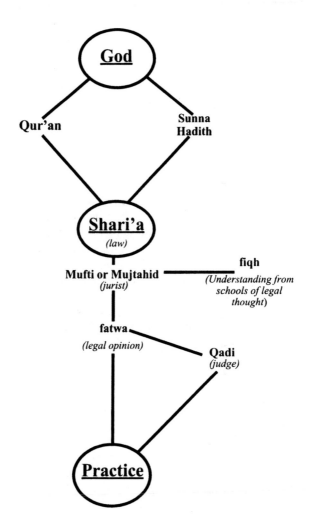

Figure 6
Derivation and Application of Sunni Islamic Law

face of the widening Islāmic world and new situations not foreseen by the Companions comes from the muftīs trained in one of the legal schools. Using their understanding, *fiqh*, gained from that school, permits the jurist to issue an opinion, a *fatwā*, on the matter at hand. This is the guide to practice. On occasion there may be some further disagreement which is settled by a judge, a *qādī*. Thus, once again, the sharī'a consists of two general sources, the divine source of the Qur'ān and sunna, and the human source coming from the muftīs guided by the *fiqh* of the schools of jurisprudence.

In the eighth and ninth centuries there was considerable development of sharī'a law, but eventually a notion developed that further innovation, *bid'a*, was becoming dangerous and that the use of independent reasoning, *ijtihād*, should be curtailed, "the door to *ijtihād* was closed". For the most part this remained so for 900 years and little new was added to sharī'a law. The 20th century saw the role of independent reasoning reappearing, but, alas, it was not coming from the ulamā or muftīs; it was coming from religious amateurs issuing *fatwās* in service of their extremist religious views. The tragedy has been that the old ulamā have been marginalized and ethically discredited as they have supported oppressive regimes, while at the same time very few new scholars have been trained to replace those dying off. Accordingly, the intellectual and spiritual vacuum left has been filled by self-interested, religiously unsophisticated, rank amateurs the likes of Osama bin Laden and Ayman al-Zawahiri of Al Qaeda. The average Muslim looking for guidance from the sharī'a and its new (mis)interpreters is often set adrift in a sea of misinformation.

It is pointless to deal with the numerous and notorious specific examples of misinterpretation and gross distortion of the sharī'a and its application just as it is with the notion of *jihād*. These examples of queer thought are easily refuted by reasonable men, Muslim and non-Muslim alike. For reassurance see the highly recommended El Fadl book, *The Great Theft*, mentioned elsewhere. However, there is no precedent for such rational thought being persuasive to the shrill believer or the gullible observer. The ambiguity of sacred texts leaves ample room for twisted justification. The great middle-ground of interested parties faced with these pathological interpretations and practices on the one hand and the moderate views of Islām on the other would do well to condemn the extremist perpetrators, not their religion. Suffice it to say that those with a wilful thirst for power masquerading as self-deluding piety have been particularly savage throughout history from the time of Abraham to the present.

Appendix C

Sūfism[144]

Long before anyone was called "Sūfī" there were Muslims who were dissatisfied with the state of affairs within the faith. Islām's primary requirement was "submission" to the will of God, indeed, Islām means submission in Arabic. For some the cold formality of this submission did not satisfy the need for a more personal and loving connection with God. And quite apart from the internal need, there was the prominently opulent lifestyle of the Umayyad leaders that seemed to fly in the face of Muhammad's simple existence. These two factors, the desire for a closer relationship with God, and the rejection of the materialism and corruption of the Umayyad caliphs, moved some to a solitary asceticism[145] that included the wearing of rough wool (Arabic *sūf*) garments. The proto-Sūfī was more than suspicious of the seductions of the material world, he believed that God abhorred it as well; thus in an early eighth-century letter by al-Hasan al-Basrī (d. 727): "Beware of this world with all wariness; for it is like to a snake, smooth to the touch, but its venom is deadly. Turn away from whatsoever delights thee in it... God has Himself sent us a warning against it...God has created nothing more hateful to Him than this world..." Al-Basrī goes on to admire the example of the Prophets Muhammad, Moses, David, and Jesus, "My daily bread is hunger, my daily badge is fear, my raiment is wool, my mount is my foot...All the night I have nothing, yet there is none richer than I!"[146]

The proto-Sūfī looked inward to discover his weaknesses for ungodly practices and materialism, and set himself the task of self-purification. He also sought to know God's will for himself and how to surrender to it. Since he believed that there was nothing outside of God and His will and creation, the seeker tasked himself with harmonizing with it. Abū-Yazīd Bistāmī (d.874) describes his mystical experience of the union with God: "I gazed upon Him with the eye of truth, and said to Him: "Who is this?" He said: "This is neither I nor other than I. There is no God but I." Then He changed me out of my identity into His Selfhood...Then I...communed with Him with the tongue of His Grace, saying: "How fares it with me with Thee?" He said: "I am thine through thee; there is no god but Thou"."[147] Thus God is loved by seeking union with Him, whereas the orthodox (mainstream Sunnī and sometimes Shī'ī) Muslim believed one demonstrated love of God by simply obeying Him. Love and union on the one hand, simple obedience on the other. Naturally enough from time to time there would be clashes over the matter.

Current scholarship believes that Sūfī asceticism developed on its own and was not appreciably influenced by the examples of Christian hermits as was thought earlier. Be that as it may, the first recorded use of the term, "Sūfī" was sometime before 776[148]; by the early ninth century Sūfism was widely known in the Muslim world, and over the next two hundred years reached its peak of influence in Islām.[149]

It was during this period that the character of the Sūfī movement changed from being individual and ascetic to communal and mystical. The stage of mystical enlightenment could be reached only under the tutelage of a master. This caused students to gather in a lodge where they were identified as a brotherhood or order. As the fame of the master and his pupils spread, the order's fame and prestige spread as well, however, for the most part, the orders were local. The followers of Sūfism might be the fully committed who would spend their lives in prayer, study, and practice, or they might be lay associates of a lodge who would follow the master's teachings much more loosely and rarely gather with the rest of the order. Residence in a lodge under a given master might be for an extended time, or as was common, at least in the beginning, the student might go from master to master. A master claimed a chain of master-student relationships stretching from himself back to Alī and thus to Muhammad. Sūfī masters were often very highly regarded by Muslims at large. This sometimes led to their elevation after death (or even before death) to a special holiness, a kind of sainthood. Their tombs became a destination for pilgrimage where miracles might be expected. Not surprisingly, the existence and veneration of Sūfī saints disturbed orthodox Muslims, since this was nearly blasphemous worship; only God was to be worshiped.

The Sūfīs accepted the Qur'ān, *hadīth*, and *sharī'a* but believed that the inner meaning was more important. They did not reject the outer practices but always gave precedence to the inner life. Though the Qur'ān was their holiest book, they saw it as more than the literal words of God, it was also the embodiment of the thought of God. It was the Sūfī desire to fathom God's thought, to discover the hidden spiritual essence of the Qur'ān. The means to this knowledge was in the mystical experience that some have described as an orgasmic-like ecstasy that was simultaneously a calmly enlightened vision, a clarity of understanding of the self, the world, and God's overarching presence in it. This stage of enlightenment might be brought on by the repetitive chant of the 99 names of God,[150] or other chants, song, or dance. The Mevlivi order of Whirling Dervishes is an example of those who chose the path of dance, though this whirling dance technique came some time after its founding in the 13th century. The order was of Turkish origin founded by the greatest of all Persian poets, Jalāl al-Dīn Rūmī (and his son). It is interesting to note that Rūmī's spiritual love poetry in worship of God, has made him a best selling poet in America, 800 years after his death.[151]

The seeker also followed a program of spiritual training under a master that included complete commitment to the master, prayer well beyond the five daily prayers of the *salāt*, exercises in breathing and proper posture, and a gradual psychological transformation. The number of psychological steps or stations in a program varied according to the master, but typically numbered several dozen. Each station must be successfully achieved before proceeding to the next. The stations typically included repentance, self-examination, silence, hope, patience, tranquility, trust in God,

Appendix C

love, and unity (with God).[152] The master also guided the pace of the disciple's progress, for it was only too easy for the seeker to misjudge his progress and prematurely imagine his loss of self and complete identity with God. This had its dangers, not only for the soul of the seeker, but for his life as well. The early tenth-century mystic Mansur al-Hallāj became so intoxicated with his imagined unity with God that he declared it openly,"I am the Truth" meaning I am the sign of God. Alas, his orthodox interrogators mistakenly thought he was saying that he was in fact God and had him tortured and crucified for blasphemy.

Of special interest are the writings of Ibn al-Arabī who lived from 1165 to 1240. His prodigious, comprehensive, and learned oeuvre on Islāmic theory and practices have earned him the sobriquet, *al-shaykh al-akbar*, the Greatest Master. He is one of the intellectual fathers of Sūfism, though it is not clear that he was ever a Sūfī himself. His writings are at once germane to core Sūfī beliefs, and to the problem of Islāmic fundamentalism and today's turmoil of ideas within Islām and without. Two names sometimes used for the Holy Qur'ān are *qur'ān* and *furqān*; a complimentary pair that reflects the wholeness and completeness of the Qur'ān, where *qur'ān* means bringing together and *furkān* means separation, differentiation, discrimination between truth and falsehood. Thus the Holy Qur'ān at once unites all things under God and discriminates all things one from another, particularly good and evil, truth and falsehood. Often in al-Arabī's writings we encounter these complimentary notions, but though he sees the necessity of both, he asserts that *qur'ān* dominates *furqān* and will, in a balanced manner, prevail. Thus, according to him and many later Sūfīs, Islām is really a religion of mercy over wrath, spiritual intoxication and intimacy over spiritual sobriety and awe, and meaning and spirit over form and letter. Nothing better highlights the contrast between Sūfism and sharī'a-minded orthodoxy; flexibility and openness v.s. rigidity and close mindedness.[153]

As mentioned elsewhere, this Sūfī flexibility has not only been the main reason for so many converts in South and Southeast Asia and elsewhere, but the main reason for so much turmoil with fundamentalists as well. Sūfī converts are just not Islāmic enough for the fundamentalists.

Sūfism

There has always been tension between orthodox Islām and Sūfism. On the one hand Sūfism has had an important influence on the mother faith, yet, its mystical dimensions have led to divergences that have sometimes brought the orthodox to condemn it as heretical. As it evolved, Sūfism became less concerned with differences in religious beliefs, seeing the multitude of outward manifestations, even of infidels, as clouding appreciation of the universal authentic inward knowledge of the one true God. This belief that at the deepest level all believed in the same God facilitated Sūfī accommodation of other religious beliefs as they made new conversions. Unfortunately for Sūfism, reformist Muslims have viewed this as too permissive and passive, and thus as time passed Sūfism was seen as weak and useless for protecting or furthering the faith. As the momentum of modern revivalism and reform has grown, the inward focus of Sūfism has been found to be irrelevant for the outwardly directed, politically active Muslim.[154] The net result is a substantial decline in the influence of Sūfism in recent centuries. Nevertheless, even today, four percent of Muslims are Sūfīs,[155] and very likely more than half the world's Muslims practice some elements of Sūfism.

Having thus summarized the historic Sūfī movement in a rather simple and linear fashion one must once again step back, and as so often happens with matters as complex as the history of Islām, caution that the reality is not so straightforward. For example, the mystical dimension has tended to decline in importance as the orders have matured. Moreover, the orders have tended to become politically active and religiously conservative, quite the opposite of early Sūfism. Through time and space the orders themselves have spanned an enormous range of practices and beliefs as we have touched on in describing Islām in Turkey, and South and Southeast Asia. Students of the subject know immediately that the Sūfism of al-Hallāj is almost unrecognizable from that of the Naqshbandī. And one would be treading on very thin ice indeed to assume that Sūfīs have not always held a paramount regard for the Qur'ān and *hadīth* and are sometimes as *sharī'a*-minded and militant as the most committed fundamentalist.

Appendix C

It is ironic that though Sūfism has been responsible for the Islāmization of more than half of the Muslim world, its flexibility and acceptance of previous religious practices among new converts has left in its tracks a popular Islām that has led to the modern trauma of revivalism in major parts of the Muslim East (Appendices E and F.)[156] Moreover, where declining Sūfism has faded in its socializing role in the community, it has left an emotional vacuum that needed filling. Trimingham notes that the early , non-militant "Muslim Brotherhood served as a substitute for the orders" in modern Egypt in providing charitable services and resistance to the West's seductions, and "a system of guidance for the individual."[157] The efficacy of this emotional vacuum for breeding discontent and providing receptive ground for fundamentalism is clear.

Appendix D

The Nizārī Ismā'īlīs[158]
(Assassins)

The history of the Assassins is imbedded in a maze of sects and subsects, of assassination and cooperation, of religious orthodoxy, of schismatic and scandalous revisionism. Figure 7 and the identities, 'Sevener = Ismā'īlī = Fātimid,' where these synonyms are the precursors of the 'Nizārīs = Assassins,' may help keep the story straight.

The sect was started by Hasan-i Sabbāh who was born in Iran in the 1050s. Though his family was Twelver Shī'a he was soon exposed to the preachings of the schismatic Seveners. The Seveners, or Ismā'īlīs, were considered extremely radical by the Abbāsids and the dominant Sunnī Seljuks, and barely less so by the orthodox Shī'a. However, the Ismā'īlīs had a home in their own Fātimid Caliphate. Though the Ismā'īlī Fātimids were active proselytizers, they were for the most part surprisingly tolerant of other beliefs, even Christian and Jewish.[159] Nevertheless, Ismā'īlī missionary zeal was manifest, particularly in the institution of the *da'wa* (summons to allegiance to the Ismā'īlī Imām) who sent out *dā'īs* (summoners) to Persia, Iraq, and Syria.

While young Hasan-i Sabbāh was a teenager in Rayy (a few miles southeast of the eventual site of Tehran) he experienced a religious epiphany and converted to Ismā'īlism. As is so often the case with the newly enlightened, he was particularly zealous and attracted the attention and admiration of the regional *dā'ī* (summoner) who appointed him an agent of the *da'wa* and sent him to the Caliph in Cairo. Unfortunately, Hasan arrived at an inopportune moment in Ismā'īlī history, for Caliph Mustansir was

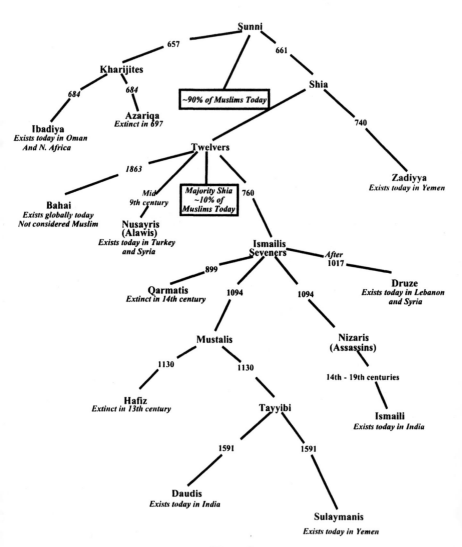

**Figure 7
Typical Fragmentation of Islam and
Christianity**

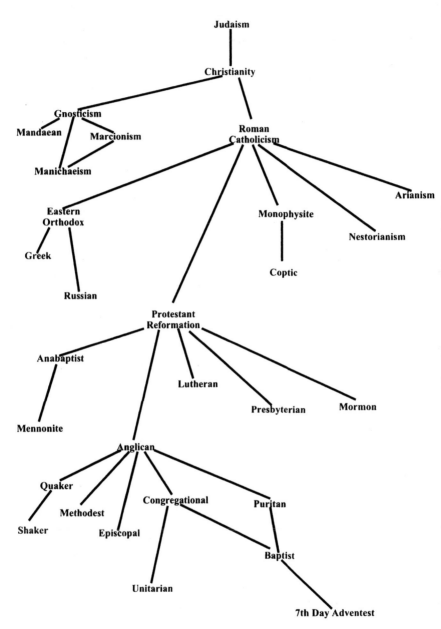

Typical Fragmentation of Christianity

weak and largely under the control of the military commander, Badr al-Jamālī.

Hasan's eagerness for the *da'wa* mission apparently came into conflict with the more conservative Badr, and he was left for three years without ever meeting the Caliph. He was deported from Egypt in 1081, returning to western Persia and his preaching and organizing, clearly with more passion than his superior, Badr al-Jamālī. Hasan's hope was that by spreading the Ismā'īlī message he could convert the Twelver Shī'as and Sunnīs, and oust the ruling Seljuk Turks and their aging Abbāsid accomplices.

There would be no question of a direct military confrontation with the overwhelmingly powerful Seljuks. Like modern terrorists, Hasan would fight their weaknesses, not their strengths, in this case the largely personal, non-institutional nature of the leadership. If one could neutralize a local or central leader it would be as effective as a military victory over thousands. Thus Hasan's success at converting the people was augmented by killing political and religious leaders.

Hasan's first victim was no less than the Seljuk vizier, Nizām al-Mulk in 1092. He was killed in a style that was to become the hallmark of the Assassins; the killer got close to Nizām by posing as a Sūfī and stabbed him with a dagger. The attack took place in public and the attacker was killed. Thus the ingredients of deception, stabbing, public action, and suicidal personal disregard, all no doubt calculated for their efficacy and psychological leverage.

Two years before in 1090 Hasan had gathered enough strength to take the mountain fortress at Alamūt just south of the Caspian sea, largely by deceit, and thereafter, for the most part by similar methods, he acquire several other mountaintop fortresses in Persia. These fortresses were by then not in hostile territory, they were among friendly, converted Ismā'īlī villages. Indeed, the overwhelming majority of Ismā'īlīs following Hasan were of a peaceful nature trying to live placid, harmless lives. They converted because they found the Seljuks oppressive and the Ismā'īlī religious message attractive. Only a very few were the dreaded *fidā'ī*, the fanatic killers awaiting the Masters evil call.

Nizārī Ismāīlīs (Assassins)

The break from the orthodox Ismā'īlīs came in 1094 when the Fātimid Caliph died, and Badr put aside the lawful successor, the older son Nizār, and engineered the succession of a younger son, al-Musta'lī. Hasan rejected Musta'lī as an interloper and continued his allegiance to the now missing Imām Nizār. This created the most serious split of the Seveners; thereafter the Fatimids were Musta'lī Ismā'īlīs and their enemies were Nizārī Ismā'īlīs led by Hasan from his headquarters at Alamūt.

The Nizārī Ismā'īlīs were now fighting everybody, on rare occasions in conventional military battles, but for the most part by the preferred method of political killings; almost fifty are known from Hasan's reign alone (1090 - 1124). Among the more prominent victims were the Fātimid and Khurāsān grand visiers, the rulers of Afamiya and Homs, and the Seljuk emir of Mosul. Islām's intense reaction to this political and religious zealotry was savage with massacres of Nizārīs in Aleppo, Damascus, Qazwīn, and Isfahān, as well as of entire peaceful Nizārī communities in many smaller towns. Nevertheless, they survived and even expanded in Khurāsān in the east and eventually into Syria in the west.

In Syria the Nizārīs struggled for almost 30 years before their place became secure beginning in 1131 with the acquisition of a number of mountain fortresses. It was about this time that the Nizārīs and their tactics first came to the attention of the Crusaders and the name Assassin began to gain currency, especially with the West. The Syrian Nizārīs were as active as their Persian parents, indeed, with Rāshid al-Dīn Sinān's takeover in 1164 they became almost independent of their Persian masters. Sinān directed the Syrian Nizārīs in a number of assassinations including two failed attempts on Saladin, and for the first time some of the targets were not only Muslims but Crusader leaders. Count Raymond II of Tripoli was killed in 1151 and Conrad of Montferrat in 1192.The fearful reputation, and myth, of the Assassins was growing even as Sinān became known as the "Old Man of the Mountain".

The Syrian and Persian branches reunited after Sinān's death in 1193. In the meantime, however, the Nizārīs were going through some startling evolutionary episodes: at Alamūt in 1162 Hasan II,

151

the third successor of Hasan-i Sabbāh, declared that he was now caliph, the *sharī'a* was no longer the guide for the Nizārīs, and the fast of Ramadan was cut in half. The sect became almost hedonistic and Muslim in name only. About half a century later a subsequent leader brought the Nizārīs back to orthodoxy - but amazingly, to Sunnī orthodoxy!

Their external relations were evolving as well. There were fewer assassinations, they began selling their services (Ibn Battuta says that in the 14th century they were called "arrows of the sultan"[160]), and they were slowly becoming less repugnant to their Sunnī brethren. Nevertheless, an assassination in service of their political/religious ends still brought joy to the true believers[161] that reminds us of the celebrations by much of the Muslim world upon the 9-11 attacks on the United States. Similar expressions of joy and pride were later expressed at the assassination of the Atabeg Qizil Arslān in 1191. The poet Hasan writing contemporaneously says in a poem, "Praise, glory, and thousands of benedictions upon the three heros ... Listen to me now, so that I may tell thee a story ... which is like princely pearls: ... the ax of vengeance got its sheath ... bringing victory and happiness ..."[162]

The idiosyncracies of leadership and external pressures eventually transformed the Syrian Nizārīs. Their absorption was completed by Baybars' Mamlūks in 1273. The Persian branch did not fare so well. When the Mongols first appeared, the Nizārīs were friendly and accommodating. They were trying to use the Mongols for their own local advantage. However, the Mongols were using them the same way. This dance of scorpions lasted for a generation until the Mongols could no longer tolerate Nizārī power in their midst and destroyed them in 1256. After two centuries not much remained of Hasan-i Sabbāh's dream.

The Nizārī Ismā'īlīs were not all co-opted by the Mamlūks or slaughtered by the Mongols. Some survived and eventually found their way east forming small communities in a large arc from Persia to India and largely out of sight of the powers. By the end of the 20th century they had long since evolved into a benign and socially constructive community with strong western links and many traces of Sūfī and Hindu practices and beliefs. Some estimate their present global population as high as 20 million.

Nizārī Ismāīlīs (Assassins)

Their current leader is the 49th Imām, the Aga Khan Prince Karim.

The history of the Nizārī Ismā'īlīs is not unique, we see in them similarities to the Khārijites of the seventh and eighth centuries and to the Islāmist movements of the 20th and 21st centuries. In the beginning they were highly motivated and absolutely certain of their beliefs. This rigid and narrow-minded certitude could brook no question, not even implicit question stemming from the mere existence of opposition. Accordingly, all opposition needed to be ruthlessly exterminated. Since in the beginning they were weak, their only recourse was violence, frequently indiscriminate and savage. Ironically, narrow-minded certitude contains the seeds of its own destruction, for where there is no flexibility, there is no ability to survive. The moment of any difference of belief, opinion, interpretation, or recollection is the moment of schism. A rigid bar easily snaps. In addition, however, there is the inevitable reaction, which can be violent as well. Sometimes the reaction defeats, sometimes it is self-defeating. Only the particular circumstances will tell. And finally, it may help us to understand the Nizārīs and similar dissenters by remembering that the general characteristics of Islāmic schismatic movements are the same as those of Christians as well.

Appendix E

Fundamentalism

The more one tries to understand the phenomenon of Islāmic fundamentalism the more unsatisfactory the word, "fundamentalism"becomes. In common use it generally denotes a practice or belief that looks back to the basics in religion. As applied to Islām before the 20th century it meant the strict and literal adherence to the Qur'ān, hadīth, and sharī'a as well as to the derived learning of one or more of the four legal schools developed in Islām's early centuries before the 'door to ijtihād closed.' A certain doctrinal rigidity and absolutism was manifest as well. Accordingly, the Sūfīs were the natural enemies of these fundamentalists. Fundamentalism specifically rejected all non-Muslim and modern law and social customs.[163] It was essentially conservative, generally apolitical, and wished to preserve what came from early Islām.[164] Things get messy as "fundamentalism" is used for 20th-century movements, and we ask 'what basics', or 'look how far back'? There is also the matter of how the belief is manifest, i.e., internally and privately, or externally and publically, passively or politically, accommodatingly or confrontationally. And of course, there is always the elasticity of interpretation and viewpoint to add further scope to the meaning of "fundamentalism." Specialists rightly tend to get touchy about the use of such a catchall and superficial term. Nevertheless, the word is in such common use that I have chosen to retain it here. Perhaps, however, the damage can be mitigated by considering some of the alternative, more finely tuned meanings of Islāmic fundamentalism, and then go on to a very brief summary of its modern history in its most important manifestations.

Appendix E

The meanings of fundamentalism are sometimes defined in an evolving historical context. For example, Choueiri[165] points out three separate movements in the past two hundred fifty years, revivalism, reformism, and radicalism. According to him, revivalism emerged in the 18th and 19th centuries typified by Wahhābism in Arabia and later the Mahdist revolt in the Sudan. Revivalism was tribal, peripheral, against religious innovation and popular (folk) practices, and frequently looked to a Mahdī for leadership. It looked inward to rectify religiously degenerate personal practices.

Reformism followed in the 19th and 20th centuries. It rejected most of historically developed Islām and accepted only the very earliest sources.[166] Nevertheless, while looking to the Islāmic community for consensus it also looked to European culture to find a way to stop Islāmic decline. Thus by mid 20th century it was often looking to, and being corrupted by, nationalism and secularism. Hassan al-Banna's founding of the Muslim Brotherhood in 1928 marked the culmination of the reform movement. Later, as the Muslim Brotherhood failed, it transformed itself and reformism into Islāmic radicalism. Reformism looked outward condemning the West's corruption and influence, but also seeking Western solutions to their weakness and humiliation. They looked to the political community for political solutions and used Islām as an integral instrument to bring this about.

Radicalism followed in the 20th century as a reaction to reformism's secular and nationalistic tendencies and the failure to fix the spiritual plight of Islām. It was significantly influenced by the Indian/Pakistani, Mawlana Mawdūdī and Egypt's Sayyid Qutb, the latter formerly of the Muslim Brotherhood. It charged the West with causing the decline of Islām, reasserted the doctrine of God's absolute sovereignty over all things, and asserted the efficacy of *jihād* (in this case, 'holy war') in service of liberation from Western influence.

One should note, however, that the names of Choueiri's categories are sometimes used differently by others thus creating a confusing terminology. For example, many scholars use "revivalism" as a general term for Islāmic resurgence. Mawdūdī is described as a revivalist as he asserts the necessity and primacy of the Islāmic state[167] His revivalism is politically active, anti-syncretic, and against corrupting popular religious practices[168]. According to Mawdūdī, modernism is an acceptable source of inspiration if limited to science, economics, and politics[169], but elsewhere should be rejected.

What clearly worries the West is called "Islāmism". It evolved out of Mawdūdī's revivalism. First before anything else it is politically very active. It is for the most part anticlerical, indeed, Islāmists are exceedingly hostile to Muslim clerics (the case of Iran excepted) seeing them as tools of essentially corrupt governments such as those of Egypt and Saudi Arabia. (By clerics I mean those with special religious training and particularly the jurists who have traditionally been the interpreters of the law, the *ulamā*.) Islāmists are for the most part young secular, semi-intellectuals[170] with no special religious training or experience. Interestingly, their rejection of Muslims who practice folk or popular Islām[171] (see Appendix F) is as ferocious as their rejection of the West. They also reject out of hand the traditional wisdom espoused by the four major legal schools and believe interpretation, *ijtihād*, 'reopened' after a thousand year hiatus. The arbitrary 'reopening' of *ijtihād* is their rationalized license to interpret Islām in any way they want.[172]   Some authors use "jihadist" or "absolutist" with a meaning similar to "Islāmist".

For this book none of the terms above seem satisfactory. "Islāmism" comes close, yet it seems to me a bit obscure and narrow. Khaled El-Fadl suggests the term, "puritan" and makes a good case for it,[173] but I think it is too evocative. John Esposito warns us about the use of "fundamentalism", because it, "...is laden with Christian presuppositions and Western stereotypes, and it implies a monolithic threat." I personally like his term, "Islāmic activism",[174]but it seems a tad too general. Another possible term is, "Islāmic extremism." It nicely catches the crux of the matter and would be my choice, except that "fundamentalism" does capture important qualities familiar to the West. Accordingly, with a respectful bow to Esposito and his caveats, I will continue to use "fundamentalism."

Appendix E

It is reasonably accurate to say that "fundamentalism" espouses political change to and through a *sharī'a* based society, its paradigm is early Islām (just how early depends on the particular advocate), and its methods are several and can be any mix of spiritual (greater *jihād*) and physical (lesser *jihād*) action.

Muslim fundamentalist movements have evolved over the past two centuries under different names driven by arguments ranging from the weaknesses of 'modern' Islamic practice, to condemnation of Western oppression, to condemnation of the West in general. With this transition has come a shift from thought to action, from introspective guilt to external attack, and from Sūfī-like flexibility to self-righteous implacable hate.

The genealogy of influential fundamentalists is quite loose, because they have been inspired by the situation of their particular time and location. These times and places are important, particularly today, because they point to two different but related causes of the Islāmic resurgence, humiliation at the hands of the West, and/or deep concern over the absence of religious purity. Thus the main target of South and Southeast Asian fundamentalists has almost always been other Muslims who they see as heretic if not apostate. Middle Eastern fundamentalists, and Pakistanis for the most part, attack the West for its cultural and economic imperialism as well. The following summary lists some important figures and their movements.

Hassan al-Bannā (1906-1949) was born in Egypt and trained as a teacher in Cairo. Egypt was a virtual colony of the British with middle and upper classes that were becoming as materialistic and morally compromised as anywhere in the West notwithstanding their superficial practice of Islām. His reaction to the situation was to call for a rejection of foreigners and foreign influence in Muslim affairs, and for his people to return to the path of pure Islām. However, it was not to be an Islām as practiced in the time of the Prophet, but as reinterpreted for modern times, yet always strictly adhering to Islāmic principles. He believed that Islām was completely sufficient for the management of a modern society; there would be no compromise with the West; Islām's world must be ruled by a totally dedicated *sharī'a* bound government. He first thought this could be attained by educating Egyptian youth and informing the larger public in proper Islāmic values, as well as providing economic and social support for the needy. To do this he founded the Muslim Brotherhood[175] in 1928. He found very shortly, however, that more was needed, and the Brotherhood became politically active. Rapid growth followed, particularly with its call for the expulsion of the British, so that by the early 1940s it claimed several hundred thousand members. Though it was essentially non-violent, a more radical wing developed that did espouse violence. Nevertheless, the violence prone were kept under control until after World War II. Thereafter, they began terrorist activity contrary to al-Bannā's wishes. In 1949, after the assassination of an important political official, the Egyptian government held him responsible and had him killed by the secret police. Though the Brotherhood supported the overthrow of the monarchy it was not welcomed into the new military government of Gamal Nasser that brought it about. Additional friction including attempts on Nasser's life led to Nasser's banning the Brotherhood and the imprisonment of many of its leaders in 1954. The tension between non-violent and violent elements is typical of protest or revolutionary organizations. We have seen it with the PLO, with Mawdūdī's Jamā'at-i Islāmī, and with the Muslim Brotherhood. It appears that frustration, impatience, and hate have more often than not driven radicalism to violent action. We shall see this shortly in Sayyid Qutb's career, but first we turn to one who has influenced Qutb and Islāmic activism arguably more than any other.

Mawlana Sayyid Abūl-Alā Mawdūdī (1903-1979) was born and lived in India, and what later became Pakistan. Like al-Bannā, he came from an unusually religious family. For much of his life he was immersed in the dual struggles of freeing India from British imperial rule, and virtually simultaneously, to free Indian Muslims from Hindu rule. The mix of deep religious belief, anti-imperialism, and rejection of the overwhelming Hindu cultural presence clearly determined the direction of his thinking. Everywhere he looked he saw unbelief, unbelief of the British imperialists with their materialism, exploitation, and low morals, unbelief of the Hindus with their scandalous practices and pantheon of gods, and even unbelief of the Muslim community that was being seduced at once by Western and Hindu values. Out of this experience he redefined the old Muslim term, *jāhilīyya,* which originally meant the ignorance of the pre-Islāmic peoples of Arabia of the one true God, to mean all un-Islāmic belief and behavior.[176] And since religious compromise led to popular practices barely recognizable as Islāmic, Mawdūdī insisted on the absolute sovereignty of God in all things (*hākimīyya*). This commitment to the absolute obedience to, and sovereignty of God cannot be overstated and is the key to his beliefs and the beliefs of those whom he influenced.

Mawdūdī felt that in a world of unbelief the only recourse was to reject *jāhilīyya* everywhere[177] and establish a pure Islāmic polity. This was top down thinking; first educate a cadre of proper believers, then have them organize a polity where the unbelievers and misbelievers could be reeducated. Nothing would be forced, success of the revolution would come about by education, and once the polity was established the people would see the light and come around peacefully.[178] However, in the process of achieving this goal he would be uncompromising in rejecting any dealings with the opposition whatsoever. They were profoundly tainted and tainting. This rigidity would later significantly weaken his local appeal in the churning, realpolitik world as India and Pakistan became independent.

Mawdūdī's religious thought, and Lenin's political thought, are disconcertingly similar. Both saw their world as profoundly corrupt, both were self-righteous, absolutist zealots, both believed in top-down social transformation, both believed in the efficacy of an elite cadre, and both naively missed the savage dimensions of well-intended power in the hands of imperfect men.

Though Mawdūdī was largely a thinker, not an activist, he did organize the Jamā'at i-Islāmī party in India in 1941. It played an influential, though scarcely decisive part in Pakistan's independence and subsequent political life. The party eventually found that Mawdudi's complete rejection of compromise with the *jāhilīyya* world got it nowhere, so it's position became somewhat more flexible. Nevertheless, it has never been a strong player in Pakistani politics, and Mawdūdī's influence was locally diluted.

Elsewhere, however, Mawdudī's influence was manifest in all subsequent notions of Muslim identity through the existence of an Islāmic polity. This polity was not so much a rejection of, or reaction to, the West alone, as it was a search for the true, pure faith. Accordingly, in the milieu of the Indian subcontinent this was motivated in large part by a fear that Islām was being diluted by popular practices originating with the Hindu majority. His solutions to the problem were taken up by others in a different context with different drivers and made part of the foundation of a greater Islāmic reaction, particularly by Sayyid Qutb in Egypt.

Qutb was a disciple of al-Bannā, but transformed al-Bannā's relatively benign activism into today's more familiar activist Islāmic extremism, largely under the influences of his experiences in the United States and with the Egyptian government, and the writings of Mawdūdī and Alexis Carrel. But before treating Qutb directly, a word on the surprising connection to Alexis Carrel.

Alexis Carrel was a French physician and winner of the 1912 Nobel Prize in Medicine and Physiology. He worked for much of his life at the Rockefeller Institute in New York. In 1935 he published *Man the Unknown* where he enumerated the degeneracies of Western civilization as he saw them, "The woman who has several children, who devotes herself to their children, who devotes herself to their education , instead of her own career, is considered weak-minded. If a man saves a little money for his wife and the education of his children, this money is stolen from him by enterprising financiers." "A rich man has every right. He may discard his aging wife, abandon his old mother to penury, rob those who have entrusted their money to him, without losing the consideration of his friends. Homosexuality flourishes. Sexual morals have been caste aside."[179] "Reason has swept away religious beliefs"[180] The body and soul are an inseparable whole[181]. Men and women are different and should be treated and trained differently.[182] The causes of this degeneracy include the misuse of science and technology and the alienation of people from the natural state of harmony found in older and simpler times. He proposed a solution including specially trained cadres to lead folks away from these seductive but degenerate practices ("Humanity has never gained anything from the efforts of the crowd. It is driven onward by the passion of a few abnormal individuals..."[183]), and suffering and death in this service are good[184].

Seyyid Qutb (1906-1966) was born in Egypt. He became a teacher and eventually a functionary in the Egyptian Ministry of Education. His public life[185], whose ramifications haunt us all even today, began with his first intimate encounter with Western civilization when he was sent by the Egyptian government to the United States for special study of American education in November 1948. The experience was staggering. When he returned to Egypt in August 1950 he was seething with indignant anger at what he saw as a vile, degenerate America. The obscenity was compounded by America's leadership of a West supporting the Zionist invasion of Palestine and the humiliating Western hegemony over the Muslim world.

Shortly after his return he joined the politically active Muslim Brotherhood,[186] and quickly rose to become one of its most influential leaders. Convicted of complicity in a plot to assassinate Nasser he was jailed in 1955. During the following nine years in prison he discovered the writings of Mawdudi and wrote many articles and books including the influential, *Signposts On the Road* in 1964.[187] He was released from prison in 1964, but was arrested again in 1965 and executed in 1966.

While in the United States he read widely including Carrel's, *Man the Unknown*. Much of Carrel's thesis was clearly in harmony with Qutb's experience. We find Carrel quoted at length in, *Islam the Religion of the Future*,[188] where Qutb agrees but in much more intense terms, for example, the separation of politics (life) and religion is a "hideous schizophrenia"[189] that is leading to the end of the "White Man's" dominance.[190]

Qutb's beliefs sound familiar in the face of Mawdūdī and Carrel, just more extreme. We have the assertion of God's absolute sovereignty in all things[191] (*hākimīyya*), we have his detestation of materialism and sexual license and general moral degeneracy, especially in America and the West, and we have his extreme condemnation of everyone, other Muslims included, in *jāhilīyya*. Mawdūdī and Carrel see the state as educator and guide to persuade the masses, Qutb sees the state as an instrument of coercion. Much stronger than Carrel's position and unlike Mawdūdī we have his belief in the necessity of *jihādic* war and martyrdom. According to Qutb a true Muslim cannot separate action from belief. But true belief entails total submission to God's absolute sovereignty and will that not only puts almost everyone in the fatal domain of unbelief but requires *jihād*, and martyrdom if necessary. Martyrdom is an inescapable personal commitment as an act of *hakimiyya* and the necessary rejection of *jahiliyya*, and it is carried out without regard to earthly consequences - God commands it, thus it shall be so. This is Qutb's message writ large on 9-11 and every suicide bombing day in Iraq.[192]

Ayatollah Ruhollah Khomeini (1902-1989)[193], was a Shī'ī Muslim, unlike all the others mentioned here who were/are Sunnī. Also unlike all the others, he was a member of the *ulamā*. He had a formal, advanced education in theology graduating in 1925 with specialties in the *sharī'a*, ethics, and spiritual philosophy. He immediately showed interest in the application of Islām to social issues and politics and wrote extensively on these matters. Not surprisingly, he saw the world through the lens of a Shī'ī Islāmic cleric. He was steeped in Shī'ī traditions of the martyrdom of Alī and his son, Husayn, to the reality and authority of the 12th Imām, the Hidden Imām. He believed in the primacy of the pure Islāmic (Shī'ī) state, rejected secularism, and objected to economic exploitation by the West with its new "capitulations", particularly in the face of later American military and oil interests. This position naturally included the complete condemnation of the Pahlavi Reza Shah government. In 1945 he was recognized as an important cleric by the title, of hojatolislam (Arabic, "proof of Islām"). He was recognized as an ayatollah (Arabic, "sign of Allāh) in 1961. His attacks against the government eventually got him exiled, but also further enhanced his religious reputation. By 1978 he had made alliances with other discontented groups including shopkeepers, intellectuals, journalists, and students. Each group had its own reasons to want the Shah gone, including his economics, and politically repressive policies, and they all worried about loss of their cultural identity to the West. Early in 1979 the Shah's regime fell and the Islāmic Republic of Iran was created. However Khomeini and his ilk very quickly jettisoned his allies who naively thought the ulamā incapable of leading the revolution or the new government it had created. This naivete was disabused when the religious zealots, students, and ulamā would not relinquish power over the neighborhoods and institutions they had taken in December.

Khomeini's contribution to revivalist thinking, in addition to that mentioned below, is rather modest and particular to Shī'ī Islām. It has been his position that political authority comes from the authority of religious jurists who get their authority from the Hidden Imām. This is clearly useless to a Sunnī, and diametrically opposed to the young firebrands who are the leading activists today.

The role of the Iranian revolution in the current surge of Islāmic activism is quite unique and should warn us against sweeping generalizations of a "clash of civilizations" or a global fundamentalist menace. Ironically, though it is the only politically successful Islāmic revolution, its success, notwithstanding its uniqueness, has been tremendously influential. The jīhadist, terrorist, fundamentalist crowd has looked with high hope at this success and dreamed of achieving it someday in their own lands; the West, the Great Satan (America) can be beaten! Otherwise, however, the Iranian revolution shares little with fundamentalist revolutionary movements elsewhere. All of the other movements are led by those who abhor the *ulamā*. All of the other movements are Sunnī.

Al-Bannā and Mawdūdī in the 1930s and 1940s laid the modern foundation for the current Islāmist revolutionary activity. Carrel provided further inspiration and validation. These currents all came together in the life and work of Sayyid Qutb. It is clearly Qutb's absolutist, violent view of fundamentalism that inspires today's activists, while Khomeini has provided the example that gives them hope of political success. Men like bin Laden, al-Zawahiri, and al-

Zarqawi are the current executors of Qutb's fundamentalist legacy. They have added nothing to the intellectual history of the fundamentalist movement and may be viewed as merely solders in the ideological and social struggle for control of Islām and its world. What they all (apart from Khomeini) share is a deep dissatisfaction and anger with their world, an appallingly superficial acquaintance with their religion that frees them to reinterpret its holy books and history as a justification for the most un-Islāmic behavior imaginable, an opportunism perfectly suited for this moment in history, i.e., an arrogant, and in their eyes, a decadent West (US), a moderate Muslim *ulamā* in near helpless opposition, and a global Muslim population driven by recent US behavior to agree with them.

In principle, this movement would be easy to neutralize, for it is profoundly vulnerable to the reality of the world. In fact, the movement is abetted by narrow Western (US) interests driven by ignorance, fear, power, and greed. And so it goes.

Permit a moment's speculation here: as one surveys the modern decline in the service of Sūfī orders, remembering the social and emotional support and comfort that they gave to their communities, one wonders if the decline has left a vacuum in popular Islām that fundamentalists exploited and successfully filled, particularly given the additional issues of disenchantment with the West's morals and imperialism. Perhaps a resurgent Sūfism, even in its conservative forms, could become a step towards a faith more in harmony with itself and the world around it.

Appendix F

Popular Religion

Religions do not exist in a vacuum. Every religion is surrounded and influenced by others. Robust and formal religions like Judaism, Christianity, Islām, Hinduism, and Buddhism are continually interacting with each other and with others less well known, as well as with those so minimal or primitive as to scarcely qualify as a religion at all. And they are interacting with other elements of the cultures they encounter as well. The results of these interactions are often called syncretic, or folk, or popular religions and religious practices. Sometimes, however, these terms are more confusing than informative, since they are often loosely used.

'Syncretic' religion combines elements of two or more religions in a coherent synthesis accepted by all the adherents, common believers and leaders alike. The key here is the religious synthesis and the breadth of acceptance, and in a formal sense as opposed to a popular and *ad hoc* sense. It could be argued that Hinduism is an example of a syncretic religion that for millennia has absorbed competitors and synthesized and expanded its belief system.

'Folk' religion is usually defined as the unsophisticated common practices of relatively primitive peoples. However, it is also often used synonymously with popular religion. Thus in *The New Penguin Handbook of Living Religions*[194] under "folk religion" we are directed to "popular religion."

'Popular' religion is usually contrasted with 'official' or doctrinally based religion as that which is actually practiced. Some specialists argue with these terms and prefer the terms 'normative' and 'operative', but the underlying key is what people actually do

167

and believe as opposed to what the religious laws, classical traditions, and leadership say they should do and believe. It is common in popular religions to incorporate beliefs or practices from the previously supplanted religions of the converted (or what might be called the partially converted.) In this book I will use the term popular religion as defined above.

Historically, popular (and folk) religion has been rather weakly held, thus its practitioners have been vulnerable to conversion. For example, the Incan, Aztecan, Mayan, and tribal religions of the Western Hemisphere were easily displaced by Roman Catholicism. Yet the new religion was a popular religion, an amalgam of pre-Christian practices and the practices of the mother church of Rome. Not surprisingly, Protestant missionaries are now having some success at converting these practitioners of popular Catholicism.

Spain was conquered by the Romanized Visigoths in the fifth century. The Arian Christianity they brought with them differed from Roman Catholicism in the beliefs that Jesus was not divine and that God was one and indivisible. The Arian heresy was eventually suppressed, but its memory remained in sufficient strength to find a brief revival shortly before the Muslim conquest in 711. Over the same period Christian religious rule was becoming more corrupt, degenerate, and unresponsive to popular needs. There was heavy persecution of the substantial Jewish and serf populations as well. The Muslim conquest was relatively easy precisely because of these factors. Conversion followed because Muslim rule, at least for the first three centuries, was very benign and tolerant and a welcome alternative to Spain's harsh and confusing Christianity then current. It is also clear that it was not as foreign as we might think given Spanish familiarity with Arian concepts so similar to the Muslim belief in the non-divinity of Jesus and the *shahādah.*[195]

In Albania the Catholic Church was a mess. There were too few clergy, sometimes only one incompetent priest to 10,000 parishioners, if any at all, and those largely illiterate and ignorant of the essentials of their own faith and its practices. Ignorant of their faith and abandoned by it, the Catholic peasantry left the faith in droves; at the beginning of the 17th century they outnumbered Muslims ten to one, but by the end of the century they were in the minority three to four.[196]

Bosnian Catholics were vulnerable to Islām while their Croatian Catholic brothers were unmoved. The difference was a dearth of clergy and the Bogomil heresy[197] that led to reduced institutional discipline. The resultant absence of formal guidance guaranteed the eventual prevalence of popular practices in Bosnia that were absent in Croatia. Thus popular Christianity in Bosnia succumbed to Islām.

The Bedouin of pre-Islāmic Arabia were easily converted to Islām, but when the center of the faith moved out of Arabia to Damascus, Baghdad, and Istanbul the Bedouin reverted to their old tribal ways and almost lost their Islāmic faith in popular practices. The 18th-century Wahhābī revival with its demands for strict adherence to the original Islām was the rectifying agent.

Islām in Southeast Asia was introduced by Sūfī traders into Hindu, Buddhist, Chinese, and local native cultures. However, the Sūfīs were only half successful, because they demanded very little of the converts, indeed so little that the converts were able to retain substantial parts of their previous religion. Here Islām is almost unrecognizable in its popular practice. Hindu, Buddhist and Chinese influences are pervasive and readily seen from the Philippines to Indonesia to Malaysia.

In India the combination of Sūfī and popular practice, and the eminence of the ever present Hindus eventually led to Mawlana Mawdudi's defensive reaction and the Islāmic state of Pakistan.

In the face of these examples it is not difficult to understand why the practitioners of the mother religion see popular practices as a threat and feel compelled to correct the matter by forcing the popular believers back to orthodoxy. Popular religion is weak by definition, since it is remote from the mother faith and lacks the mother faith's institutional power. In the case of Islām, the popular faith is uncomfortably widespread. It is vulnerable to indifference, if not indeed conversion.[198] Thus the first target of reformist/Islāmist Islām is popular Islām. This is seen especially in South and Southeast Asia. It is worth repeating here that fundamentalist activity throughout the Muslim world is multidimensional, and that much of it that is grouped by the US into a single threat is in fact a largely unrelated internal affair trying to correct popular practices.

Glossary

Pronunciation Guide for Arabic Words
(a): Short "a": between the vowel sounds of "hat" & "fur."
(ā): Long "a": (ā): like a in "hard."
(i): Short "i": as in "pit."
(ī): Long "i": (ī): like vowel sound in "feet."
(u): Short "u": as in "hook."
(ū): Long "u": (ū): as in "clue."
('): Hamza or glottal stop (') as where "t's" should be in "bottle"
as it is pronounced by many New Yorkers.
The emphasis goes on the long vowel.

Glossary

Abbāsid: as in the Abbāsid Caliphate, of or related to the house of
    al-Abbās.
al-īlāh: pre-Islāmic name for one of the principal gods of the
    Arabs.
Alawis: Influential in ruling Ba'th party in Syria, and the religion
    of the late Syrian president, Hafaz al-Assad.
Amir: commander, governor, or prince, usually a nonreligious
    leader.
Anatolia: the Asian part of what is now Turkey.
ayatollah: from the arabic, *ayat allāh*, meaning token, or sign of
    God; a Shī'ī religious leader.
Azāriqa: the most violent of the branches of the Khārijites existing
    briefly from 684 to 698. Its extremely narrow view of

171

Glossary

Islām was manifest it its belief that those Muslims who did not agree with its beliefs should be killed on sight, men, women, and children.

Bahā'ī: a modern religion stemming from a 19th-century Shī'ī schism in Iran. Not considered Muslim.

Balkans: countries occupying the peninsular area between the Adriatic Sea and the Black Sea; recently, Albania, Yugoslavia, Bulgaria, Rumania, Greece, and European Turkey.

bayt al-hikma: "House of Wisdom", an institution in Baghdad during the Abbāsid caliphate where it is thought translations into Arabic of classical Roman and Greek texts were carried out. This library was thought to have existed in some form in the pre-Abbāsid times of Sasanian Persia. It may have been the center of translation efforts as early as the caliphate of al-Mansūr, though there is, however, some disagreement among specialists as to its true functions.

Bengal: northeast area of Indian subcontinent roughly centered on the mouths of the Ganges river, and Calcutta.

bid'a: an innovation for which there is no precedent in early Islām and thus should be avoided. Some Muslims made a distinction between acceptable innovation and unacceptable.

bismillah: the invocation of Allāh's aid found at the beginning of all but one of the Qur'ān's *surāhs*: "In the name of Allāh, the beneficent, the merciful."

caliph: from the arabic, *khalīfa,* meaning successor, in this context, successor of the Prophet (a religious/secular leader).

Chistī: relatively flexible Sūfī order founded in Rajasthan in 13th century and very influential with the early Mughuls.

dā'ī: a summoner to the true faith. Used as a title for the leaders of several schismatic Shī'ī sects including the Nizārī Assassins.

Daudis: a schismatic sect that split from the Tayyibi in 1591 over the leadership succession.

Glossary

da'wa: a wide range of meanings centering around the idea of the call, or the organization or movement making the call, to unbelievers to join the true faith according to the caller (*dā'ī*).

Deccan: southern area of Indian subcontinent sometimes limited to the Indian peninsula and sometimes used to include a portion directly north of India's waist as well.

Devanāgarī: a script used to write several Indian languages, including Hindi and Sanscrit. Written from left to right it is characterized by a continuous, long horizontal bar from which the individual letters seem to hang.

Druze: a distinct religion with their own scripture originating in the 11th century as a small offshoot of the Ismā'īlī Shīā and surviving today mostly in Lebanon.

Fātamid: as in the Fātamid Caliphate, of or related to Fātima, the daughter of Muhammad and wife of Alī, the fourth caliph.

fatwā: a legal opinion issued by a religious scholar on the meaning and application of the *sharī'a.*

fidā'ī: a devotee of a cause or individual (sometimes even to giving up one's life.)

fiqh: scholarly knowledge used in interpreting the *sharī'a.*

furqān: to distinguish or separate (good from bad). A term whose meaning is still not settled.

hadīth: reports, traditions and sayings of the Prophet, also applied by the Shī'ā toAlī.

Hafiz: short lived schismatic group that split the Musta'līs in 1130.

hajj: pilgrimage to Mecca; the third of five pillars of faith.

hakimiyya: the absolute sovereignty of God in all things, the sole ruler, the sole authority. The slightest deviation from this is unbelief and condemnable in the harshest terms. This particularly characterizes the position of Mawdudi and Qutb.

Hanafī: the largest and most liberal Sunnī school of law found over much of the Muslim world.

Hanbalī: the most conservative Sunnī school of law found almost solely in Saudi Arabia.

Glossary

hanīf: heathen monotheists preaching in Arabia at the time of Muhammad.

hijra (or hegira): emigration, withdrawal; Muhammad's emigration from Mecca to Medīna in 622.

Ibadiya: the more moderate wing of the Khārijites springing from its split with the Azāriqa in 684. They were more flexible in the face of differing Islāmic religious views, even permitting marriage, unlike the Azāriqa, outside of their sect. Still in existence today.

ijmā: consensus of the community of Islamic scholars (with some flexibility in the terms "community" and "scholars.")

ijtihād: special intellectual effort in service of reaching a ruling in ambiguous areas of the law of Islām.

imām: leader or exemplar, prayer-leader, a spiritual leader of the community; in Shī'ī Islām, the divinely inspired successor to the Prophet.

Islāmism: practiced by those who believe in their freedom to interpret the Qur'ān and hadīth as they wish. Islāmism rejects Muslim institutional authority and has little respect or tolerance for Muslim traditions after the Companion Caliphs.

Ismā'īlis: a major sect of the Shī'ā that followed the Seventh Imām. They are also known as the Seveners.

istihsān: judging best; making the best judgement for society among plausible alternatives as a *mujtahid* rules on the *sharī'a.*

istislāh: a process of juridical judgement about the *sharī'a* giving consideration to public good.

Jafarī: a Shī'ī school of law.

jāhilīyya: term used for the "time of ignorance" that existed in Arabia before the coming of the Prophet Muhammad. Always a pejorative, in late 20th century times it has been extended to a state embracing all, Muslim and non-Muslim alike, who do not subscribe to a particular radical fundamentalist view and thus merit death.

174

Glossary

Jaxartes: now called the Syr Darya; the eastern-most of the two great rivers flowing into the Aral Sea, it originates near Tashkent in Uzbekistan.

jihād: exceptional effort or struggle on behalf of Islām. It can be applied to the internal struggle of a believer to be a better Muslim, or to the efforts of missionary work, or more commonly in recent years, to the struggle to defend Islām from its enemies (usually, the West.) See Joseph E. B. Lumbard's *Islam, Fundamentalism, and the Betrayal of Tradition*, Chapter 1, "The Myth of a Militant Islam", by David Dakake, and Bernard Lewis' extended but flawed consideration of the concept in, *The Crisis of Islam*, Ch II.

Ka'bah: the central shrine of Islām, a roughly cubic building in the Grand Mosque in Mecca

Khārijites: the first schismatics disagreed with both the Sunnīs and the Shī'ās on matters of the qualifications to be Caliph. They were particularly savage with those who disagreed with them. Eventually they split into the Ibadiya and Azāriqa.

Khwārezmia: also Khwārezm, area just south of the Aral Sea astride the Oxus river.

madrasa: a free Islāmic school originally for higher religious studies, but in the 20th century expanded to teaching Islām to all grades.

mahdī: the awaited one or specially guided one who will be the returning "hidden Imām"; divinely inspired leader to bring perfect justice to the world just before its end.

Malikī: a Sunnī school of law found largely in Africa.

Mamluke: military caste of slaves who ruled Egypt in medieval times.

maslahah: the public good to be divined through *istislāh* in interpreting the *sharī'a.*

mawālī: plural of *mawla;* client, helper, freed slave; non-Arab Muslims in the early centuries of Islām.

Mesopotamia: the region in modern Iraq astride the Tigris and Euphrates rivers.

Glossary

Moors: a mixed North African (Berber) and Arab people.

mufti: an extensively trained Muslim jurist. Roughly equivalent to *mujtahid*.

Mughul: a Muslim dynasty, originally Mongols, that ruled India from the 16th to the 18th centuries.

mujtahid: a Muslim jurist fully qualified by virtue of long training to issue rulings and interpretations (*fatwā*) of Islāmic law (*sharī'a*.) The training includes the Qur'ān and *sunna*, and all the subtle analytical techniques for their analysis, as well as full mastery of the classical Arabic language and its fine points of grammar to assure proper reading of the original texts.

Musta'līs: Egyptian faction that with the Nizārīs, Iranian faction, split the Ismā'īlīs Shī'ā over the succession of a Fātamid caliph.

Naqshbandī: conservative Sūfī order, very widespread and active (except in Arab lands), founded in central Asia in the 14th century. Though especially important in Turkey and India, it has little or no transnational, institutional coherence.

Nazārīs: see Musta'līs.

Nejd: the rocky, central plateau region of Arabia bounded on the north and south by the sandy Nafūd and Rub al-Khali deserts respectively.

Nusayris: a Shī'ī sect formed about 873 that still exists for the most part in Syria.

OPEC: Organization of Petroleum Exporting Countries; organization which tries to regulate crude oil production and prices.

Ottoman: the name given to a long line of Turkish Sultans who ruled much of the Muslim world beginning in the 13th century with Osman I.

Oxus: now called the Amu Darya; the western-most river entering the Aral Sea flows 1,600 miles from the mountains of Afghanistan.

Punjab: northernmost area of the Indian subcontinent immediately east of Pakistan.

qādī: a judge who makes rulings in court using the *sharī'a*; administers law as distinguished from a *mufti* who helps make law.

Qarmatīs: split from the Ismā'īlis in 899 remaining committed to Isma'il as the true *mahdī*. This sect was particularly prone to military violence. At one time they occupied Mecca during the hajj, slaughtered the pilgrims, and made off with the Black Stone.

qiyās: analogical reasoning used in interpreting the Qur'ān and *hadīth* for the purpose of applying the *sharī'a*.

qur'ān: the word used for the Muslim holy book (Qur'ān) but uncapitalized. There is some disagreement among scholars as to its origin and meaning. One the one hand we have, 'recite', or 'the act of reciting', or 'read' and on the other we have it meaning, 'joining', especially with the form "*qurān*" without the hamza (').

radicalism: the indifferent results of reformism, even as it became aggressively politically active, spawned this latest and most violent phase of Islāmic fundamentalism. The various forms of Islāmic radicalism are characterized by a peculiar vision of early Islām, a deep commitment to *jihād* in its most extreme form, and a vision of the absolute and universal role of Islām for all the world. See also, "Islāmism."

Rajasthan: northwest quarter of the Indian subcontinent immediately east of Pakistan.

ra'y: the use of expert, personal opinion in interpreting the *sharī'a*.

reformism: a 19th and 20th century evolutionary development out of the failed Islāmic revivalism. Reformism was a response to the growing awareness of European encroachment on Muslim political and social beliefs and institutions. At the same time Muslim reformers were also aware of the backwardness of their culture in governmental, economic and technological areas compared to Europe. Thus the reformers looked to a synthesis of some European values in these areas with core Islāmic values to reassert their independence of the

West. Reformism was as much outward-looking as inward-looking. See also, "radicalism."

revivalism: general term for early modern (18th and 19th centuries) attempts to purify Islām of superstition and religious innovation. Revivalism objected not only to Western influences, but to Hindu, Buddhist, and popular/folk religious influences as well. Wahhābism was a revivalist movement in Arabia aimed at rectifying the substantial return of tribal pagan traditions. Revivalism was largely an inward-looking movement. See also, "reformism."

Safavid: Persian dynasty that ruled Iran from the 16th to the 18th centuries, changed the country's religion from Sunnī to Shī'ā and gave it a national consciousness that eventually made it an important power.

salāt: prayer made five times daily; the second of the "five pillars" of Islāmic faith.

Sanskrit; an ancient language of India still in use, and the mother tongue of all Indo-Aryan languages today.

Sassanid: Persian dynasty founded 400 years before it was destroyed by the Arabs in the mid seventh century.

sawm: the fast from sunup to sundown during the month of Ramadan and the fourth pillar of Islām.

Seljuk: dynasty coming from Turkic tribes in central Asia ruling the central and eastern regions of Islām, particularly later in Anatolia as the Sultanate of Rum.

Sevener: name often given to the Ismā'īlī sect of Shī'ā Islām that split with the Twelvers over who should be the seventh *imām*.

Shafī'i: moderately conservative Sunnī school of law found mostly in Southeast Asia.

shahādah: the first of the "five pillars" of Islām, the declaration of faith; "There is no god but Allāh, and Muhammad ishis Prophet."

sharī'a: unchanging Muslim law, derived from God's word through the Qur'ān, governing all aspects of life; religious, secular, public, or private.

Glossary

shī'a:: from the arabic, *shī'at*, party or follower (of Alī), those who believe that the successors to the Prophet should be of his family through his nephew Alī and his daughter (and Alī's wife), Fātima.

shī'ite: synonymous with *shī'a* or *shī'ī*.

Sūfī: of or pertaining to a Muslim mystic, Sufis were very effective missionaries for Islam.

Suhrawardī: relatively conservative Sūfī order originating in Iraq in the 12th century and politically active in Mughul northern India.

Sulaymanis: a sect of the Tayyibi Shī'ā identifiable as early as 1591.

sultan: "authority", used from the time of the Seljuks for the political head of state.

sunnī: one who believes in the consensus of the Muslim community and leadership, historically, the Caliph; about 90 percent of Muslims are sunnī, about 10 percent shī'ā.

surāh: general name for a chapter in the Qur'ān.

taqīyah: "caution," "dissimulation," "prudential concealment," a fundamental shī'ite tenant, the practice of concealing one's commitment to shī'ism; historically, often a necessary tactic for survival amidst the sunnī majority; also sanctioned and practiced by sunnīs when individually under serious threat by non-Muslims.

Tayyibi: a branch of the Musta'līs founded in 1130 that later (1591) split into the Daudis and Sulaymanis.

Transoxania: the region between the Oxus and Jaxartes rivers.

Twelver: sect of shī'ī Islām that split with the Seveners over who should be the seventh *imām*. Their line of *imams* ended with the disappearance of the twelfth *imām* in the ninth century. Sect has strong messianic tradition awaiting the return of the Twelfth, or "hidden" *imām,* the *mahdī*. Twelver shī'ism became the state religion of Persia under the Safavids.

ulamā: the class of religious scholars and leaders.

Umayyad: of or pertaining to the dynasty of Umayyah beginning with the first Umayyad caliph, Mu'āwiyah in 659.

Glossary

umma: the community of all Muslims.

Urgench: ancient city of Khwarizm about 100 miles south of the Aral Sea on the west bank of the Oxus river. Modern Urgench is about 80 miles southeast of the ancient city.

vizier: (or wazier) chief minister.

Wahhābism: very strict monotheistic beliefs put forward by Muhammad Abd al-Wahhāb in Arabia in the late 18th century reacting to the lax Islāmic practices of the Arabs. In particular Wahhāb rejected saint worship as well as smoking and going clean-shaven. Wahhābism is a *sunnī* system that rejects all innovation in Islām after the third century A.H.

Wallachia: a region approximating the southern half of modern Romania.

Zadiyya: founded by a great great grandson of Muhammad (grandson of Husain) about 740 and the first to attempt (unsuccessfully) the overthrow of the Umayyads. Were particularly anti-Sūfī in their rejection of mysticism.

zakāt: alms, the fifth of the "five pillars" of Islām.

Zoroastrianism: pre-Islāmic religion of Persia founded in the sixth century B.C. has had important influence on Judaism, Christianity, and Islām. Largely destroyed in Persia by the   Muslims, still exists in small groups, mostly in India.

Bibliography

Ali, Maulana Muhammad, *trans.,A Manual of Hadith*, The Ahmadiyya Anjuman Ishaat Islam, Lahore, undated.

Ali, Maulana Muhammad, trans., *The Holy Qu'rān*, 5th ed., The Ahmadiyya Anjuman Ishaat Islam, Lahore, Inc., USA. 2002.

al-Suhrawardy, Allama Sir Abdullah al-Mamun, *The Sayings of Muhammad*, Carol, Secaucus, 1999.

Anonymous, *Through Our Enemies' Eyes: Osama bin Laden, Radical Islam, and the Future of America,* , Brassey's, Washington, 2002, pp. 90-92.

Arberry, A. J., *Sufism: An Account of the Mystics of Islam*, Dover, Mineola, 2002.

Arnold, T. W., *The Preaching of Islam*, Low Price Publications, Delhi, 1913 (2001).

Asad, Muhammad, trans., *The Message of the Qu'rān*, Dar Al-Andalus, Gibraltar, 1984. Also a later edition printed by The Book Foundation, Bristol, 2003.

Babinger, Franz, *Mehmed the Conqueror and His Time*, trans. Ralph Manheim, Princeton University Press, New York, 1978.

Bibliography

Babur, *The Baburnama: Memoirs of Babur, Prince and Emperor*,
W. M. Jr. Thackson, trans., Random House, New
York, 2002.

Bakalla, M. H., *Arabic Culture Through Its Language and
Literature*, Kegan Paul International, London, 1984.

Barakat, Halim, *The Arab World: Society, Culture, and State*,
University of California Press, Berkeley, 1993.

Barber, Noel, *The Sultans*, Simon and Schuster, New York, 1973.

Barrett, David, et al, *World Christian Encyclopedia: A
Comparative Survey of Churches and Religions - AD 30
to 2200*, 2nd. edition, 2 vols. Oxford University Press,
Oxford, 2001.

Bary, William Theodore de, Stephen N. Hay, Royal Weiler, and
Andrew Yarrow, *Sources of Indian Tradition*,
Columbia University Press, New York, 1958.

Battuta, Ibn, *The Travels of Ibn Battuta*, trans. H. R. A. Gibb,
Goodword Books, New Delhi, 1929 (2003).

Battuta, Ibn, *Ibn Battuta: Travels in Asia and Africa: 1325 - 1354*,
trans. H. A. R. Gibb, Routledge, London, 1929.

Berger, Morroe, *The Arab World Today*, Doubleday, Garden City,
1962.

Blair, Sheila S., and Janathan M. Bloom, *The Art and Architecture
of Islam 1250 - 1800*, Yale University Press, New Haven,
1994.

Bibliography

Bhaskaranahda, Swami, *The Essentials of Hinduism: A Comprehensive Overview of the World's Oldest Religion, 2nd ed.*, Viveka Press, Seattle, 2002.

Bulliet, Richard W., *Conversion to Islam in the Medieval Period: An Essay in Quantitative History*, Harvard, Cambridge, 1979.

Burton, Richard F., *The Book of the Thousand Nights and A Night*, 3 vols., Heritage Press, New York, 1962.

Chejne, Anwar G., *Succession to the Rule in Islam: with Special Reference to the Early Abbasid Period*, Ashraf, Lahore, 1960.

Chejne, Anwar G., *The Arabic Language: Its Role in History*, The University of Minnesota Press, Minneapolis, 1969.

Choueiri, Youssef, *Islamic Fundamentalism*, revised edition, Pinter, London, 1997.

Cleary, Thomas, trans., *The Wisdom of the Prophet: Sayings of Muhammad*, Shambala, Boston, 2001.

Corbin, Jane, *al-Qaeda: The Terror Network that Threatens the World*, Nation Books, New York, 2002.

Dakake, David, Chapter 1 in, *Islam, Fundamentalism, and the Betrayal of Tradition*, edited by Joseph E. B. Lumbard, World Wisdom, Bloomington, 2004.

Dawood, N. J., *The Koran*, Penguin Books, New York, 1990.

Douglass, Susan L., ed., *World Eras, vol. 2, The Rise and Spread of Islam 622 - 1500*, Gale, Detroit, 2002.

Bibliography

Dunn, Richard S., *The Age of Religious Wars: 1559 - 1689*, Norton, New York, 1970.

Durant, Will, *The Age of Faith,* Simon and Schuster, New York, 1950.

El Fadl, Khaled Abou, *The Great Theft*, Harper-Collins, New York, 2005

Encyclopaedia Britannica, 15th ed., Benton, Chicago, 1977.

Encyclopaedia of Islam, New Edition, 11 vols., eds. H. A. R. Gibb and others, Brill, Leiden, 1960 <2005>

Ernst, Carl, W., *The Shambhala Guide to Sufism*, Shambhala, Boston, 1997.

Esposito, John L., *The Islamic Threat: Myth or Reality?*, Oxford University Press, New York, 1992.

Esposito, John L., editor, *The Oxford History of Islam*, Oxford, New York, 1999.

Ettinghausen, Richard, Oleg Grabar, and Marilyn Jenkins-Madina, *Islamiic Art and Architecture 650 - 1250*, Yale University Press, New Haven, 2001.

Ezzati, A., *The Spread of Islam: The Contributing Factors*, 4th ed., Islamic College for Advanced Studies, London, 2002.

Fitzgerald, Edward, *Rubaiyat of Omar Khayyam*, 5th ed.

Fuller, J. F. C., *A Military History of the Western World*, 3 vols., Funk & Wagnalls, New York, 1954.

Gellner, Ernest, *Muslim Society*, Cambridge University Press, New York, 1983.

Bibliography

Gibb, H. A. R. ed., *The Encyclopaedia of Islam*, New Edition, Luzac, London, 1960.

Gibbon, Edward, *The Decline and Fall of the Roman Empire*, 3 vols., Heritage Press, New York, 1946.

Goffman, Daniel, *The Ottoman Empire and Early Modern Europe*, Cambridge University Press, New York, 2002

Goodwin, Jason, *Lords of the Horizons*, Holt, New York, 1998.

Gunaratna, Rohan, *Inside Al Qaeda: Global Network of Terror*, Columbia University Press, New York, 2002.

Gutas, Dimitri, *Greek Thought, Arabic Culture: the Greco-Arabic Translation Movement in Badhdad and Early Abbāsid Society (2nd-4th/ 8th-10th centuries)*, Routledge, New York, 1998.

Halil, Inalcik, *The Turkish Impact on the Development of Modern Europe*, in "The Ottoman State and Its Place in World History," vol. XI of Social, Economic and Political Studies of the Middle East, edited by Kemal H. Karpat. E. J. Brill, Leiden, 1974.

Hall, D. G. E., *A History of South-East Asia, 4th ed.*, St. Martin's Press, New York, 1981.

Hefner, Robert W., and Muhammad Kasim Zaman, eds., *Schooling Islam: The Culture and Politics of Modern Muslim Education*, Princeton University Press, Princeton, 2007.

Heitzman, James, and Robert L. Worden, *Bangladesh: A Country Study, 2nd. ed.*, Area Handbook Series, United States Government, Washington, 1989.

Bibliography

Hiro, Dilip, *Holy Wars: The Rise of Islamic Fundamentalism*, Routledge, New York, 1989.

Hodgson, Marshall G. S., *The Venture of Islam*, 3 vols., University of Chicago Press, Chicago, 1974.

Hodgson, Marshall G. S., *The Secret Order of the Assassins: the Struggle of the Early Nizārī Ismā'īlīs Against the Islamic World*, U Penn Press, Philadelphia, 2005.

Hosen, Nadirsyah, "Religion and the Indonesian Constitution: A Recent Debate," *Journal of Southeast Asian Studies*, 36, (3), October, 2005. Available on web at: eprint.uq.edu.au/archive/00002795/01/hosen-JSEAS.pdf

Huntington, Samuel P., *The Clash of Civilizations and the Remaking of World Order*, Simon & Schuster, New York, 1996.

Hupchick, Dennis P., *The Balkans: from Constantinople to Communism*, Palgrave, New York, 2002.

Ivanow, W., "An Ismaili Poem in Praise of Fidawis", Journal of the Bombay Branch of the Royal Asiatic Society (New Series), v. 14, 1938.

Juvaini, 'Ata-Malik, *The History of the World Conqueror*, 2 vols., trans. John Andrew Boyle, Harvard, Cambridge, 1958.

Kennedy, Hugh, *When Baghdad Ruled the Muslim World: the Rise and fall of Islam's Greatest Dynasty*, Da Capo, New York, 2004.

Kepel, Gilles, *Jihad: The Trail of Political Islam*, trans. Anthony F. Roberts, Harvard, Cambridge, 2002.

Bibliography

Khaldūn, Ibn, *The Muqaddimah*, trans. Franz Rosenthal, Princeton University Press, Princeton, 1969.

Khan, Muhammad Hameedullah, *The schools of Islamic Jurisprudence: A Comparative Study, 2ⁿᵈ. ed.*, Kitab Bhavan, New Delhi, 1997.

Khayyam, Omar, *The Rubāiyāt of Omar Khayyām,: comprising the metrical translations by Edward fitzgerald and E. H. Whinfield, and the prose version of Justin Huntly McCarthy: with an appendix showing the variations in the first three editions of Fitzgerald's rendering*, Thomas Nelson, NY, 1926

Kinross, Lord, *The Ottoman Centuries*, Morrow Quill, New York, 1979.

Lapidus, Ira M., *A History of Islamic Societies*, Cambridge University Press, New York, 1988.

Lavoie, Louis, *The Limits of Soviet Technology*, Technology Review, Vol. 88, No. 8, p. 68, Nov/Dec (1985).

Lavoie, Louis, *The Limits of Technology Transfer*, Military Logistics Forum, Vol. 2, No. 7, p. 35, April (1986).

Lawrence, Bruce, *Messages to the World: The Statements of Osama bin Laden,* trans. James Howarth, Verso, New York, 2005.

Lewis, Bernard, *The Arabs in History*, Harper & Row, New York, 1966.

Lewis, Bernard, *The Assassins: A Radical Sect in Islam,* Oxford, New York, 1967.

Bibliography

Lewis, Bernard, *The Emergence of Modern Turkey*, 2nd. ed., Oxford, New York, 1968.

Lewis, Bernard, ed., *The World of Islam: Faith, People, Culture*, Thames and Hudson, London, 1976.

Lewis, Bernard, *The Political Language of Islam*, University of Chicago Press, Chicago, 1988.

Lewis, Bernard, "License to Kill", *Foreign Affairs*, November-December, 1998

Lewis, Bernard, *The Crisis in Islam*, The Modern Library, New York, 2003.

Loeffler, Reinhold, *Islam In Practice: Religious Beliefs in a Persian Village,* State University of New York Press, Albany, 1988.

Lumbard, Joseph E. B., ed., *Islam, Fundamentalism, and the Betrayal of Tradition*, World Wisdom, Bloomington, 2004.

Manchester, William, *A World Lit Only By Fire*, Little, Brown and Company, New York, 1993.

Masood-ul-Hasan, Syed, trans., *110 Ahadith Qudsi: Sayings of the Prophet Having Allāh's Statements*, Darussalam, NY, 2003

Metcalf, Barbara Daly, *Islamic Revival in British India: Deoband, 1860 - 1900*, Oxford University Press, New York, 1982.

Morgan, David, *The Mongols*, Blackwell, Cambridge, 1987.

Bibliography

Morgan, Kenneth W., *The Religion of the Hindus*, Ronald Press, New York, 1996.

Moussalli, Ahmad S., *Radical Islamic Fundamentalism: The Ideological and political Discourse of Sayyid Qutb*, American University of Beirut, Beirut, 1992.

Nasr, Seyyed Vali Reza, *Mawdudi & the Making of Islamic Revivalism*, Oxford, New York, 1996.

New York Times, Armageddon View Prompts A Debate, Oct. 24, 1984:A1.

Oxford Encyclopedia of the Modern Islamic World, 4 vols. ed. John Esposito, Oxford University Press, New York, 1995.

OPEC Web site: http://www.opec.org.

Pati, Raphael, *The Arab Mind*, Scribners, New York, 1983.

Pearson, Charles H., *The Early and Middle Ages of England*, Kennikat Press, London, 1971.

Pires, Tomé, *The Suma Oriental of Tomé Pires*, edited by Armando Cortesao, 2 vols., Asian Educational Services, New Delhi, 2005.

Polo, Marco, *The Travels of Marco Polo*, Orion Press, New York, 1958.

Prawdin, Michael, *The Mongol Empire: Its Rise and Legacy,* trans. Eden and Cedar Paul, Allen and Unwin, London, 1940.

Bibliography

Rahim, Abdur, *Principles of Islamic Jurisprudence*, 2nd. ed., Revised ed., Kitab Bhavan, New Delhi, 1994.

Ratchnevsky, Paul, *Genghis Khan: His Life and Legacy,* trans. Thomas Nivison Haining, Blackwell, Cambridge, 1992.

Risso, Patricia, *Merchants of Faith: Commerce and Culture in the Indian Ocean*, Westview Press, Boulder, 1995.

Rizvi, Saiyid Athar Abbas, *A History of Sufism in India*, 2 vols., Manoharlar, New Delhi, 2003.

Said, Edward W., *Orientalism*, Vintage Books, New York, 1978.

Stetkevych, Jaroslav, *The Modern Arabic Literary Language: Lexical and Stylistic Developments*, The University of Chicago Press, Chicago, 1970.

Toffler, Alvin, *Future Shock*, Random House, New York, 1970.

Toynbee, Arnold, *A Study of History*, 12 vols., Oxford University Press, New York, 1961.

Tritton, A. S., Materials On Muslim Education in the Middle Ages, Luzac, London, 1957.

Trimingham, J. Spencer, *The Sufi Orders in Islam*, Oxford, New York, 1998.

Wei, Kuei-sun, *The Moghuls: Chingizid and Timurid, Connections and Differences*, The Asiatic Society, Calcutta, 1997.

Williams, Paul L., *Al Qaeda: Brotherhood of Terror*, Alpha, no city, 2003.

Whinfield, E. H., see Khayyam, Omar.

End Notes

1.

   Said, Edward, *Orientalism*, Vintage Books, New York, 1978, and more recently and succinctly, *The Clash of Ignorance*, The Nation, (New York), vol. 273, no. 12, October 22, 2001, pp. 11 - 14.

2.

   Huntington, Samuel P., *The Clash of Civilizations and the Remaking of World Order*, Simon & Schuster, New York, 1996.

3.

   Lapidus, Ira M., *A History of Islamic Societies*, Cambridge University Press, New York, 1988.

4.

   Khaldūn, Ibn, *The Muqaddimah*, trans. Franz Rosenthal, Princeton University Press, Princeton, 1969.

5.

   Gibbon, Edward, *The Decline and Fall of the Roman Empire*, Ch 3.

6.

The shape and site of the Ka'bah date from antiquity, however the structure has been rebuilt several times.

7.

Ali, Maulana Muhammad, *A Manual of Hadith*, The Ahmadiyya Anjuman Ishaat Islam, Lahore, undated.   Ch. I:2.

8.

The Muslim calendar uses the lunar year of twelve lunar months equaling 354 days. Since the solar year on which the Gregorian calendar is based has about 365 1/4 days the Muslim calendar gains a year every 32 ½ years.

9.

A 'sixth pillar', *jihād*, is sometimes included, but it is not universally accepted as are the other five. *Jihād* is taken to be the obligation of every Muslim to exert his best efforts in the service of Islām, often incorrectly interpreted as 'holy war.' See Appendix A.

10.

There are many translations of the Qur'ān, a touchy matter as indicated shortly. Many, especially those dating from the19th and early 20th centuries are not very good. A later attempt may be found in N. J. Dawood, *The Koran*, Penguin Books, New York, 1990. However, Arab scholars tend to scoff at all Western translations, see for example, Asad's Forward in the endnote 13 reference. Asad's translation has a useful accompanying commentary, as has Maulana Muhammad Ali's translation, *The Holy Qu'rān*, 5th ed., The Ahmadiyya Anjuman Ishaat Islam, Lahore, Inc., USA. 2002, and Abdullah Yusuf Ali, *The Qur'an*, Tahrike Tarsile Qur'an, Elmhurst, 2005. A very readable new translation without commentary or accompanying Arabic text is Thomas Cleary's, *The Qur'an*, Starlatch, 2004.

11.

The Qur'ān; 26:192-195.

12.

Also, the form of the revelation, i.e., its original language, the Arabic of Muhammad's time, is as much meaning-laden as the content. And since it is Allāh's message to Man, its form and content are of Allāh and not to be changed. Thus, one best approaches His message only through intimate knowledge of its classical Arabic idiom, and by reading it in that idiom. Translations, therefore, are merely representations of Allāh's message, and inescapably limited. It would be bad enough to read the Qur'ān in the original Arabic without attending to the subtlety of its Arabic meanings, but it would be foolhardy and empty to do the same with a translation. Reading the Qur'ān in English is almost pointless and meaningless without recourse to an extensively and authoritatively annotated text. But this is no novelty; Christian church-goers know that every Sunday they will hear similarly beneficial elaborations of the Gospels. It should be noted here that the vast majority of the world's Muslims do not understans Arabic; they simply read or recite sounds of the Arabic script before them.

13.

Some Muslim scholars tell us that the *sūrahs* are, "...arranged in accordance with the inner requirements of its message as a whole..." See Muhammad Asad, trans., *The Message of the Qu'rān*, Dar Al-Andalus, Gibraltar, 1984. p. i. There is a beautiful later edition of this work with expanded commentary and Arabic transliteration from The Book Foundation, Bristol, 2003.

14.

Ali, Maulana Muhammad, *A Manual of Hadith*.

15.

The Qur'ān minces no words on the matter in The Unity, the four line Surāh 112. "...He, Allāh, is One...He begets not, nor is He begotten..." Thus Islām rejects the Christian Trinity and the divinity of Jesus.

16.

Before the 20th century it was common to refer to Muslims and Islām as 'Muhammadans' and 'Muhammadanism', terms inherently offensive to Muslims and expressly forbidden by Muhammad himself as recounted in the *hadīth*: "The Prophet said, "Do not lavish praise on me as the Christians have lavished praise on the son of Mary; for I am only a slave. So call me God's slave and messenger."" Thomas Cleary, trans., *The Wisdom of the Prophet: Sayings of Muhammad*, Shambhala, Boston, 2001, p. 19.

17.

Alī was fighting for power with Mu'āwiyah over the succession to the caliphate after the murder of Uthmān. When the two sides met in battle at Siffīn in 657 they decided to put the issue to arbitrators rather than continue having Muslims slaughtering Muslims. The group who were eventually called the Khārijites objected to human arbitration of what they believed to be a theological matter, i.e., the succession to the caliphate. They believed that the Qur'ān required the matter should have been settled by God through a trial of arms. In addition, they believed that any Muslim was eligible to be caliph, contrary to the Shī'a who thought only descendants of Alī eligible, and the Sunnīs, who thought only those of the Prophet's tribe, the Quraysh, eligible. Accordingly, they objected not only to the recent caliphate of Uthmān and his supporter, Mu'āwiyah, but to Alī's pretensions as well. Any who disagreed with them were labeled infidel or apostate and deserved to be killed, with their families, on the spot. Though Alī later destroyed a large part of the Khārijite army, the sect still survived, indeed, it was a Khārijite who murdered Alī in 661. Internal schisms, so common with absolutists, as well as external defeats, eventually weakened them. The main legacy of the Khārijites was the unrest that contributed to the downfall of Alī's caliphate, and later to the downfall of the Umayyads as well. Perhaps too, they remind us of the common characteristics of absolutist and extremist ideologies, Muslim and non-Muslim: they are exceedingly inflexible and self-righteous in their beliefs, and utterly savage with those who do not agree with them.

18.

Toynbee, Arnold, *A Study of History*, 12 vols., Oxford, New York, 1961.

19.

Bulliet, Richard W., *Conversion to Islam in the Medieval Period: An Essay in Quantitative History*, Harvard, Cambridge, 1979, p.146. He tells us of a poem of the time that, "...likes miscegenation of Arab and non-Arab to Arab women fornicating with donkeys and mules."

20.

Abu Al Abbās's speech at the mosque announcing his leadership and al Saffāh title to the people is recorded in, *Succession to the Rule in Islam: with Special Reference to the Early Abbasid Period* by Anwar G. Chejne, Ashraf, Lahore, 1960. pp. 66 - 68. However, there seems to be a considerable range of interpretation of the meaning of "al Saffāh." *The Encyclopaedia of Islam*, New Edition, H. A. R. Gibb, ed., Luzac, London, 1960, vol. 1, p. 103, tells us that al Saffāh means "the bloodthirsty" or "the generous". Professor John Woods at the University of Chicago informs me that the term is "never complimentary," and since al Abbās's first task as caliph was to destroy all trace of potential Umayyad pretenders there is little room for the nicety of "the generous."

21.

Language is so often a window on history. The Arabs and Arabic encountered the Sāsanids speaking their Middle Persian (Pahlavi) language written in an Aramaic script right to left. The result after the 9th century was a Persian script very similar to Arabic script (see Figure 3), and Persian would become almost as important as Arabic in the middle Asian Muslim world. Similarly, we shall the Persian - Hindi encounter spawn Urdu in Chapter 4.

22.

Burton, Richard F., *The Book of the Thousand Nights and A Night*, 3 vols., Heritage Press, New York, 1962. p.3847. Edward Gibbon, *The Decline and Fall of the Roman Empire*, 3 vols., Heritage Press, New York, 1946. pp. 1868-9 tells us of considerably larger Muslim libraries of this time and later centuries. In Bernard Lewis', *The World of Islam: Faith, People, Culture*, Thames and Hudson, London, 1976, p. 228, we are told of Caliph al-Hakam II's Cordoban library of 400,000 volumes in 976! We find in A. S. Tritton's, *Materials On Muslim Education in the Middle Ages*, Luzac, London, 1957, (pp. 99-100) reference to a Baghdad library of more than 10,000 volumes in 991. Elsewhere (p. 152) Tritton notes a ninth century relocation by a private individual that required 600 loads to move the library; and other public and private libraries are noted on page 196 from 5,000 to 100,000 volumes. The modest European libraries of the time, overwhelmingly in monasteries, were often lost by the late Middle Ages due to fire, war, and neglect. One senses the cultural gap by noting that six centuries after Vizier Ibn Abbād European libraries of consequence could typically claim but a few hundred books. In the 15th century Humphry, duke of Gloucester, had 600, the king of France had 910, and Christ Church priory of Canterbury had 2,000 to 5,000, though at the beginning of the14th century it had but 698 volumes. See Charles H. Pearson, *The Early and Middle Ages of England*, Kennikat Press, London, 1971, p.452; William Manchester, *A World Lit Only By Fire*, Little, Brown and Company, New York, 1993, p. 95; Will Durant, *The Age of Faith,* Simon and Schuster, New York, 1950, pp. 908-909.

23.

Oxford History of Islam, John L. Esposito, ed., Oxford, New York, 1999, p. 272. However, in the same work (p.160) we find reference to a slightly different founding in the time of Hārūn al-Rashīd. Hugh Kennedy in his, *When Baghdad Ruled the Muslim World*, Da Capo, New York, 2004, p. 246 takes a somewhat more conservative position about the House of Wisdom choosing to follow Dimitri Gutas' argument (admittedly controversial) that the evidence in this matter is weak; *Greek Thought, Arabic Culture,* Routledge, New York, 1998, pp. 54 - 60. We shall leave these arguments to the specialists.

24.

  Rosenthal, Franz, *The Classical Heritage in Islam*, trans., Emile and Jenny Marmorstein, U. Cal Press, Berkeley, 1975, p. 49

25.

  Bernard Lewis, ed., *The World of Islam: Faith, People, Culture*, especially Chapter 2. Also, Ettinghausen, Richard, Oleg Grabar, and Marilyn Jenkins-Madina, *Islamiic Art and Architecture 650 - 1250*, Yale University Press, New Haven, 2001, and Blair, Sheila S., and Janathan M. Bloom, *The Art and Architecture of Islam 1250 - 1800*, Yale University Press, New Haven, 1994.

26.

  The Oxford English Dictionary Supplement gives the Arabic translation of *fidā'ī* as "one who undertakes perilous adventures." The Encyclopaedia of Islam, New Edition, v. II, p. 882, says, "One who offers up his life for another, a name used of special devotees in several religious and political groups." Clearly *fidā'ī* is the source of the modern "fedayeen," the Arab guerillas who have attacked their enemies from Israel in the 1950s to the US in 2003 (the "Fedayeen Saddam,") as well as the Iranian domestic terrorists active in the 1940s and 1950s.

27.

  Lewis, Bernard, *The Assassins: A Radical Sect in Islam,* Oxford, New York, 1967, pp. 10-12, 48, 112.

28.

  The modern survival and transformation of this once extremist sect is nicely described and analyzed in Ernest Gellner's, *Muslim Society*, Cambridge University Press, New York, 1983, pp. 105 - 109.

29.

Edward Fitzgerald, fifth edition translation, quatrain XII. Fitzgerald's translation has often been cited as exceedingly loose compared to the original. Nevertheless, references to "wine" and "drink" are encountered throughout the Rūbaiyat not only in his translation but in the translation of others such as E. H. Whinfield's. There is, however, a good deal of learned commentary, especially on Persian Sūfī poetry, that suggests references to wine and drinking are really metaphorical allusions to spiritual intoxication. Nevertheless, there is no disagreement about the use of wine during the Umayyad caliphate and thereafter by many of the elites of Islām.

30.

The Arabic prose of Osama bin Laden and his associates (Bruce Lawrence, *Messages to the World: The Statements of Osama bin Laden*, trans. James Howarth, Verso, New York, 2005) has been described by Bernard Lewis ("License to Kill", *Foreign Affairs*, November-December, 1998) as "magnificent", "eloquent", and "poetic." Lawrence describes it as powerfully lyrical and an important part of bin Laden's appeal.

31.

Issawi, Charles, "European Loanwords in Contemporary Arabic Writing," *Middle Eastern Studies*, 3:110-133, 1967. By comparison Issawi finds three times as many loanwords in Persian and 10 times as many in Turkish. However, this resistance to loan words from other languages is a characteristic of classical and literary Arabic. The lexicon of spoken or modern Arabic has yielded to the modern world, technology and all. See for example, Bakalla, M.H., *Arabic Culture Through Its Language and Literature*, Kegan Paul International, London, 1984, Ch. IX; Stetkevych, Jaroslav, *The Modern Arabic Literary Language*, University of Chicago Press, Chicago, 1970, Ch. 3; Chejne, Anwar G., *The Arabic Language: Its Role in History*, The University of Minnesota Press, Minneapolis, 1969, Chs. 1, 4, 9.

32.

Almost all Arabic words are formed from a three consonant root. The three consonant root has a meaning out of which additional words and meanings are constructed by inserting different vowels, prefixes, and suffixes. The new words have different primary meanings, but they are always subtly linked to the root meaning. For example, in the *bismullah* (an invocation of Allāh's aid found in the Qur'ān, see Glossary), we find the words, *rahmān* and *rahīm*, both from the root **rhm** = womb, kinship. In Islāmic intellectual history these words, *rahmān* and *rahīm*, in this context, have received an immense amount of attention. Though from the same root, *rahmān* is interpreted as reflecting a quality intrinsic to

197

Allāh, i.e., beneficence, compassion, or most gracious, and _rahīm_ as the action of Allāh, merciful or dispenser of grace. Same root; deep, subtle currents of meaning. A less weighty example is, **ktb** = mark or inscribe; _kitāb_ = book, _katīb_ = writer, _maktab_ = desk, _maktaba_ = library, etc.. Because of this linkage, every word brings with it not only its primary meaning, but a subtle interplay of additional meanings all connected with the root group. The difficulty, if not impossibility, of succinct translation is obvious, and puts upon the translator, whether Qur'ānic or diplomatic, a considerable burden and responsibility.

33.
Pati, Raphael, _The Arab Mind_, Scribners, New York, 1983. Ch. IV. Also see Bernard Lewis, _The Arabs in History_, Harper & Row, New York, 1966, pp. 131-132. Berger, Morroe, _The Arab World Today_, Doubleday, Garden City, 1962, p. 139.

34.
For original material available in English translation see, Juvaini, 'Ata-Malik, _The History of the World Conqueror_, 2 vols., trans. John Andrew Boyle, Harvard, Cambridge, 1958. For secondary materials see, Prawdin, Michael, _The Mongol Empire: Its Rise and Legacy_, trans. Eden and Cedar Paul, Allen and Unwin, London, 1940. For more recent works see, Ratchnevsky, Paul, _Genghis Khan: His Life and Legacy_, trans. Thomas Nivison Haining, Blackwell, Cambridge, 1992, and Morgan, David, _The Mongols_, Blackwell, Cambridge, 1987.

35.
Battuta, Ibn, _Ibn Battuta: Travels in Asia and Africa: 1325 - 1354_, trans. H. A. R. Gibb, Routledge, London, 1929. pp. 171 - 174.

36.
Toynbee, Arnold, _A Study of History_, 12 vols., Oxford University Press, New York, 1961. IV:42-3, XII:474-5.

37.
Occasionally, there were still leaders who assumed the title of Caliph in various places in the Muslim world, but never again would the title have the cachet of Abbāsid times or earlier.

38.

The term originated in January, 1853. Russia's Nicholas I was discussing 'The Eastern Question', i.e., how to handle the decaying Ottoman Empire and remarked to the British Ambassador Sir Hamilton Seymour that they had, "...a sick man on our hands," hence the later term, "sick man of Europe." See Kinross, Lord, *The Ottoman Centuries*, Morrow Quill, New York, 1979, p. 483.

39.

For example, Khaldūn, vii - ix.

40.

Trimingham, J. Spencer, *The Sufi Orders in Islam*, Oxford, New York, 1998, p. 69-70, 99.

41.

The expansion of the Muslim religion into Central, South, and Southeast Asia carrying with it a range of political power varying from almost nothing to almost everything was substantially complete by the 17th century.

42.

In recent years it is frequently said that Islām is the most rapidly growing religion in the world. However plausible this may be, there is little credible evidence one way or the other. The best available data are of uncertain quality and often self-admittedly no more than estimates. Moreover, the 'rapid' growth comes largely from the higher birthrates common in Muslim countries, not conversions, and in no way represents an Islāmic virulence that the West likes to worry about. This problem has been exacerbated recently by wildly inflated population numbers of 1.2 to 1.5 billion, again without any evidence whatsoever. (In 2006 Time produced a pretentious special entitled, "The Middle East: The History, The Cultures, The Conflicts, The Faiths" telling us that there were 1.5 billion Muslims globally. Sigh.) Indeed at this moment Christians outnumber Muslims about two billion to one billion, and 11% of Christianity's growth does come from conversions. See David Barrett et al, *World Christian Encyclopedia: A Comparative Survey of Churches and Religions - AD 30 to 2200*, 2nd. edition, 2 vols. Oxford University Press, Oxford, 2001, p. 4. See also Samuel P. Huntington, *The Clash of Civilizations and the Remaking of World*, pp. 64 - 66. It is interesting to note that Islāmic virulence apparently has not touched Buddhist Burma (Myanmar) since its estimated Muslim fraction has remained at 4% for several decades notwithstanding its highly porous borders with the

199

overwhelmingly Muslim Malaysia and Bangladesh.

43.

A common element of Ottoman vassalage frequently required the local rulers to send their sons to live and be educated at the Ottoman court, more or less as high level hostages. The young Vlad III (Tepes) of Wallachia, born in 1431, the same year Joan of Arc was burned at the stake, passed his teenage years in the court of Murad II as a companion to his son, the future conqueror of Constantinople, Mehmed II. His abilities were recognized, and he was promised his father's throne when the time arrived. However, his patriotism wasn't seduced, for when he returned to Wallachia and became ruler he was among the most vigorous in asserting independence from the Ottomans. (Alas, patriotism, as so often the case, did not preclude cruelty; "Tepes" means "The Impaler," and Vlad III is known in history by his given name, Dracula.)

44.

Hupchick, Dennis P., *The Balkans: from Constantinople to Communism,* Palgrave, New York, 2002. pp. 47, 49.

45.

Long before the Ottomans came to the Balkans history was setting the stage there for many of the troubles of the 20th century. The wanderings of the Slavic peoples found the South Slavs settling in the Balkans about the same time as the ancestors of the Russians, the East Slavs, settled in the area of the Ukraine.

The initial conversion of the heathen, Balkan Slavs went according to their proximity to a particular religious context. The subgroups later known as the Croatians and Bosnians became Catholic. However, Bosnian Catholicism was weak because of the popular practices of the Bosnian Catholic Church and the differences with Rome in what was known as Bogomilism.

The popular practice of religion is common in history; it is characterized by its flexibility and easy incorporation of congenial elements of other encountered religions as well as of local beliefs and practices which can be heathen or even animistic. Popular religions are often weak and relatively easy to supplant when faced by a strong and highly organized religion. It is fascinating to note that much of the Muslim world today practices popular Islām. This is true from Bosnia to Indonesia and is due to the efficacy of Sūfī missionaries that were rather easygoing in their requirements of converts often letting them keep whatever they liked of their old religion. The concomitant weakness of popular Islām has modern Islāmic fundamentalists very upset as we will see later. For more on popular religion see Appendix F.

46.

The 13th-century conquests of Jenghis Khan created an empire stretching from China to the Mediterranean. The empire eventually devolved to the grandsons who had not the unity of interest of their grandfather. The major part went to Kublai Khan in China. Though he was the nominal head of the entire Mongol Empire he was largely ignored by his cousins, one of whom, Batu Khan, was the first Khan of the Golden Horde that occupied or controlled European Russia and Siberia east to the Ob river. Later the Golden Horde broke into several sub-hordes, one in the Crimea. The Crimean Khanate was the last survivor of the world empire of Jenghis Khan.

47.

Babinger, Franz, *Mehmed the Conqueror and His Time*, trans. Ralph Manheim, Princeton University Press, New York, 1978. p. 375.

48.

The dividing line in this Treaty of Tordesillas cut north south through Brazil, thus to this day all of South America west of 49 degrees speaks Spanish leaving only Brazil speaking Portuguese.

49.

Inalcik, Halil, *The Turkish Impact on the Development of Modern Europe*, p.52. In "The Ottoman State and Its Place in World History", vol. XI of Social, Economic and Political Studies of the Middle East, edited by Kemal H. Karpat. Leiden: E. J. Brill, 1974.

50.

Ibid. 53.

51.

Some historians have set the beginning of the Ottoman decline with Suleiman's son, the perfectly inept Selim II (1566 - 1574) known to history as Selim the Sot.

52.

Fuller, J. F. C., *A Military History of the Western World*, 3 vols., Funk & Wagnalls, New York, 1954, vol. 1, pp. 559 - 578. On the European side Cervantes received a wound in his left hand that he was proud to display for the rest of his life.

53.

Dunn, Richard S., *The Age of Religious Wars: 1559 - 1689*, Norton, New York, 1970, p. 59. The same attitude is illustrated when the Grand Vizier says, "What does my master care, if the Dog worry the Hog, or the Hog the Dog, but that his Head is safe?," Jason Goodwin's, *Lords of the Horizons*, Holt, New York, 1998, p. 264. And a few years earlier the Sultan directs his Grand Vizier to admit the Venetian ambassador, "Feed and clothe the dog and bring him into me," Noel Barber, *The Sultans*, Simon and Schuster, NY, 1973, p.102. And on and on, the Grand Vizier just before getting trounced by the Russians in 1672, "Such is the strength of Islam, that the union of Russians and Poles matters not to us," Barber, 103.

54.

Some scholars see this infatuation more seriously claiming that this was the first opening of the Ottoman mind to what the West had to offer. This is true, but it was a very small opening that grew exceedingly slowly.

55.

An indication of the power shift away from the Sultan is seen in the name for the seat of Ottoman power. Like the reference to the "White House" in the United States, the Ottoman government was referred to as the "Porte" or "Sublime Porte" from the French words for the 'high gate' entrance to the Grand Vizier's palace.

56.

In the 1630s Kadizade Mehmed, the imām of the Hagia Sofia, citing the *hadīth*, was preaching against Ottoman innovative and condemning un-Islāmic practices from religious endowments to drinking wine and coffee, "every innovation is heresy, every heresy is error, and every error leads to hell." Daniel Goffman's, *The Ottoman Empire and Early Modern Europe*, Cambridge, New York, 2002, p. 117. Mehmed's position on innovation (*bid'a*) was more conservative than most. Muslim jurists have recognized that there are 'good' innovations and 'bad' innovations. Yet good and bad are often in the eye of the beholder, and the more extreme the beholder the less tolerant he is for deviation from the religious practices of Muhammad's time. Such conservative preaching would be perfectly at home in today's Saudi Arabia and in too much of the rest of the Muslim world.

57.

However, presses in foreign languages had been established earlier in Constantinople: a Jewish press in 1493 or 1494, Armenian in 1567, and Greek in 1627, Bernard Lewis, *The Emergence of Modern Turkey*, 2nd. ed., Oxford, New York, 1968, p.50. Eildert Mulder argues differently about why an Arabic press was so long delayed in the Ottoman Empire; he believes the problem was more in the nature of a calligraphic limitation. A given Arabic letter will take on many different shapes depending on where it appears in a word and what the adjacent letters are. According to him this made an adequate typeface impossibly large. However, the limitation he alludes to is more stylistic than substantive and thus not very persuasive. See Eildert Mulder, *Keyboard Calligraphy*, Saudi Aramco World, July/August, 2007, pp. 34 - 39.

58.

Perhaps a bit too superficial, for there is ample room to contest this so called 'loss of vigor' in western Islām. The Ottomans began and flourished thru the first 400 years of our story of the Islāmic east, and to a lesser degree the Safavids of Persia somewhat later. Nevertheless, in the broadest strokes the picture remains that over the centuries the Islāmic east was rising as the Islāmic west was static or declining.

59.

This is not to suggest that between 711 and 1206 there were no Muslim armies or political powers in the Subcontinent. Indeed, there was a notable presence in the north of the Ghaznavids in the Punjab and the Sind as well as a relatively brief Ghūrid presence just before the Delhi Sultanates.

60.

Of course I speak of the subcontinent as a whole, for there were always areas with Muslim majorities, particularly in the north and centrifugally manifest in the 20th century by the countries of Bangladesh and Pakistan.

61.

There were also in the area at the time several similar but distinct offshoots from Hinduism, i.e., Buddhism, Jainism, and Sikhism, that are interesting theologically and meaningful in Asian history but do not significantly impact our story except perhaps the Buddhists in Bengal which we will leave for the curious to discover elsewhere.

62.

A common metaphor for this illusion of the false distinction of self from the universal ALL says that the self is like a drop of water momentarily tossed from the turbulent sea of the ALL only to fall back and rejoin it as one of its indistinguishable parts.

63.

Hindu history and beliefs are widely treated; I have used Kenneth W. Morgan's, *The Religion of the Hindus*, Ronald Press, New York, 1996, and William Theodore de Bary et. al., *Sources of Indian Tradition*, Columbia University Press, New York, 1958. See also Swami Bhaskaranahda;s *The Essentials of Hinduism: A Comprehensive Overview of the World's Oldest Religion, 2nd ed.*, Viveka Press, Seattle, 2002.

64.

Battuta (Gibb trans., 1929), 191, 244, 250. Marco Polo, *The Travels of Marco Polo*, Orion Press, New York, 1958, pp. 282, 284, 287.

65.

Indeed, Trimingham (p. 219) remarks, "Sūfism could take root in India , since in a sense it was already there..."

66.

Scholars differ on the matter, some saying the Chishtis originated in Chisht, Afghanistan; but all agree that their 13th century appearance in India had a major influence there as no where else. See for example, Rizvi, Saiyid Athar Abbas, *A History of Sufism in India*, 2 vols., Manoharlar, New Delhi, 2003, vol 1, ch 2.

67.

Christian revivalists are familiar with this experience. The author attended as a youth in the 1940s tent meetings in the rural Midwest of Pentecostal "Holy Rollers" who would fall to the ground in religious ecstacy after repetitive prayer and dancing.

68.

"Urdu" comes from the Turkish word for camp which further reflects the fusion of cultures. See A. Ezzati, *The Spread of Islam: The Contributing Factors*, 4th ed., Islamic College for Advanced Studies, London, 2002.

69.

However, the principle of an egalitarian *umma* was rarely seen in practice. Recall how the *mawālī* were seen as second class citizens during the Umayyad Caliphate and the racial snobbery of the early Arab Muslims. Indeed, even some low-caste Hindu converts were excluded from the mosque on occasion.

70.

Time beclouds so much; even here there is conflicting opinion, for Wie insists (as others do) that, "Bābur's maternal grandfather, Yunis Khan, was of the race of Chaghatai Khan." (Emphasis added.) Wei, Kuei-sun, *The Moghuls: Chingizid and Timurid, Connections and Differences*, The Asiatic Society, Calcutta, 1997, p. 23. On the other hand, S. A. A. Rizvi in Lewis (1976), p. 302, suggests ancestry traceable to Jenghis himself. Since it is common for rulers, no matter how humble their pedigree, to legitimize their position by claiming august ancestry, we may reserve judgement and move on.

71.

Clearly, "Mughul" derives from "Mongol". The spelling of "Mughul" is hopeless; it appears variously as, Mogol, Mughol, Moghul, Mughal, etc.. About as confusing as "Jenghis" Khan: Gengis, Genghis, Tchenghis, Chingiz, etc.!

72.

I am indebted to Dr. Muhammad Isa Waley, Curator of Persian and Turkish Collections at the British Library, who informs me that the miniature dates from about 1590. Indian miniatures of this time were done solely on the sponsorship of the Emperor, in this case Akbar, thus the theme of this miniature is clearly the intellectual product of Bābur's descendent who had no reason to diminish the luster of his heritage.

73.   Babur, *The Baburnama: Memoirs of Babur, Prince and Emperor*, W. M. Jr. Thackson, trans., Random House, New York, 2002.

74.

"Jahāngīr's liberalism" was only relative. Like all rulers he abhorred instability. Sirhindī's threat was from the religiously conservative side. At the same time Jahāngīr was dealing with the emerging Sikhs in 1606 by arresting and torturing to death Arjan Das, a Sikh holy man and 'fifth guru.'

The Sikhs believed in the efficacy of a teacher, a spiritual guide, a guru. The guru had many of the characteristics of the Sūfī master, and the Shī'ī Imām, and like the Seventh and Twelfth Imāms there was a tenth and last Guru. Indeed, the parallel is not surprising, since the Sikh movement (religion) clearly was a syncretic creation out of Hinduism and Islām (reincarnation and karma with monotheism for example.)

The Sikhs have always been famous as warriors; the killing of Arjan Das precipitated a militant defensiveness that eventually gave Sikhs a well deserved reputation for military prowess. However, in 1849 they were forced to submit to the British, and in the act, gave over the celebrated Koh-i-noor diamond. Re-cut to 109 carats it now resides with the British crown jewels prominently displayed afront the queen's state crown. Their honor bound them to their conquerors so much that they fought on the side of the British during the Sepoy Mutiny. Thereafter, they were consistently considered by the British as the most reliable, devoted, and effective police constabulary in the Subcontinent. The partition of India in 1947 split the Sikh Punjab homeland and they became a persecuted religion by both Muslims and Hindus. Today there are 20 or 30 million Sikhs world wide, most in the Punjab of India.

In the late 20th century, following the current fashion, every petty tyrant with any claim whatsoever has demanded the return of the Koh-i-noor, including the Taliband in Afghanistan and Indian Sikhs. Perhaps fortunately, the endless claims to rectify history have largely neutralized themselves and the status quo remains.

75.

Indeed, when the British had realized what they had done, they 'ungreased' the bullets, but too late.

76.
   "Mutiny" applied here has a familiar self-serving ring. Reminds one of the appellation, "terrorists" for Palestinians fighting for their rights, or "battle" as originally applied to the1890 slaughter of the Sioux at Wounded Knee, SD.

77.
   For the general historic context as well as Islam's appearance and influence see, D. G. E. Hall's *A History of South-East Asia.*

78.
   Scholars lament at the absence of evidence for early Sūfī activity in Southeast Asia. But there is a dearth of evidence here for much more, so in this case let us remember that, 'Absence of evidence is not evidence of absence.'

79.
   Risso, Patricia, *Merchants of Faith: Muslim Commerce and Culture in the Indian Ocean,* Westview Press, 1995, p. 43.

80.
   Pires, Tomé, *The Suma Oriental of Tomé Pires,* edited by Armando Cortesao, 2 vols., Asian Educational Services, New Delhi, 2005, p. 228. The vibrant trade world of early 16th century Southeast Asia is presented to us through the words of Tomé Pires in one of the most remarkable and reliable records of that century. Pires was sent to India in 1511, and to Malacca in 1512 where he was the Portuguese King's commercial representative. He was there for two years before being sent to China as ambassador. Unfortunately, some members of the party behaved so arrogantly that Pires was jailed and after many years died in a Chinese prison. His secret report to the Portuguese King, *The Suma Oriental* (Account of the East), concerning trade and its networks provide us with the earliest reliable evidence not only of the trade networks in the Indies but of the merchandise that was profitable, and of Islām's influence and distribution. In addition it contains the first European description of Malaysia, the islands east of Java, the Celebes, the first European mention of the Philippines and Acheh, the first use of the word 'Japan', and the first European description of chopsticks.

81.

The strength, influence, and repercussions of popularized Islām have in my view been considerably underestimated here by modern Western politicians.

82.

For example, contrary to Qur'ānic prohibition (2:221) it was accepted custom for heathen Malaccan men to marry Muslim women. Pires, 243.

83.

Though we speak here of "Southeast Asia," the historic and cultural situations differed in Malaya, Sumatra, Java, and the rest of the area. Nevertheless, all were economically exploited netting much to Europe and little to the natives.

84.

Unintended consequences of Western invasions of Muslim lands continue to this day: Israeli pressure on the Palestinians has begun to transform the largely secular Palestinian resistance into a religious affair, witness the growing role of Hamas, especially in the Gaza Strip in 2007. Note also the appearance of Al-Qaeda in Iraq, an organization that did not even exist before the US invaded Iraq.

85.

The Shattārī order was founded in India in the 15th century. It was perhaps the most Hindu-like of all the Sūfī orders with strong mystical leanings and belief in the efficacy of yoga practices. Coming from Gujarat in northwestern India they came to Southeast Asia where they became strong in Sumatra and were the first Sūfīs in Java.

86.

Dutch hegemony was so complete after this war that the East Indian archipelago began to develop a unified sense of identity that led to the eventual formation of the Indonesian state after World War II.

87.

The military has often led the way in bringing to society new techniques and technologies, for example, the semiconductor integrated circuit revolution with the Minuteman ICBM, the development of radar in WWII, plastic surgery after WWI, and sensor technology in modern guided missiles.

88.

Hefner, Robert W., and Muhammad Kasim Zaman, eds., *Schooling Islam: The Culture and Politics of Modern Muslim Education,* Princeton University press, Princeton, 2007, p. 2. Hefner cites here an article in "Foreign Policy", 133, (Nov/Dec 2002), pp. 13-20, by Husain Haqqani that also says there are an estimated six million madrasas students globally (p.18). By any arithmetic this constitutes less than 1 % of all school age Muslims in the world!

89.

Hefner, 5, 93.

90.

Hefner, 28.

91.

Hefner, 179.

92.

Metcalf, Barbara Daly, *Islamic Revival in British India: Deoband, 1860-1900,* Oxford University Press, New York, 1982.

93.

Hefner, 100.

94.

Metcalf, 136.

95.

Heitzman, James, and Robert L. Worden, *Bangladesh: A Country Study, 2nd*. *ed.*, Area Handbook Series, United States Government, Washington, 1989 p. 12.

96.

The Muslim League, know at the beginning as the All-India Muslim League, was founded in 1906 by the Agah Khan III, leader of the   world's Ismailis, the benign descendants of the fearful 11th - 13th century Assassins. (see Appendix D.)

97.

The name was created in 1933 by Muslim students at Cambridge University who were urging partition with a Muslim state to be created in the northwest consisting of Punjab, Afghania (otherwise known as the North-West Frontier Province), Kashmir, Sind, and Baluchistan. Bengal was not mentioned. Heitzman, p.16.

98.

The merit of Bengali literature can be gauged by its most illustrious writer, the 1913 Nobel Laureate in literature, Rabindranath Tagore.

99.

One should not make too much of this change; recall that in 1956 "In God We Trust" was made the national motto of the United States. "In God We Trust" has also appeared on our coinage since 1864 and on our paper money since 1957. Also recall the change to our Pledge of Allegiance in 1954 with the addition of,"Under God."

100.

For example, Google, *Library of Congress Country Studies, Bangladesh, Structure of Government, Constitution.*

101.

Though Indonesia extends 3,000 miles west to east and 1,000 miles north to south comprising more than 17,000 islands, just five islands make up more than 84% of its land area: Sumatra, Java, Kalimantan (Indonesian part of Borneo), Sulawesi (Celebes), and Irian Jaya (the western half of New Guinea.) More striking is that these five islands hold more than 90% of the population with Java home to comfortably more than half of Indonesia's total.

102.

This policy proposed by Christiaan Snouck Hurgronje could with great benefit be adopted today by the US government.

103.

Hosen, Nadirsyah, "Religion and the Indonesian Constitution: A Recent Debate," *Journal of Southeast Asian Studies*, 36, (3), pp 419-440 October 2005. This article puts in sharp historical perspective the role of Islām in Indonesia and is very highly recommended for those who wish to break free of the hysterical Western reactions to Islām. Available on the Web at, eprint.uq.edu.au/archive/00002795/01/hosen-JSEAS.pdf

104.

Hosen, 427.

105.

OPEC members as of 2003 are: Algeria, Indonesia, Iran, Iraq, Kuwait, Libya, Nigeria, Qatar, Saudi Arabia, United Arab Emirates, and Venezuela.

106.

From OPEC's official Web site: http://www.opec.org.

107.

My first knowledge of the fear SAVAK invoked came when a female American colleague at the University of Minnesota who was married to an Iranian graduate student refused to discuss the Shāh's regime in any way, even

211

privately, for fear of SAVAK overhearing us. She worried about SAVAK agents in Minneapolis in 1977!

108.
The attempt failed largely because the United States opposed it.

109.
The Ba'th (Renaissance or Resurrection) Party was founded in 1943 in Damascus by a Christian school teacher, Michel 'Aflaq. He believed that the Arab peoples should unite as one nation and free themselves from European dominance. 'Unity, freedom, and socialism' was the Ba'th organizational cry. The West often mistook "socialism" for "communism" but the Ba'th Party was very suspicious of the communists and generally avoided them. Though the party was secular it was not anti-Islām. Its pan-Arabic aspirations failed, though it succeeded independently as a national party in Iraq and Syria. However, the 'freedom' it espoused was absent from domestic political representation, witness the preposterous 2002 'reelection' of Saddam Hussein in Iraq with 100% of the vote.

110.
Esposito, John L., *The Islamic Threat: Myth or Reality?*, Oxford University Press, New York, 1992. Esposito is not comfortable with the term "fundamentalism" and ably explains why on pp. 7-8 preferring the term "Islāmic revivalism." However, I have chosen to retain "fundamentalism" and more carefully define it in the following paragraphs.

111.
Hiro, Dilip, *Holy Wars: The Rise of Islamic Fundamentalism*, Routledge, New York, 1989, p. 61.

112.
Hiro, 63.

113.

Bernard Lewis discussing a similar idea in *The Political Language of Islam*, University of Chicago Press, Chicago, 1988, pp. 2-5 disagrees. He notes that the source of authority in Islām is not separable into the spiritual and temporal (religion and politics) as it is in the West, and this is true in principle. But it leaves the implication that there can be no confrontation between the two within Islām. However, this does not appear to be the case in practice. Examples of Muslim internal political turmoil belying the idea of the inseparability of religion and politics abound. The clearest examples are the Abbāsid overthrow of the Umayyads, the Turkish intertribal wars between the time of the Seljuks and Ottoman, and the Iraqi Shī'a fighting the Iranian Shī'a in the Iran/Iraq War. Many other confrontations could be listed that are sometimes explained by supposing a failure of religious legitimacy, but the explanations seemed contrived to salvage the principle in the face of the practical fact.

The Biblical injunction, "Render to Caesar the things that are Caesar's and to God the things that are God's" has an insight that the idealism of Islām overlooks, ignores, or condemns. In practice religion always eventually yields to politics in matters of this world, and though we are considering Islām we can make the same assertion for any religion. The focus of religion is on the hereafter, whereas the focus of politics is on the here and now. For the most part people's primary concern is with matters of the moment, food, shelter, clothing, safety, freedom, and the like, and the need of the moment takes precedence.

114.

Fundamentalist activity elsewhere in the Muslim world is not entirely, nor even largely an export from the Middle East and Mawdudi's Pakistan. The Philippines, Indonesia, Bosnia, Malaysia, and Sri Lanka are typical areas where Muslim fundamentalists fear for an Islām of such casual or popular practice as to be offensive to purists and vulnerable to non-Muslim missionaries.

115.

The understandable reaction of the United States to Al Qaeda is nevertheless approaching hysteria. Al Qaeda is now invested with all the sinister power we were accustomed to give the old Soviet Union. Threat inflation is rampant and ridiculous. Al Qaeda, like the Soviets in the past, poses a real but manageable threat with an intelligent foreign policy. Typical of this hysterical assessment is Rohan Gunaratna's, *Inside Al Qaeda: Global Network of Terror*, Columbia University Press, New York, 2002. Indeed, the American reaction to even a hint of Al Qaeda affiliation is so powerful that any terrorist group wanting to increase its impact makes the claim. Meanwhile the true incoherence of the numerous terrorist groups is suggested by the killing of the Director of CARE Iraq, Margaret Hassan, on November 16, 2004 by an independent Iraqi terrorist group. This was done contrary to the publically stated wishes of the important Al Qaeda leader, Abu Musab Zarqawi. The Islāmic fundamentalist world is full of loose cannons. For a reflection on some aspects of Cold War threat inflation see the author's *The Limits of Soviet Technology*, Technology Review, Vol. 88, No. 8, p. 68, Nov/Dec (1985) and *The Limits of Technology Transfer*, Military Logistics Forum, Vol. 2, No. 7, p. 35, April, 1986.

116.

Conditions in both Turkey and Saudi Arabia have recently become more tense due in part to pressure from fundamentalist or Al Qaeda groups. Turkey seems to be successfully accommodating some change. The jury is still out for Saudi Arabia where pressure is more intense.

117.

Though none of these is very satisfying or reliable one may take a look at: Corbin, Jane, *al-Qaeda: The Terror Network that Threatens the World*, Nation Books, New York, 2002; Williams, Paul L., *Al Qaeda: Brotherhood of Terror*, Alpha, no city, 2003; as well as Gunaratna's, *Inside Al Qaeda* (ref. 47). They are all characterized by poor documentation, vague references to "linked to" etc. and near hysterical threat inflation not seen since the darkest days of the Cold War. Unfortunately, the available government data are not much better.

118.

There exist many implausible beliefs about bin Laden's combat record in Afghanistan including his thrice being wounded. This all seems very unlikely, especially when one views the well known video of him holding an AK-47. He is clearly not at home holding a weapon; his body language reminds one of a woman holding a firearm for the first time. Nevertheless, some reliable sources say otherwise, see for example, *Through Our Enemies' Eyes: Osama bin Laden, Radical Islam, and the Future of America,* Anonymous, Brassey's, Washington, 2002, pp. 90-92.

119.

This ridiculous figure is cited on page 8 of Gunaratna's, *Inside Al Qaeda* (ref. 47). More judicious estimates range from 7,000 to 10,000, but I would guess that even these are a bit on the high side. A more discerning look at the numbers and motives of those going to Afghanistan for 'training' is found in Gilles Kepel's *Jihad: The Trail of Political Islam*, Harvard University Press, Cambridge, 2002, pp. 147-8 where he notes that young Saudis would go to Afghanistan on "jihād tours" of several weeks. These may be viewed as similar to going on the pilgrimage to Mecca, the *hajj,* as a one-time pious act and then one moves on in life, a sort of 'getting your ticket punched' in demonstrating your commitment to

Islām. Extremely few of these young Saudis ever took up arms thereafter.

120.

Michael Scheuer, the former head of the CIA's bin Laden task group recently said that Osama bin Laden probably has a nuclear weapon of some kind and plans to use it in the United States. CBS 60 Minutes interview November 14, 2004.

121.

One may take considerable issue with my characterization of post 9-11 times as reflecting an "absence of terrorist activity in the United States." There is one possible exception, the attempted destruction of an American Airlines flight over the Atlantic on December 22, 2001 by the 'shoe bomber' Richard Reid. The State Department on their web site (www.state.gov/s/ct/rls/pgtrpt) lists in their Chronology of Significant Terrorist Incidents 124 terrorist incidents globally in 2001 and 139 in 2002. But 40% of these are in India and have little to do with the terrorism we fear, certainly not of Al-Qaeda's doing. Similarly, the on-going Intifada attacks in Israel have nothing to do with Al-Qaeda, and most of the remainder are remote, trivial, and nonthreatening. Under any other circumstances they would be completely disregarded. The attacks against a French ship in Yemen on October 6, 2002, the night club attacks in Bali, Indonesian on October 12, 2002, against foreign civilian compounds in Riyadh, Saudi Arabia on May 12 and November 8, 2003, and two synagogues in Istanbul on November 15, 2003 may or may not be part of a global, coherent Islāmist challenge. The issue is similarly cloudy with the train attacks of March 11, 2004 in Madrid and the subway bombings in London on July 7, 2005. The evidence in the case of the London bombing suggests a rather amateurish, independent enterprise. As for the anthrax scare, it was clearly unrelated and of some peculiarly domestic origin. It did illustrate, however, how easily Al- Qaeda could have driven the US into a paralyzing and devastating hysteria. That Al-Qaeda has not done this or something like this should tell us something. Therefore, the fact remains that there have been no attacks of any kind whatsoever by Islāmists within the United States, and abroad the attacks have been against Muslims as much as against Americans or Westerners.

122.

This is certainly not the view of Huntington in *The Clash of Civilizations and the Remaking of World Order* who makes a very interesting and thought provoking case for a new paradigm which includes an implied monolithic Muslim civilization. Nevertheless, there is much evidence to suggest that his thesis overstates the real religious or civilizational unity of Islām.

123.

The Taliban in Afghanistan were typical of another form of fundamentalism where the motive was less a break from Western influence and more a desire to purify what they believed was a corrupted practice of popular Islām. Recall, for example, the Taliban's destruction of the two giant statues of Buddha, hardly a reaction to the West!

124.

Nasr, Seyyed Vali Reza, *Mawdudi & the Making of Islamic Revivalism*, Oxford, New York, 1996. It is fascinating how Mawdudi, one of the spiritual fathers of the revivalist/Islamist movement could not resist the 'wiles' of Western thought and culture even as he fought valiantly to resist and condemn them.

125.

These figures are only approximate, and for good reason. The analysis of future petroleum resources is loaded with political bias, shoddy technical calculations, and booby traps of terminology. It is safe to say that the figures given here are probably not far off.

126.

The flurry of reports at the time was a classic case of threat inflation. Well over a decade later there has been no confirming evidence of such a deal, not even a behavioral change hinting at its secret possession. New anxieties about an offensive Iranian nuclear threat developed in 2005. This seems to miss the natural interest Iran must have in a defensive nuclear posture given the American invasion of a non-nuclear Iraq on the one hand and a virtually benign reaction to an ostensibly nuclear North Korea, the other members of Bush's "Axis of Evil."

127.

Armageddon View Prompts A Debate. *New York Times*, Oct. 24, 1984:A1. President Reagan's view of the potential imminence of Armageddon was shared by several Cabinet members and senior military officials.

128.

Of course this list is not intended to imply that none of these behaviors have ever occurred, but like human nature in general there were many responses, and the varieties no worse than the behaviors of the West and America, and at times notably better.

129.

A fine treatment of this subject is presented in Chapter 1, "The Myth of a Militant Islam," by David Dakake in the book, *Islam, Fundamentalism, and the Betrayal of Tradition*, edited by Joseph E. B. Lumbard, World Wisdom, Bloomington, 2004. Very highly recommended, especially as one tries to understand what the Qur'ān and *hadīth* are saying about the matter. Also worth looking at is Khaled Abou El Fadl's, *The Great Theft*, Harper-Collins, New York, 2005, particularly Chapter 11.

130.

However, this scandalous representation appears only in secular, non-religious architecture and objects such as monuments, hospitals, palaces, caravansaries, mausoleums, citadels, and bazars, as well as in ceramics, metal work, printed matter, and textiles. For examples of animal and human images in Muslim art see Richard Ettinghausen's *Islamic Art and Architecture 650 - 1250*. As for religious prohibitions of intoxicants, see the Qur'ān, 2:219, and for prohibition of portraying animal life see, Syed Masood-ul-Hasan, trans., *110 Ahadith Qudsi: Sayings of the Prophet Having Allāh's Statements*, Darussalam, NY, 2003, p. 101. Note that 'hadith qudsi' are especially weighty sayings of the Prophet because they are the Prophet's words accounting Allāh's commands to him., whereas, the Qur'ān is directly Allāh's words. The hadith are the Prophet's own words and actions.

131.

Bulliet, Richard W., *Conversion to Islam in the Medieval Period: An Essay in Quantitative History*, Harvard, Cambridge, 1979. For a nice summary of the matter, see Susan Douglass', *World Eras, vol. 2, Rise and Spread of Islam 622 - 1500*, Gale, Detroit, 2002.

132.

These words were written in the first edition, and I choose to leave them here notwithstanding the phenomenal change directly attributable to the Bush policies of 2000 - 2008. Some may feel uncomfortable with this clearly political statement, but it can not be avoided, since it is how the Muslim world feels. Thus I beg the messenger's license here. I choose to leave the statement unchanged because I believe it reflects the essential truth.

133.

Loeffler, Reinhold, *Islam In Practice: Religious Beliefs in a Persian Village*, State University of New York Press, Albany, 1988. I know of no work that better illuminates the views of most Muslims, at least until the 1990s, about the West. If I would recommend just one book about the Muslim world for Westerners to read it would be this one.

134.

Toffler, Alvin, *Future Shock*, Random House, New York, 1970. Toffler tells us that when things around us change faster than we can deal with we encounter "future shock." One reaction is "obsessive reversion to previously successful adaptive routines that are now irrelevant and inappropriate." pp. 359-360 (Bantam edition.)

135.
Bukhari, Vol. 4, Book 52, Number 46. Available at www.islammuslim.com.

136.

Lewis, *The Crisis of Islam*, p. 30.

137.

See, for example, verses 2:218; 8:72,74; 9:73 16:110; 25:52; 66:9 in: Rodwell, J. M., *The Koran*, Guernsey Press, London, 1987; Dawood, N. J., *The Koran*, Penguin, New york, 1990; Shakir, M. H., *The Qur'an*, Tahrike Tarsile Qur'an, Elmhurst, 2004; Asad, Muhammad, *The Message of the Qur'ān*, Dar Al-Andalus, Gibraltar, 1984; Ali, Abdullah Yusuf, *The Qur'an: Text, Translation and Commentary*, Tahrike Tarsile Qur'an, Elmhurst, 2005; Ali, Maulana Muhammad, *The Holy Qur'ān*, Ahmadiyya Anjuman Isha'at Islam Lahore, Dublin, 2002; Cleary, Thomas, *The Qur'an*, Starlatch, 2004.

138.
The Encyclopaedia of Islam, New Edition, v. II, p.538.

139.

The Encyclopaedia of Islam, New Edition, v. II, p.539.

140.

Lumbard, Joseph E. B., ed., *Islam, Fundamentalism, and the Betrayal of Tradition.*

141.

Of the 600,000 examined by al-Bukhārī (d. 870) only 7,397 were included in his celebrated compendium of *hadīth.*

142.

A useful source for understanding the sharī'as legal schools is, Muhammad Hameedullah Khan's, *The Schools of Islamic Jurisprudence: A Comparative Study, 2ⁿᵈ. ed.*, Kitab Bhavan, New Delhi, 1997. Naturally enough, since it is by an Indian Muslim, there are some nonstandard spellings for the more or less familiar Arabic terms, there is a moment's difficulty in following the text, but this is quickly resolved.

143.

See for example: Rahim, Abdur, *The Principles of Islamic Jurisprudence*, 2ⁿᵈ. Revised ed., Kitab Bhavan, New Delhi, 1994.

144.

Trimingham, J. Spencer, *The Sufi Orders in Islam*, Oxford, New York, 1998.

145.

Because of this asceticism and renunciation of material things, the early Sūfīs were known as "the poor", which in Arabic is *faqīr* and Persian is *darvīsh*, from which we recognize fakir and dervish.

146.
    Arberry, A. J., *Sufism: An Account of the Mystics of Islam*, Dover, Mineola, 2002, pp. 33-35.

147.
    Hodgson, Marshall G. S., *The Venture of Islam*, 3 vols., University of Chicago Press, Chicago, 1974, vol.1, The Classical Age of Islam, p. 404.

148.
    Arberry, 35.

149.
    Hodgson, v. 1, 395.

150.
    Ernst, Carl, W., *The Shambhala Guide to Sufism*, Shambhala, Boston, 1997, pp. 82-84.

151.
    It goes without saying that the modern western concept of love imagined in Rūmī's poetry is not what he had in mind. New Age ideas as well as old fashion heterosexual love are the drivers behind Rūmī's 20/21st century popularity in America.

152.
    Ernst, 104-106.

153.
    The Holy Qurān, Maulana Muhammad Ali, trans., Sura 25, "Al-Furqān". Also see his footnoted commentaries 53a, p. 27, and 1a, p. 717. *The Encyclopaedia of Islam*, New Edition, and the entries on "Furkan", "al-Kur'ān",

and "Tasawwuf" found in volumes II, V, and X respectively.

154.
There is an interesting dynamic and exception here. In post Ottoman Turkey one of the important reasons Islām is reemerging out of Ataturk's reforms is the persistence and influence of the relatively un-mystical Nakshbendi Sūfī order.

155.
World Christian Encyclopedia, 4.

156.
I quote Trimingham (228-9) at length here not only for its relevance to the Sūfī experience, but because this point of view is essentially pertinent to what we may learn from *Anger in the East* as well. "It is a step towards understanding to remind ourselves that the world in which the order-shaikhs and their devotees lived is incomprehensible to modern man. As Wilhelm von Humboldt has said in connection with the language problem: "Each language draws a magic circle round the people to which it belongs, a circle from which there is no escape save by stepping out of it to another." We, however, are trapped within a circle from which there is no genuine escape. No attempt will be made in this fact-centered book even to enter into that world imaginatively, for this can be done only within the context of a study of Muslim life as a whole, but we should at least draw attention to the fact that the people about whom we are writing were living in an entirely different dimension from that likely to be experienced by readers of this book. They believed, not merely in the reality of the supernatural world, but in it as an ever-present reality. Should we hear someone say that he had found himself in the actual presence of the Prophet, who had called him to a mission, we might feel embarrassed and take him to be suffering from visual and auditory hallucinations. It is the same when we read the lives of the Sufis. Accounts of 'states', moments of epiphany, and evidences of *karāmāt* (special spiritual power) will be meaningless unless one projects oneself into their atmosphere. We have to remember that each one of us is enveloped in a world of unconscious assumptions which give structure and meaning to our experience, shaping our way of expressing that experience in words. We, today, living in an entirely different atmosphere from that of Sufis, falsify our historical view when we question their experience in that vision (the ultimate question is the reality of the source of that experience), the honesty of their accounts, or their mental stability. We are questioning a view of the world of which we have no experience, as well as showing our lack of historical imagination. Our view of life is just as much conditioned as theirs."

157.
   Trimingham, 251.

158.
   For the most thorough treatment of the Nizārīs see the recently reissued, *The Secret Order of the Assassins: the Struggle of the Early Nizārū Ismā'īlīs Against the Islamic World*, Marshall G. S. Hodgson, U. Penn. Press, Philadelphia, 2005.

159.
   Unfortunately, the Fātimids got bad press because of their extremist relatives, the Qarmatīs and Nizārīs. The Qarmatīs, a branch of the Ismā'īlīs, appeared about 875 and did not support the Fātimids. They attacked pilgrim caravans and even Mecca itself in 930 killing large numbers of pilgrims and residents. Then they carried off the Black Stone that was only ransomed in 951 by the Abbāsid Caliph. Qarmatī influence and power gradually declined through the eleventh century as they were haltingly reabsorbed by the Fātimids. Sunnīs and Twelver Shī'as looked at these physical and spiritual atrocities and said 'a curse on you all'. Alas, they unfairly included the Fātimids as well.

160.
   Ibn Battuta, *Travels of Ibn Battuta*, trans, H. A. R. Gibb, Goodword Books, New Delhi, 2003, p. 61.

161.
   When the Abbāsid Caliph al-Rāshid was assassinated in 1138 there was seven days of celebration, Hodgson, op. cit, p.143.

162.
   Ivanow, W., "An Ismaili Poem in Praise of Fidawis", Journal of the Bombay Branch of the Royal Asiatic Society (New Series), v.14, pp.63 - 72, (1938).

163.
   Lewis, Bernard, *The Political Language of Islam*, p. 118.

164.

   Roy, Oliver, *The Failure of Political Islam*, tr. Carol Volk, Harvard, Cambridge, 1994, pp. 30-1.

165.

   Choueiri, Youssef, *Islamic Fundamentalism*, revised edition, Pinter, London, 1997. In this revised edition Choueiri (in the "Introduction to the Revised Edition") makes a more erudite case for "fundamentalism" than I make here.

166.
   Roy, 30-1.

167.
   Nasr, 3, 32-33.

168.
   Nasr, 122.

169.
   Nasr, 102-3, 107, 115-16.

170.
   Roy, 36

171.
   Roy, 22.

172.
Specialists take issue with the notion that the 'door to *ijtihād*' had ever closed. Nevertheless, this appears to be simply an argument of degree of 'closure.' See for example, *The Oxford Encyclopedia of the Modern Islamic World*, ed. John Esposito, Oxford University Press, New York, 1995. vol. 2, pp. 178 - 181.

173.
El-Fadl, 18-20.

174.
Esposito, John, *Islamic Fundamentalism*, Britannica Online.

175.
Ikhwan al-Muslimin. Also variously called The Society of Muslim Brothers, or the Muslim Brethren.

176.
The term has since become a general pejorative used to cohdemn those who disagree in any way with the radical speaker.

177.
Mawdūdī's condemnation of un-Islāmic belief included virtually all of Islāmic history after the first four, Rightly Guided, Caliphs.

178.
Some have described Mawdudi as a violent revolutionary which is clearly not the case. By revolution he meant a gradual reform.

179.
Carrel, Alexis, *Man the Unknown*, 56 ed., Harpers, New York, 1935, p. 153. This lament has a disconcerting relevance to events 70 years later.

180.

Carrel, 15.

181.

Carrel, 60.

182.

Carrel, 60, 92.

183.

Carrel, 141.

184.

Carrel, 308.

185.

He had been a well known literary figure and political critic before this. His criticism of the government is said to have inspired the government to send him to America so that he could see for himself how wonderful America and the West were, and by association, how wonderful the Egyptian government.

186.

There is some debate on the date ranging from 1951 to 1953. See Ahmad Moussalli, *Radical Islamic Fundamentalism: The Ideological and Political Discourse of Sayyid Qutb*, American University of Beirut, Beirut, 1992, p. 61.

187.

Few of Qutb's works have been translated into English, but this has under the title of, *Milestones*, by Kati Publishers, 1993.

188.
 Qutb, Seyyid, *Islam the Religion of the Future,* Delhi, Markazi Maktaba Islami, 1974.

189.
 Qutb, 37.

190.
 Qutb, 79.

191.
 "Islām is a system for practical human life in all its aspects." Qutb, 7.

192.
 The irony of all this is how un-Islāmic it is, for the Qur'ān and *hadīth* are very specific and unambiguous on the matter of suicide: Qur'ān (4:29) "do not kill yourselves", and *hadīth* (Bukhari 4.23.445) "Allāh said: My slave has caused death on himself hurriedly, so I forbid Paradise for him."

193.
 Sources differ on his birth date; May 17, 1900, or September 24, 1902.

194.
 Hinnells, John R., ed., *The New Penguin Handbook of Living Religions*, 2nd. edition, Penguin Books, New York, 1998. p. 868. Similar usage elsewhere for example in Gellner (pp. 4-5), Barakat (p. 125), and the Encyclopaedia Britannica (v. 9, pp. 922-23)

195.
 Arnold, T. W., *The Preaching of Islam*, Low Price Publications, Delhi, 1913, Ch. V.

196.
　　Arnold, 183 - 185.

197.
　　Bogomilism rejected worship of the Virgin Mary, the crucifixion of Christ, baptism, the priesthood, the cross and other religious symbols. The Bogomils led very austere lives, disliked bells, condemned drinking alcohol, prayed five times a day and five times a night, and had very unadorned churches. With so much in common with Islām, it is not surprising that they were easily converted.

198.
　　However, there are exceptions, the best example being the resilient and persistent popular Islam of the Turks. Ataturk was completely unsuccessful in cleansing the Turkish people of their "backward" religious beliefs based on the widespread influence of the *tarikatlar* (Turkish Sufi brotherhoods.) That they were not easily converted to secularism might be explained by the totally unsatisfactory alternative, an emotionally barren secularism.

Index

Bosnians, 45, 46
Bosporus, 5, 91
Boudiaf, Muhammad, 104
Bouteflika, Abdelaziz, 104
Brazil, 46
Britannia, 5, 73
British Admiralty, 77
British colonial era, 56
British East India company, 64, 71
British navy, 77
brocade, 68
brotherhood, 96, 97, 99, 142, 146, 156, 159, 162, 190
Brothers Karamazov, 121
Buddha, 107n
Buddhism, 55, 167
Buddhist Wesak Day, 89
Bukhara, 20, 36
Bulgaria, 45, 74, 172
Burma, 45, 64
Bush, George, 118
Byzantine Empire, 6, 20, 31, 45, 46
Byzantium, 5, 6, 9, 14, 27, 43, 106

C

Cabral, Pedro Alvarez, 70
Caesar, 12
calendar, 12, 78
Calicut, 56, 63, 70
California, 42, 182
caliph, 16, 17, 19, 21, 23, 24, 26-32, 38, 40, 80, 147, 150-152, 172, 173, 175, 176, 179
Caliph al-Hakam II's Cordoban library, 29
calligraphic limitation, 51n
Camel, Battle of the, 21
Canterbury, 29
Cape of Good Hope, 70
Capitulations, 47, 74
CARE, 49, 98
Carrel, Alexis, , 161
Caspian sea, 150
caste, 59, 87, 161, 175
Catholic schools in Northern Ireland, 84
Caucasus, 91
cave, 10, 11
caveat, 40
Celebes, 68, 71, 89
ceramics, 68, 115
Cervantes, 48n.52
Ceylon, 30
Chaghatai Khan, 61

challenge and response, 25
Charlemagne's grandfather, 20
Charles "Chinese" Gordon, 111
Charles Martel, 20
Charles V, 47
Charter for Peace and National Reconciliation, 104
Chief Turk, 79
China, 9, 20, 24, 29, 30, 38, 46, 65, 67, 68, 112
Chishtīs, 57, 58
cholera, 88
chopsticks, 68n
Christ Church priory, 29
Christian Bible college, 84
Christian fundamentalism, 95
Christian proselytization, 89
Christian Trinity, 17
Christians, 10, 13, 16, 17, 21, 45, 89, 95, 111, 113, 114, 131, 153
clash of civilizations, 2, 45, 106, 113, 186
climate, 121
cloves, 68
coal fired steam propulsion, 77
coffee, 50, 71
Columbus, 30, 61
command good and forbid evil, 133
commerce, 6, 9, 43, 46, 49, 50, 67, 68, 77, 190
Commodus, 5
common legal school, 67
Companion, 20, 45, 174
concept of zero, 29
Conrad of Montferrat, 151
conservatism, 43, 49, 50, 63, 85, 124
Constantine, 5
Constantinople, 29, 41, 44, 45, 47, 48, 51, 95, 118, 186
Constantinople fell, 45
constitution, 87, 88, 90, 97, 186
conversion to Islām, 56, 118
conversions, 44, 45, 59, 87, 145
convert, 44, 64, 77, 113, 150
Cordoba, 41, 95
Cordoban library, 29
corrupting effect, 95
corruption, 47, 48, 50, 78, 95, 127, 141, 156
Count Raymond II of Tripoli, 151
cousin of Muhammad's first wife, 10
Crimean Tatars, 46
Croatian Catholic, 169
Croats, 45, 46
Crusaders, 31, 114, 151
Crusades, 31
cutting off the hand, 134

D

Dakake, David, 114, 131, 175
Damascus, 9, 10, 23, 27, 94, 95, 151,
    169
damask, 68
Dark Ages, 20
darvīsh, 141n.145
Das, Arjan, 63n
Daudis, 172, 179
David, 36, 45, 114, 131, 141, 175, 182,
    183, 188
David Dakake, 114, 131, 175
dā'ī, 147, 172, 173
da'wa, 32, 147, 150, 173
Dead Sea, 81
death of al-Assad, 105
Deccan, 53, 61, 62, 173
declaration of faith, 14, 178
Decline and Fall of the Roman Empire,
    5, 29, 118, 185
decline in tourism, 104
Deepavali, Hindu, 89
deification of Jesus, 17
Delhi Sultanate, 53-6, 61
Deobandi madrasa, 83
dervish, 141n.145
Dervishes, Whirling, 143
Devanāgarī, 59, 173
Devil, 12
dhikr, 57, 58
Diodorus Siculus, 7
Diogo Lopes de Sequeira, 70
Director of CARE, 98
disrespect of their children, 95
dissemblance, 108
dissimulation, 31, 44, 179
distaste of worldly, 57
divinity of Jesus, 17, 168
divorcees, 57
djihād" (jihād), 130
Do I not know, 49
Dome of the Rock, 29
Domitian, 5
Dr. Husain Nasar, 107
draconian punishments, 134
Dracula, 45n.43
Druze, 32, 173
Duke of Gloucester, Humphry, 29
Dutch, 63, 71, 72, 89
Dutch colonial policy, 89
Dutch East India Company, 71

E

East and West Pakistan, 87
East Indies, 30
East Pakistan, 87, 88
East Slavs, 46n.45
Eastern Orthodoxy, 45
Eastern Question, 41n.38
Eastern Roman Empire, 5, 6
ebb and flow, 51, 121, 122
economic destruction, 124
ecstasy, 143
education, 29, 49, 83-86, 109, 160-163,
    185, 190
Edward Gibbon, 5, 29
Edward Said, 1, 130
Egypt, 6, 20, 21, 23, 24, 29-31, 38, 41,
    42, 46, 51, 73,
    74, 82, 84, 91,
    93, 94, 96, 98,
    101, 103, 104,
    115, 122, 126,
    127, 146, 150,
    157, 158, 161,
    162, 175
Egyptian Dark Age, 42
Egyptian Islamic Jihad, 99
Eighth Amendment to the Constitution,
    88
elasticity of Sūfī demands for
    conversion, 69
electronic news media, 118
elite cadre, 160
emancipation of women, 95
Emirates, 92
Encyclopaedia of Islam, 26, 32, 112,
    130, 131, 144,
    184, 185
England, 29, 46, 73, 74, 130, 134, 189
erroneous beliefs about Islām, 113
Euclid, 29
Euphrates, 6, 175
Europe, 6, 20, 24, 25, 28, 38, 41,
    44-48, 50, 70,
    73, 84, 177,
    185
European Dark Age, 5
European libraries, 29

F

failures, 2, 49
faker, 141n.145
faqīr, 141n.145
fast of the month of Ramadan, 14

232

Fātima, 19, 173, 179
Fātimid caliphate, 24, 30-32, 96, 147
fatwā, 138, 173, 176
Feisal, King, 94
Fertile Crescent, 53, 56
fidā'ī (devotee), 32
Fifth Guru, 63n
fine woods, 68
fiqh, 138, 173
FIS, 103, 104
five pillars, 14, 178, 180
five pillars of Islām, 106
flexibility, 46, 59, 63, 125, 128, 134,
          144, 146, 153,
          158, 174
flower displays, 49
France, 29, 46, 47, 73, 74, 76, 77, 79,
          81
Francis I, 46
Fundamentalism, vii, 91, 93, 95-98,
          101, 103, 104,
          106-109, 114,
          121, 124, 127,
          131, 144, 146,
          155-157, 162,
          164, 175, 177,
          183, 186, 188,
          189
Fundamentalists, 2, 46, 87, 89, 90, 95,
          96, 98,
          103-105, 107,
          108, 113, 115,
          121, 124, 127,
          131, 144, 155,
          158, 165
furqān, 144n, 173
future petroleum resources, 109

G

Gabriel, 11, 14, 15, 35
Galen, xi, 29
Gallia, 6
Gama, Vasco da, 63, 70
Gamal Abdul Nasser, 93, 120
Gamal Nasser, 159
Gandhi, Mahatma, 86
gasoline prices, 91
Gaza Strip, 70, 94
Genesis, 121
geography, 7, 65, 121
geology, 7, 121
George Bush's Washington, 118
German, 48
Ghatafān, 7
Gibbon, Edward, 5, 29
Gibbon's farewell, 118
Gibraltar, Straights of, 20

glass objects, 68
Gloucester, 29
Goa, 70
Good Hope, Cape of, 70
gold, 50, 71
Golden Horde, 46
Gordon, General Charles "Chinese",
          111
Gothic horde, 6
Granada, 29, 41, 42, 95
Grand Inquisitor, 121
Grand Mosque in Mecca, 126, 175
Grand Seraglio, 49
Grand Vizier, 28, 48-50
Grand Vizier's palace, 50
Great Britain, 44, 76, 81
Great Satan, 122
Greater jihād, 114, 129, 131, 158
Greatest Master, 144
Greece, 6, 29, 45, 74, 79, 172
green flag, 28
Gregorian calendar, 12, 78
Groupe Islamique Arme, 104
Guantanamo Bay, 103
Gujarat, 72n.85
Gulf of Lepanto, 48
Gulf States, 97
Gulf War, 99, 100, 126
guru, 63n

H

hadīth, 11, 15, 17, 17n.16, 42, 50, 58,
          84, 85, 95, 96,
          101, 111, 114,
          127, 129, 130,
          133, 134, 143,
          145, 155, 163,
          173, 174, 177
Hafez al-Assad's Syria, 98
Hagia Sofia, 50
hākimīyya, 160, 162
Hamas, 70, 97, 126
Hamilton Seymour, 41
Hanafī, 67, 136, 173
Hanbalī, 134, 136, 173
hanīf, 10,120 174
Hapsburgs, 46, 47
Hārith, 7
Hārūn al-Rashīd, 27-29
Hārūn al-Rashīd's Baghdad, 118
Hasan II, 151
Hasan-i Sabbāh, 147, 152
Hāshemite Kingdom of Jordan, 9
Hāshim, Banū, 9
Hāshim, 9, 21
hashish, 32
hashshsāhīn, 32

Hassan al-Bannā, 158
Hassan al-Banna's founding, 156
Hassan, Margaret, 98
Hawāzin, 7
hedonistic, 152
hegira, 12, 174
Henry VIII, 46
Herat, 36
Herodotus, 6
Herzl, Theodore, 74
Hezbollāh, 97
Hidden Imām, 31, 32, 111, 175
hijra (hegira), 12
Hindi, 28n, 59, 88, 173
Hindu, 55-59, 61-64, 67, 69, 72, 83,
        85-89, 152,
        159-161, 167,
        169, 178, 189
Hindu beliefs and customs, 55
Hindu Deepavali, 89
Hindu god Oladevi, called by Muslims,
        Olabibi, 88
Hinduism, 55, 59, 61, 62, 63, 64, 167,
        183
Hippocrates, 29
Hispania, 6
historic changes, 118
historic social experiment, 100
Hitler, Adolph, 81
Hizb al Islāmi, 97
hojatolislam, 163
Holland, 49
Holy Rollers, 58n
homeland for the Jews, 74
Homs, 151
honorific title, 23
hope, 2, 12, 70, 101, 117, 127, 143,
        150, 164
House of Wisdom (bayt al-hikma), 29
Hulagu, 38
Humayun's Tomb, 62
humiliation, 94-96, 98, 99, 101, 104,
        106, 156, 158
Humphry, duke of Gloucester, 29
Hun, 6
Huntington's Clash of Civilizations, 2
Husayn, 23, 111, 163
Hussain, King, 9
Hussein, Saddam, 44
Hussein, Sharif, 76
hysteria, 98, 100, 110

I

Ibadiya, 174, 175
Iberian Peninsula, 44
Ibn Abbād, 28, 29
Ibn al-Arabī, 144

Ibn Battuta, 36, 57, 152, 182
Ibn Khaldūn, 5, 25, 121, 123
Ibn Khaldūn's analysis, 50
Ibn Khaldūn's Muqaddimah, 29
Ibn Sa'ūd, 42
ijmā, 174
ijtihād, 138, 155, 157, 174
Ikhwan al-Muslimin, 159n
Iltutmish, 58
imām, 15, 16, 23, 24, 28, 30-32, 40,
        43, 50, 63,
        111, 147, 151,
        153, 163, 164,
        174, 175, 178,
        179
Imāmate, 23, 32, 40
Imāms, 23, 30, 32, 63, 84
Impaler, 45n.43
Incan, 168
incense, 68
India, 9, 20, 24, 29, 30, 34, 41, 53,
        55-59, 61,
        63-65, 67, 68,
        70-73, 84-88,
        100, 152, 159,
        160, 169, 176,
        178-180, 188,
        190
Indian cotton textiles, 68
Indian miniatures, 61
Indian National Congress, 86
Indies, 68
Indonesia, 25, 46, 65, 84, 89, 90, 92,
        98, 114, 125,
        169
Indus, 53
industry, 49, 50, 77
In God We Trust, 88n.99
Inquisitor, Grand, 121
international Communist conspiracy,
        112
intertribal blood feuds, 10
Intertribal conflict, 7
Iowa, 7
Iran, 12, 15, 21, 31, 32, 43, 47, 83,
        91-93, 95,
        97-99,
        105-107, 109,
        110, 112, 115,
        120, 122, 125,
        147, 157, 164,
        172, 178
Iran/Iraq War, 21, 97, 105
Iranian Plateau, 6
Iranian Soviet Socialist Republic, 91

235

Khomeini, Ayatollah Ruholla, 43, 93, 163-165
Khurāsān, 151
Khwārezmia, 36, 38, 175
Khyber Pass, 55, 61
King Feisal, 94
King Hussain, 9
Kitchener, 111
Koh-i-noor diamond, 63n
Köprülü', Ahmed, 49
Köprülü, Mehmed, 48
Kosovo, 45
Kublai Khan, 46
Kufā, 23
Kurds, 80
Kuwait, 78, 92, 99

L

Lahore, 11, 14, 26, 53, 56, 130, 181, 183
Lake Balkhash, 38
language, xi, 14, 28n, 34, 35n.31-32, 59, 62, 85, 88, 97, 99, 131, 146, 155, 176, 178, 182, 183, 188, 190
largest naval battles in history, 48
law, ix, 15, 19, 24, 26, 30, 59, 69, 83, 87, 89, 95, 126, 134, 136, 138, 155, 157, 173-178
lawyers, 16, 47
League of Nations, 77, 81
League of Nations Mandate, 77
Lebanon, 6, 32, 76, 82, 97, 104, 173
Lenin's political thought, 160
Lepanto, Battle of, 48
lesser jihād, 114, 129, 131, 158
Lewis, 29, 32, 35, 36, 51, 61, 97, 112, 130, 155, 187, 188
library, iv, xi, 29, 35, 61, 85, 88, 172, 188
Libya, 82, 92, 94, 120
literature, 15, 35, 43, 62, 88, 114, 121, 182
lodge, 24,142
London, 26, 29, 35, 36, 59, 100, 130, 156, 182-185, 188-190
Lord Nelson's appearance off Alexandria, 73
Lord Rothschild, 75
Louis XIV's ambassador, 49

M

mace, 68
MAD, 110
Mahdī, 31
Madīnat al-Salām (City of Peace), 27
madrasa, 83-85, 90, 175
Madrid, 100
Mahatma Gandhi, 86
mahdī, 31, 32, 108, 111, 112, 128, 156, 175, 177, 179
Majles (National Consultative Assembly, i.e., Parliament), 82
Malacca, 65, 67, 68, 70, 71, 121
Malacca Strait, 65, 67, 68, 121
Malay ethnic identity, 89
Malay peninsula, 65, 68
Malaysia, 45, 65, 68, 89, 98, 169
Mali, 84
Malikī, 136, 175
Mamlūk Egypt, 41
Mamlūks, 38, 42, 152
Man the Unknown, 161, 162
Manat, 11
Mandate, 76, 77, 81
Mansur al-Hallāj, 144
Mao Zedong, 123
Marco Polo, 30, 57, 68, 189
Marcus Aurelius, 5
Margaret Hassan, 98
Martel, Charles, 20
martyrdom, 23, 163
Marx, Karl, 121
maslahah, 175
Masters evil call, 150
Mataram state, 70
mathematics, 29
Maufal, Waraqah ibn, 10
Mauretania, 6
mawālī, 26, 59, 93, 175
Mawdūdī's religious thought, 160
Mawlana Mawdūdī, 63, 156
Max Plank, 26
māyā, the illusion of the existence of self, 55
Mayan, 168
McCarthy, Joseph, 112
Mecca, 7, 9-14, 16, 21, 23, 31, 65, 100, 126, 147, 173-175, 177
media, 1, 3, 112, 118, 119
Medīna, 10, 13, 14, 16, 31, 115, 133, 174
Mediterranean, 1, 2, 27, 44, 46, 48
Mehmed, 45, 46, 48, 50, 181
Mehmed II, 45n.43

Q

qadī, 57
Qādira, 58
qādis, 16
Qājār dynasty, 82
Qarmatīs, 147n.159, 177
Qatar, 92
Qazwīn, 151
qital, 130
Quraysh, 7, 9, 21n
Qur'ān, 10-12, 14n.10, 15, 17n.15, 21, 23, 31-35, 42, 58, 84, 95-97, 101, 113-115, 127, 129, 130, 133, 134, 136, 138, 143-145, 155, 163, 174, 176, 177-179
Qutb, Sayyid, 156, 161, 162, 164, 189

R

racial arrogance, 26
radicalism, 156, 159, 177
rainfall, 7
Rajas of Rajasthan, 61
Rajisthan, 57
Rājputs, 61, 62
Ramadan, 14, 152, 178
rapidly growing religion, 45n.42
Raymond II, Count of Tripoli, 151
Rayy, 147
ra'y, 177
Reagan, President Ronald, 112, 112n
Reality is a brick on the side of the head, 119
rebellions, 72
Red Sea, 6, 9, 31
Reformation, 46, 47, 83
reformers, 34, 53, 177
reformism, 65, 156, 177, 178
reformist, 71, 85, 145, 169
reformist/fundamentalist movement, 71
Reid, Richard, 100n.121
reincarnation, 61, 63
religious and ethnic tolerance, 114
religious school, 84
Renaissance, 29, 46, 94
Render to Caesar, 12, 98n
repetitive chanting (dhikr) of the names of Allāh, 57
Republic of Kazakhstan, 110
revivalism, 72, 95, 108, 145, 146, 156, 157, 177, 178, 189

Rezā Khān, 82
Rezā, Shāh Muhammad, 43
Richard Reid, 100
Rightly Guided, 20, 111, 160
rigid and archaic practices of early, 107
Rita, 34
Roman Catholicism, 168
Roman Empire, 5, 6, 29, 118, 185
Roman polytheism, 5
Romania, 45, 77, 180
Romanized Visigoths, 168
Rothschild, Lord, 75
Rub' al-Khālī, 7
Rubaiyat of Omar Khayyam, 34, 184
Rule, Britannia! Britannia, rule the waves, 73
Rūmī, Jalāl al-Dīn, 143
Rushdie, Salman, 12
Russia, 38, 44, 46, 47, 51, 73-75, 77, 79, 82, 91, 112
Russian Emperor, 120

S

Sadat, Anwar, 98
Saddam Hussein, 21, 44, 35, 94, 103, 105, 111, 120, 126
Safavid Persia, 41
Safawī, 44
Said, Edward, 1, 130
sainthood, 143
saints, 16, 57, 58, 63, 69, 143
Saladin, 30, 151
salāt, 14, 143, 178
Salman Rushdie 12
samā, 58
Samarkand, 20, 36, 61
Samudra, 68
sandalwood, 68
Sanskrit, 59, 178
Sasanian dynasty, 6
Sasanid Persia, 6, 20
Satanic Verses, 12
sātī, 57
satin, 68
Sa'ūd, Ibn, 42
Saudi Arabia, 15, 43, 50, 78, 82, 90, 92, 94, 95, 98-100, 103, 112, 125, 134, 157, 173
SAVAK, 93
sawm, 14, 178
Sayyid Qutb, 156, 161, 162, 164, 189
schools of jurisprudence, 138
secret police, 93, 98, 159
sectarian viewpoints, 97

239

secular Arab nationalism, 91, 93, 94
secular powers, 16
secular state, 88
secularism, 94, 95, 101, 156, 163, 169
secularist governments, 98
Selim II, 48n.151
Selim the Sot, 48n.151
Seljuk, 30, 31, 36, 38, 41, 45, 150,
        151, 178
sell nuclear materials, 110
selling their services, 152
separate action from belief, 163
Sepoy Mutiny, 63n, 64, 83
Sequeira, Diogo Lopes de, 70
Seraglio, Grand, 49
Serbia, 45, 74
Serbians, 45
Sevener Imamate, 30
Seveners, 30, 32, 147, 151, 174, 178,
        179
seventh century, 6, 65, 83, 106, 120,
        123, 131, 178
Seventh Imām, 31, 32, 174, 178, 179
Seymour, Sir Hamilton, 41
Seyyid Qutb, 162
Shabab Muhammad, 97
Shāfi'ī, 67, 136
Shāh Muhammad Rezā, 43
Shāh Rezā Pahlavī, 83, 120
Shah Waliallah, 63
shahādah, 14, 168, 178
Shakyh Muhammad Ahmed, 111
Sharif Hussein, 76
sharī'a, vii, ix, xi, 4, 16, 26, 58, 59,
        62, 63, 69, 84,
        87-90, 95, 115,
        133, 134, 136,
        138, 143-145,
        152, 155, 158,
        163, 173-177
sharī'a-based Islāmic state, 88
Shattārī, 72, 72n.85
Shaykh Ahmad Sirhindī, 63
Shī'a Amal, 97
Shī'a of Iran, 12
Shī'ī, 15, 21, 23, 28, 30-32, 40, 41, 43,
        44, 51, 96, 98,
        105, 108, 111,
        123, 126, 171,
        172, 174, 179
Shī'a, 19, 21, 43, 80, 97, 115, 147, 179
Sick Man of Europe, 41
sickness of the culture, 49
Siculus, Diodorus, 7
siege of Vienna, 48
Siffīn, 21n
Signposts On the Road, 162
Sikhism, 55
Sikhs, 63
silk, 11, 68

Sinai, 9, 94
Sinān, 151
Singapore, 65, 70
Sir Hamilton Seymour, 41
Sirhindī, Shaykh Ahmad, 63
sixth pillar, 14n.9
Slavs, 46
Smith, Joseph, 16
Social authority in the villages, 69
social conservatism, 124
socialism, 101, 103
Society of Social Reform, 97
South and Southeast Asia, vii, 2, 4, 53,
        65, 83, 90,
        144, 145, 169
South Asia, ix, 55, 56
South China Sea, 65, 67
South Dakota, 7
South Slavs, 46n.45
Southeast Asia, vii, ix, 2, 4, 44, 53, 65,
        67-69, 72, 83,
        89, 90, 121,
        144, 145, 169,
        178
Soviet Union, 91, 92, 94, 98, 99, 109,
        110
Spain, 7, 20, 24, 26, 41, 42, 44, 46,
        61, 114, 168
Spanish Muslims, 44
Spanish Umayyad Caliphate, 26
Spanish Umayyads, 30
spice trade, 9, 71
spices, 68
spiritual competence, 55
Sri Lanka, 98
State of Israel, 81, 82, 90, 91, 106
statues of Buddha, 107
stone building, 7
stoning to death, 134
Straights of Gibraltar, 20
Strait of Malacca, 65
strive hard, 129
Subcontinent's history, 56
Sublime Porte, 50n.55
submission/surrender, 11
Suez, 73, 93
sūf, 24, 141
Sūfī, 24, 34, 42-44, 46, 56-59, 63, 64,
        67, 69, 72, 80,
        85, 87, 115,
        128, 141-146,
        150, 152, 158,
        165, 169, 172,
        176, 179, 180
Sūfī accommodation of other religious
        beliefs, 145
Sūfī missionaries, 46n.45, 87
Sūfī orders, 43, 44, 57, 58, 72, 85, 165
Sūfī saints, 63, 143

240

241

242